STUDIES IN ENGLISH LITERATURE

Volume LXXIV

INGELD AND CHRIST

Heroic Concepts and Values in
Old English Christian Poetry

by

MICHAEL D. CHERNISS

University of Kansas

1972

MOUTON

THE HAGUE · PARIS

LIBRARY OF CONGRESS CATALOG CARD NUMBER: 72-88189

Printed in The Netherlands by Mouton & Co., Printers, The Hague.

CONTENTS

1

INTRODUCTION

The visitor to the British Museum may view among the relics of British antiquity one of the most famous examples of Anglo-Saxon art, the Franks Casket. Over seventy years ago, W. P. Ker drew attention to the analogy between the heterogeneous subject matter portrayed on this eighth-century artifact and the heterogeneous nature of the Germanic poetry preserved from the same period. Here is Ker's description of that emblem of the "literary chaos" of the time:

Weland the smith (whom Alfred introduced into his *Boethius*) is here put side by side with the Adoration of the Magi; on another side are Romulus and Remus; on another, Titus at Jerusalem; on the lid of the casket is the defense of a house by one who is shooting arrows at his assailants; his name is written over him and his name is *Ægli* – Egil the master-bowman as Weland is the master-smtih, of the Northern mythology. Round the two companion pictures, Weland on the left and the Three Kings on the right, side by side, there go wandering runes, with some old English verses about the "whale", or walrus, from which the ivory for these engravings was obtained. The artist plainly had no more suspicion than the author of *Lycidas* that there was anything incorrect or unnatural in his combinations. It is under these conditions that the heroic poetry of Germania has been preserved; never as anything more than an accident among an infinity of miscellaneous notions, the ruins of ancient empires, out of which the commonplaces of European literature and popular philosophy have been gradually collected.[1]

Like the carvings on the Franks Casket, the poems which form

---

[1] W. P. Ker, *Epic and Romance* (New York, Dover Publications, Inc., 1957; original edition 1896), pp. 48-49.

the corpus of Old English verse treat both Germanic and Christian subjects. Indeed, one finds within single poems both Germanic and Christian concepts and motifs. This phenomenon is not surprising since, as Ker suggests, whatever Germanic literary remains we have were recorded at a time when Christianity – and with Christianity the Roman alphabet – was steadily obliterating the traditions of the heroic past in the North. The mixing of Germanic and Christian elements in Old English verse has been noted and discussed by scholars for nearly a century; it is duly acknowledged by Greenfield, in the very first paragraph of his recent history of Old English literature:

Quid Hinieldus cum Christo? "What has Ingeld to do with Christ?" Alcuin's famous remonstrance to Hygebald, Bishop of Lindisfarne, in a letter of 797, concerning the monks' fondness for listening in the refectory to heroic song rather than to spiritual wisdom, is for several reasons a suitable prolegomenon to a history of Old English literature. For one thing, the context of the statement suggests something of the significance of cultural, political, social, and linguistic forces that are involved with the literature. The fact that Lindisfarne was founded by the Irish bishop Aidan from Iona calls attention to the Celtic force in the complex structure of the Anglo-Saxon society, while Alcuin's words themselves attest to the pagan Germanic and Christian Latinic concepts that either dramatically confront each other, as here, or else harmoniously fuse in the culture and literature of this earliest English era.[2]

That most Old English poems contain both Christian and pre-Christian heroic elements is a fact beyond dispute, and attempts have been made to show how these sometimes disparate elements have been combined by the poets. The earliest, and most successful, of these attempts was published by Arthur R. Skemp in 1907; the most recent by Benno J. Timmer in 1944.[3] These scholars and others, however, have neglected to draw valid distinctions between the ways in which individual poets have integrated these elements

---

[2] Stanley B. Greenfield, *A Critical History of Old English Literature* (New York, 1965), p. 1.
[3] A. R. Skemp, "The Transformation of Scriptural Story, Motive and Conception in Anglo-Saxon Poetry", *MP* IV (1907), 427-470; B. J. Timmer, "Heathen and Christian Elements in Anglo-Saxon Poetry", *Neophil.* XXIX (1944), 180-185.

in particular poems, and have failed to evaluate the varying degrees of success which they achieve. Scholars have either contented themselves with making simple statements about the 'mixed' or 'hybrid' nature of Old English verse or if, like Skemp and Timmer, they actually have examined the ways in which the elements of 'paganism' are used in the Christian poetry, they treat this poetry as a single, uniform body, and do not attempt to distinguish between individual poems.

The purpose of the present investigation is to show how inadequate general, all-encompassing statements about the use of pre-Christian elements in Old English Christian poetry are, and to illustrate some of the different ways in which Anglo-Saxon poets use these elements in their poems. It would, of course, be impossible in a work of this scale to deal with all of the Christian poems in Old English, or to discuss all of the ways in which Christian elements appear in them, but a close examination of a few exemplary poems should suffice to make it clear that distinctions between them do exist and are worthy of attention. Thus we may emerge from this discussion with a fuller knowledge of how Anglo-Saxon poets accommodate a double tradition, Christian and pre-Christian, of subject matter, concepts and motifs, which they inherit from the Germanic and Latin past.

G. K. Anderson has noted that "We are probably justified in assuming this threefold material – classical, Biblical, and native – to have been the stock-in-trade of English writers of the period before the Norman Conquest." [4] We need not concern ourselves here with classical material, if indeed any is actually present, in Old English verse. Whatever classical material one might discover in Old English poetry would have been transmitted together with the Biblical material as a part of the tradition of Latin Christianity, and it is of course this tradition which is of primary importance to Christian poetry in the vernacular.

Although Christianity had been introduced into Roman Britain around the year 200, and had persisted in parts of the island through the period of heathen Saxon invasion and settlement, it

[4]   G. K. Anderson, *The Literature of the Anglo-Saxons* (Princeton, 1949), p. 80.

was not until 597, when Pope Gregory the Great sent Augustine
to reconvert Britain to Roman doctrine, that Orthodox Latin
Christianity began to gain ascendancy there. Two generations
later, the orthodox faith was firmly established in England by
Theodore and Hadrian, and with the Synod of Whitby in 664 the
Roman Church became the undisputed Church of the English.
During the next two centuries many of the literary materials of
Christianity, principally stories from Scriptures and apocryphal
documents, and Saint's Lives, were transformed from their original
Latin into Old English vernacular verse, presumably for the edifi-
cation of the mass of people to whom Latin was unintelligible. By
the year 1000, about the time when the poetry with which we are
dealing was written down, it is extremely unlikely that any verse
extant in England had not been at least touched by the literary
tradition of Latin Christianity. This tradition furnished the plots
and ideals which appear in most of the vernacular poetry which
has been preserved from the period before 1066. Before the
establishment of Roman Christianity in England, another poetic
tradition held what must have been uncontested precedence. The
Germanic heroic tradition, whose basic technique and subject
matter is generally assumed to have been common to all of the
various heathen Germanic tribes of Europe, had its roots in the
Heroic Age of the fourth, fifth and sixth centuries. A large body
of heroic narrative poetry, much of it now completely lost, dealt
with stories, perhaps originally historical, of the kings and heroes
of the great period of Germanic migrations. These stories survived for many centuries in Europe, appearing in the twelfth
century in such works as the Old Norse *Thedrik Saga* and *Vol-
sunga Saga* and, with Christian trappings, in the Middle-High
German *Nibelungenlied,* and in the thirteenth century Icelandic
manuscript known as the Poetic Edda.[5]

We have, as Greenfield observes, "ample evidence" that these
primarily Continental stories were known in England.[6] Two fragments of a poem in Old English about Walter of Aquitane are

---

[5] H. Munro Chadwick, *The Heroic Age* (Cambridge, Eng., 1912), remains
the most extensive treatment of this tradition.
[6] Greenfield, p. 80.

extant, *Beowulf* contains numerous allusions, not all of them intelligible to us today, to the famous warriors of the Heroic Age, and
Widsith, perhaps the earliest Old English poem extant, is a veritable catalogue of the tribes, kings and stories of the Germanic
past. While we cannot know with any certainty how long these
heroic, pre-Christian stories themselves remained current in England after the reconversion of the island to Christianity, the heroic
tradition which they embodied left an indelible mark upon Old
English verse. Greenfield further remarks, "Perhaps more important for Old English poetry as a whole than the particular figures
of the Heroic Age were the spirit and code of conduct they
embodied, for these were to endure down to the Norman Conquest", in the verse, one might add, if nowhere else.[7] The poem
which recounts the story of *The Battle of Maldon* in 991 would
in its heroic spirit have been intelligible and congenial to the same
audience that, in *Beowulf,* listened to the presumably pagan songs
about Sigemund and Fitela or Finn and Hengest.

The preservation and dissemination of the heroic stories and
the heroic spirit was the function of the Germanic *scop.* The
primary ambition of the Germanic hero was to win praise (*lof*)
among men and have his glory (*dom*) preserved forever. The
praise and glory he won by deeds of valor and by his generosity,
but the poet was, in the absence of written records, necessary to
the preservation in song of the hero's reputation.[8] Thus, after
Beowulf has slain Grendel's mother, Hrothgar's *scop* extempo-
rizes a song about Beowulf's great deed, and recalls the deeds
of another, earlier, monster-slayer, Sigemund:

> Hwilum cyninges þegn,
> guma gylphlæden,   gidda gemyndig,
> se ðe ealfela   ealdgesegena
> worn gemunde,   word oþer fand
> soðe gebunden;   secg eft ongan
> sið Beowulfes   snyttrum styrian
> ond on sped wrecan   spel gerade,
> wordum wrixlan;   welhwylc gecwæð,
> þæt he fram Sigemundes   secgan hyrde

[7]   Greenfield, p. 80.
[8]   See Chadwick, pp. 77-100.

> ellendædum,   uncuþes fela
> Wælsinges gewin,   wide siðas . . . .   (867–877)[9]

Later, at the great banquet, the *scop* retells another old story of heroic deeds, that of Finn and Hengest (1063-1159).

Widsith is the most complete and most provocative account in Old English of the Germanic poet and his calling. In its final form in the seventh or early eighth century, [10] the poem is ostensibly the first-person narrative of the travels and adventures of a *scop* among the Germanic tribes of continental Europe. That this account should not be understood literally is evident from the fact that three of the kings that Widsith mentions as his patrons, Eormanric, Gutthere and Ælfwine, all historical persons, died respectively about the years 375, 435 and 572. After a brief introduction in the third person, Widsith begins with a catalogue of kings and the tribes they ruled (10-49).[11] He then catalogues the tribes which he claims to have visited (50-87), and then shifts to a somewhat more detailed account of the particular kings he claims to have served (88-130). The poem concludes with some general remarks about the life of a wandering minstrel (131-143).

Early critics of *Widsith* concerned themselves primarily with questions of the origin and composition of the poem. R.W. Chambers, the greatest scholar of Widsith, rejects as late interpolations all Biblical and classical references in the catalogues and, because of certain inconsistencies between earlier and later portions of the poem (that is, between the "Catalog of Kings", 10-49, and the "Ealhild-Eormanric lay", 50-130) concludes that the "Catalog of Kings" is earlier than the rest of the poem, which must therefore be of composite origin. He describes *Widsith* as follows:

. . . a phantasy of some man, keenly interested in the old stories, who depicts an ideal wandering singer, and makes him move hither and

---

[9]   *Beowulf and the Fight at Finnsburg*, ed. Fr. Klaeber, 3rd ed. (Boston, 1950). All citations in my text are to this edition.
[10]   See, e.g., R. W. Chambers, *Widsith: A Study in Old English Heroic Legend* (Cambridge, Eng., 1912), p. 150. The most important modern edition is that of Kemp Malone (London, 1936).
[11]   The text of *Widsith* used in this study is that of G. P. Krapp and E. V. K. Dobbie, eds., *The Exeter Book* (New York, 1936), pp. 149-153.

thither among the tribes and the heroes whose stories he loves. In the names of its chiefs, in the names of its tribes, but above all in its spirit, *Widsith* reflects the heroic age of the migrations, an age which had hardly begun in the days of Ermanaric.[12]

For Chambers, the real value of the poem is that "it shows us what was the stock-in-trade of the old Anglian bard; and if Widsith be of composite origin, this only makes the evidence more representative".[13]

A more recent critic, W. H. French, takes issue with some of Chambers' conclusions, and in so doing offers a more satisfactory interpretation of the poem as an organic whole:

It is simply this: that the writer was a scop; that his learning was merely professional; that his object in displaying it was not to teach or to construct a rhapsody on heroic themes; that far from being in retirement, he was striving to remain in active service; and that his ultimate aim in composing the poem or in reciting it subsequently was to interest a patron in supporting him.[14]

These conjectures are almost certainly correct. If one ignores for the moment the antiquarian interest of the various catalogues, he is immediately struck by the heavy emphasis upon the virtue of generosity in the kings singled out for special praise, and particularly upon their generosity toward Widsith himself. The catalogues must, as Chambers indicated, present the 'stock-in-trade' of the scop whose advertisement this poem is, but it is unnecessary to exclude as spurious Biblical and classical references, since a seventh-or eighth-century English poet might easily have heard and added stories of Alexander and of the Israelites to the Germanic stories in his repertory. Further, whatever contradictions concerning persons, places or events there are in the poem[15] can be accounted for if one bears in mind that such contradictions would no doubt be found within the group of stories known to the poet. Thus, that two sets of rulers are given for the Burgundians indicates only that Widsith knows stories associated with

---

12 Chambers, *Widsith*, pp. 5-6.
13 Chambers, *Widsith*, p. 181.
14 Walter H. French, "Widsith and the Scop", *PMLA* LX (1945), 623-630.
15 Chambers, *Widsith*, p. 133ff.

two groups of rulers who are supposed to have ruled this same tribe, not necessarily at the same time.

This proposed reading of *Widsith* leads us to some very definite conclusions about the role of the *scop* in the Germanic poetic tradition. The *scop,* or at least some *scops,* must have traveled extensively among the tribes of Germania. Even if one discounts as fiction the catalogues of kings and places Widsith claims to have visited, the references to his travels are too frequent to be ignored. He is described as *se þe monna mæst mægþa ofer eorþan, / folca geondferde* (2-3), and he himself says, *Swa ic geondferde fela fremdra londa / geond ginne grund* (50-51). The peregrinations of minstrels during the Heroic Age would account for the wide dissemination of tales among tribes remote geographically from the heroes and tribes treated in the poems – minstrels told the stories they knew wherever they went, and learned new stories in turn. Through continual intercourse with foreign tribes a mature minstrel might accumulate a repertory of considerable size, and if at first glance Widsith's repertory seems incredibly large, one need only consider that any scholar whose business, like Widsith's, is poetry knows at least as many stories as the *scop* mentions in this poem. Nor should the heterogeneity of Widsith's poetic material disturb us since, by the time the poem was composed, any poet in England would have had ample opportunity to hear stories of Biblical and classical, as well as Germanic, origins. A good story is worth retelling, whether it be of "Alexandreas" or "Eormanrice," of "Israhelum" or "Creacum" or "Hunum".

The numerous allusions in *Widsith* make it apparent that the *scop* was usually attached to the court of a Germanic chieftain upon whom he depended for his livelihood. Widsith tells in some detail about the patronage he received from Guthhere (66), Ælfwine (70), Eormanrice (88), Eadgils (93) and Ealhhild (97) in return for his services as a *scop* (*songes to leane* – 67), and even though no one could have lived long enough to have seen all of these rulers, the prevalence of the custom of patronage need not be questioned. It would, however, be slighting the Germanic bard to think of him as a mere paid entertainer, for *Widsith* makes it clear that the poet has a more exalted view of his role in Germanic society. Widsith says that he has received, and suggests that he would like to receive, rich gifts from generous patrons, but he offers in return far more than just the pleasure of hearing his repertory. Widsith builds gradually to an explicit statement of his higher function, beginning obliquely with the simple remark that Guthhere was not a *saene cyning* since he *forgeaf glœdlicne maþþum / songes to leane* (66-67). A few lines later we learn that Ælfwine had *leohteste hond lofes to wyrcenne* (72). The reference to Guthhere relates generosity to kingly virtue, while the reference to Ælfwine goes further by relating this generosity directly to the praise (*lof*) which such virtue earns. When he comes to speak of Ealhhild, the poet states his function in less ambiguous terms:

> Hyre lof lengde geond londa fela,
> þonne ic be songe secgan sceolde
> hwær ic under swegle selast wisse
> goldhrodene cwen giefe bryttian. (99–102)

Emphasis is equally divided between poet and patroness here. The poet is himself both the recipient of generous gifts and the singer of the patroness' praises in the many lands through which he travels. *Widsith* ends with a generalized statement of this function in the clearest possible terms:

> Swa scriþende gesceapum hweorfað
> gleomen gumena geond grunda fela,
> þearfe secgað, þoncword sprecaþ,
> simle suð oþþe norð sumne gemetað
> gydda gleawne, geofum unhneawne,
> se þe fore duguþe wile dom aræran,
> eorscipe æfnan, oþþæt eal scæceð,
> leoht ond lif somod; lof se gewyrceð,
> hafað under heofonum heahfæstne dom. (135–143)

A Germanic warrior-king is eager to hear songs about other heroes and to have his glory (*dom*), like theirs, enshrined in song. He proves his worth to the poet by his generosity, and the poet makes this worth known among men by singing songs in praise (*lof*) of the hero, thus ensuring that the hero's glory will be spread abroad and will live after him. If the glory of Guthhere and

Ælfwine lives on after them, it is only because they, through their generosity as well as their valor, won the admiration of poets who then made songs to praise them. So it is that the *scop* becomes the sole preserver and transmitter of the heroic spirit and matter of Germanic tradition.

As long ago as 1912 H. M. Chadwick expressed the opinion that the Germanic heroic tradition in poetry was preserved and transmitted orally,[16] and until 1953 scholarly opinion seems to have agreed with Chadwick in a vague, general way while denying that particular extant poems were the works of oral poets. The primary obstacle to any wholehearted acceptance of theories of oral transmission was the total ignorance of scholars as to how this oral transmission might be achieved. It seemed quite reasonable to argue, for example, that a poetic text as long as *Beowulf* could not be memorized and recited accurately over a long span of time, and that, therefore, the text which we have must have been composed with pen in hand by a literate poet. In 1953, however, Francis P. Magoun, Jr., suggested in a seminal article that *Beowulf* may have been composed by a method similar to, if not identical with, the method discovered through the now well-known research of Millman Parry and Albert B. Lord.[17] Parry and Lord studied the techniques of composition employed by unlettered poets in Yugoslavia, and from these studies emerged an oral-formulaic theory of composition which they later successfully applied in order to demonstrate the oral nature of the Homeric epics.[18] Briefly, Lord and Parry discovered that unlettered poets compose narrative verse at the time that they recite it by using a large stock of metrical formulas which they have learned in the course of their training as oral singers of tales. The oral poet does not memorize the texts of his poems; he

[16] Chadwick, pp. 30-40.
[17] Francis P. Magoun, Jr., "The Oral-Formulaic Character of Anglo-Saxon Narrative Poetry", in *An Anthology of Beowulf Criticism*, ed. Lewis E. Nicholson (Notre Dame, Indiana, 1963), pp. 189-221, hereafter cited as "Nicholson". Originally published in *Speculum* XXVIII (1953), 446-467.
[18] Albert B. Lord, *The Singer of Tales* (New York, 1965; original edition Cambridge, Mass., 1960) is the most recent and readily available summary of the research of Parry and Lord.

rather uses metrical formulas to construct a finished poem upon the framework of events of a story which he knows.

Magoun adopts the theory of Parry and Lord almost without reservation and, finding that over seventy percent of the first fifty verses of *Beowulf* are found elsewhere in the limited corpus of Old English verse, concludes that, because "Oral poetry ... is composed entirely of formulas, large and small, while lettered poetry is never formulaic",[19] *Beowulf* is indeed an orally-composed poem. Subsequently, several scholars have attempted to modify portions of the oral-formulaic theory as it is applied to Old English verse. The primary strictures placed by these scholars upon Magoun's exposition of the theory are concerned with the question of whether formulaic diction necessarily implies oral composition (as opposed to literary, pen-in-hand composition), and whether a lettered poet might not compose formulaic poetry.[20] The oral-formulaic theory has steadily gained acceptance until today very few scholars would deny that most Old English verse is largely, if not entirely formulaic, and therefore has its origins in oral poetic tradition, even if it was not orally composed. Recent studies have demonstrated the formulaic quality of the diction of *The Dream of the Rood*,[21] the signed poems

[19]   Magoun, p. 190.
[20]   See, esp., Magoun, p. 212; Claes Schaar, "On a New Theory of Old English Poetic Diction", *Neophil.* XL (1956), 301-305; Arthur G. Brodeur, *The Art of Beowulf* (Berkeley, 1959), pp. 1-38; William Whallon, "The Diction of *Beowulf*", *PMLA* LXXVI (1961), 309-319; Frederic G. Cassidy, "How Free Was the Anglo-Saxon Scop?", *Franciplegius: Medieval and Linguistic Studies in Honor of Francis Peabody Magoun, Jr.*, ed. Jess B. Bessinger, Jr. and Robert P. Creed (New York, 1965), pp. 65-85; Larry D. Benson, "The Literary Character of Anglo-Saxon Formulaic Poetry", *PMLA* LXXXI (1966), 334-341; Michael Curschmann, "Oral Poetry in Mediaeval English, French and German Literature: Some Notes on Recent Research", *Speculum* XLII (1967), 36-52. A thorough and judicious critique of the oral-formulaic theory as applied to Old English poetry is Ann Chalmers Watts, *The Lyre and the Harp: A Comparative Reconsideration of Oral Tradition in Homer and Old English Poetry* (New Haven and London, 1969).
[21]   Robert E. Diamond, "Heroic Diction in *The Dream of the Rood*", *Studies in Honor of John Wilcox*, ed. Wallace A. Doyle and Woodburn O. Ross (Detroit, 1958), pp. 3-7.

of Cynewulf,[22] and the 'elegiac' poems.[23] Greenfield states at the outset that "The Old English poets utilised their word hoard formulaically", and adds a bit later the qualification that "the formulaic-thematic habit also carried over into written compositions as well . . .".[24] For our purposes here, one need accept the oral-formulaic theory only half-heartedly; that is to say, he need accept only certain aspects of this theory and need only assume that certain portions of the poems to be treated are formulaic. He need not assume that the poems were composed orally. The reasons why such equivocation is possible should become apparent shortly.

While a complete, detailed recapitulation of the findings of Lord and Magoun is both unnecessary and impractical here, a few major points must be touched upon, since they are necessary to account for the mixture of elements found in Old English Christian poetry. Lord describes oral narrative poetry as follows:

Stated briefly, oral epic song is narrative poetry composed in a manner evolved over many generations by singers of tales who did not know how to write; is consists of the building of metrical lines and half lines by means of formulas and formulaic expressions and of the building of songs by the use of themes . . . By formula I mean "a group of words which is regularly employed under the same metrical conditions to express a given essential idea." This definition is Parry's. By formulaic expression I denote a line or half line constructed on the pattern of the formulas. By theme I refer to the repeated incidents and descriptive passages in the songs.[25]

The 'formula pattern' is the basic unit used to construct poetic lines; once the poet has learned the formulaic technique, he is free to substitute other words in the formula patterns, thus altering the meanings of those formulas.[26] Out of these individual formulaic lines the oral poet creates what Lord calls "themes" – clusters of lines or formulas which are always found together

[22]   Robert E. Diamond, "The Diction of the Signed Poems of Cynewulf", *PQ* XXXVIII (1959), 228-241.
[23]   W. A. O'Neill, "Oral-Formulaic Structure in Old English Elegiac Poetry", unpublished dissertation (Wisconsin, 1960).
[24]   Greenfield, pp. 74-75.
[25]   Lord, p. 4.
[26]   Lord, p. 36.

because as a unit they express frequently needed ideas or situations.[27] These themes are, in turn, the blocks from which entire poems are built. The poet builds a particular poem from his store of formulas and themes as he recites it. "Singer, performer, composer, and poet are one under different aspects *but at the same time*. Singing, performing, composing are facets of the same act." [28] Each written text is therefore unique since, if it has not been altered by an editor, it records a single performance by an oral poet.[29]

Lord does not believe in the existence of "transitional" texts; texts composed in part by oral-formulaic techniques and in part by written techniques. "The two techniques are . . . contradictory and mutually exclusive." [30] An oral poet can, however, be literate and write down his own poems as he composes them; so long as he is not producing a text verbatim from memory the technique remains oral. The poet becomes a 'literary' artist when he ceases to use the formulaic technique and constructs metrical lines which are regular but free of the old formulaic patterns:

An *oral* text will yield a predominance of clearly demonstrable formulas, with the bulk of the remainder "formulaic", and a small number of nonformulaic expressions. A *literary* text will show a predominance of nonformulaic expressions, with some formulaic expressions, and very few clear formulas. The fact that nonformulaic expressions will be found in an oral text proves that the seeds of the "literary" style are already present in oral styles; and likewise the presence of "formulas" in "literary" style indicates its origin in oral style. The "formulas" are vestigial. This is not surprising. We are working in a continuum of man's artistic expression in words. We are attempting to measure with some degree of accuracy the strength and mixture of traditional patterns of expression.[31]

This passage contradicts, or at least tempers, Lord's earlier remarks on the improbability of "transitional" texts, and his statement that "The formulas in oral narrative style are not limited to

---

[27] Lord, pp. 58, 68-69.
[28] Lord, p. 13.
[29] Lord, pp. 101-102.
[30] Lord, p. 129.
[31] Lord, p. 130.

a comparatively few epic 'tags', but are in reality all pervasive. There is nothing in the poem that is not formulaic." [32] If formulas in oral style are "all pervasive", how could an oral text have even a "small number of nonformulaic expressions" and yet not be in some measure "transitional"? And surely a "continuum of man's artistic expressions in words" must include a transitional phase as it moves from one technique to another; it is not a continuum otherwise. Magoun likewise retreats from the dictum that "Oral poetry ... is composed entirely of formulas, large and small, while lettered poetry is never formulaic",[33] when he concedes that "Cynewulf was surely a lettered person" whose poetry might not be entirely formulaic.[34]

The foregoing qualifications are important for our purposes because when we come to discuss Christian Old English poems we shall not need to assume that they are totally formulaic or orally composed so long as we can agree that they are heavily influenced by the tradition of oral-formulaic composition. Cynewulf is certainly a lettered poet, whose "runic signatures ... depend on a knowledge of spelling and reading for their efficacy",[35] while the anonymous poets of many of the other Christian poems could have been literate. Lord points out that a literate oral poet is in a position to introduce changes in the ideas and themes of his oral poetry. "Eventually, however, writing will free [the poet] from the need of the themes for purposes of composition. This will mean not only a freer opportunity for new themes, but also greater freedom in consciously combining and recombining themes." [36] As we shall see, when the literate Christian tradition comes in contact with the previously illiterate Germanic tradition, just such changes as these do occur in Old English verse.

The oral-formulaic technique of poetic composition, in whatever language it may appear, develops slowly through many gen-

---

[32] Lord, p. 47.
[33] Magoun, p. 190.
[34] Magoun, p. 212; on the subject of "transitional" texts see especially the works of Schaar, Benson, Curschmann and Watts cited above (note 20).
[35] Magoun, p. 212.
[36] Lord, p. 131.

erations of singers, and for this reason it is, when matured, highly traditional and not receptive to change. The singer, says Lord, "makes no conscious effort to break the traditional phrases and incidents; he is forced by the rapidity of composition in performance to use these traditional elements".[37] The singer may, of course, learn new stories – even from books [38] – and add them to his repertory, but since he uses the same stock of formulas to put all of his stories into verse,[39] the tendency is for the technique to control the subject matter rather than for the subject matter to alter the technique. Individual formulas are extremely stable, and the stock of them known to the largest number of singers at any given time necessarily expresses the most common and useful ideas in the poetic tradition.[40] New formulas sometimes arise to express new ideas, "But the process of building formulas is so quiet and unspectacular and so slow that it is almost imperceptible."[41] By the same token, formulas which have lost their vitality are preserved by the tradition, and "meaning in them [becomes] vestigial, connotative rather than denotative".[42] Themes, since they are composed of these rather inflexible formulas, tend to preserve traditional ideas perhaps even more rigidly than do the individual formulas; the elimination of a single formulaic element, even though it were moribund, might conceivably cause an entire theme to disintegrate.

The early Anglo-Saxon poet who wished to tell Christian stories in the vernacular had to employ a conservative oral-formulaic tradition of composition like the one outlined above. He had no alternative. Early English Christians, like early Christians in the Roman Empire, had to convert their native literary heritage to Christianity.[43] That, in the case of the Anglo-Saxons, the oral tradition was by its very nature not readily susceptible to new ideas was no doubt an obstacle, but not an insurmountable one.

[37]   Lord, p. 4.
[38]   Lord, p. 23.
[39]   Lord, p. 24.
[40]   Lord, p. 49.
[41]   Lord, p. 43.
[42]   Lord, p. 65.
[43]   On the Christian assimilation of Classical literary tradition see Henry

Magoun refers to "a long tradition, running back to the Continental homeland and into a distant common Germanic heritage,
a tradition of at least seven centuries and probably more", citing
Tacitus and "allusions by authors from late antiquity", to support
the contention that Old English verse partook of a tradition of
oral-formulaic verse long before the influence of Christian letters
was felt in England.[44] On the other hand, however, Magoun later
demonstrates that "*Christ and Satan*, a poem of appreciably later
date than *Beowulf* and mainly telling a story of Christ's harrowing
of hell, exhibits plainly the formulaic character of the language." [45]
As one might expect from the foregoing discussion of the conservative qualities of oral-formulaic technique, a change in the subject matter of the verse seems to have preceded any changes in
the manner of its composition. The oral poet needs only the outlines of a story in order to make a poem, so long as the ideas
incorporated in the story can be brought into harmony with
those ideas which the formulas that the poet has at his command
have been developed to express. New formulas capable of expressing new ideas develop very slowly, while formulas expressing old
ideas are very stable and persist in the poetry. Themes, too,
persist in oral poetry so long as the ideas which they express
remain useful in the telling of the poet's stories.[46]

The strikingly Germanic flavor of the diction of Old English

Osborn Taylor, *The Emergence of Christian Culture in the West* (New
York, 1958 – original ed. 1901); and Ernst Robert Curtius, *European Literature and the Latin Middle Ages*, trans. Willard R. Trask (New York, 1963).
[44]   Magoun, p. 191.
[45]   Magoun, p. 205.
[46]   For discussions of some of the more common themes in Old English
poetry, see Stanley B. Greenfield, "The Formulaic Expression of the Theme
of 'Exile' in Anglo-Saxon Poetry", *Speculum* XXX (1955), 200-206; Francis
P. Magoun, Jr., "The Theme of The Beasts of Battle in Anglo-Saxon Poetry",
Neuphilologische Mitteilungen LVI (1955), 81-90; Adrien Bonjour, "*Beowulf* and the Beasts of Battle", *PMLA* LXXII (1957), 563-573; D. K.
Crowne, "The Hero on the Beach", *Neuphilologische Mitteilungen* LXI
(1960), 362-372; Robert E. Diamond, "Theme as Ornament in Anglo-Saxon
Poetry", *PMLA* LXXVI (1961), 461-468; George Clark, "The Traveller
Recognizes His Goal: A Theme in Anglo-Saxon Poetry", *JEGP* LXIV
(1965), 645-659; Paul Beekman Taylor, "Themes of Death in *Beowulf*",
Old English Poetry: Fifteen Essays, ed. Robert P. Creed (Providence, 1967),
pp. 249-274.

Christian poetry has been duly noted by scholars for so long that by the time of Magoun's article, comments like the one by R. W. Chambers in 1912 that "whenever the theme of loyalty is touched, the gospel stories of the *Heliand,* or the legends of the apostles, become for the moment war-songs",[47] had become commonplaces of Old English literary criticism. Lord, in his discussion of oral-formulaic tradition, gives us a clearer, more abstract idea of how this mixing of traditions comes about. In this passage he could easily be speaking about the presence in the native, formulaic *Beowulf* of Christian, "literary" elements:

In most countries of Western Europe where there are traces of a change from an oral to a literary tradition having at least started, the development seems to have come about through the intermediary of those trained to some degree in a literary tradition that has itself entered from foreign sources. In other words the stimulus has come from an already existent, originally nonnative, literary tradition. Some member or members of that group applied the ideas of written literature to the native oral literature.[48]

Magoun applies the theories of Parry and Lord directly to *Christ and Satan,* and draws some general conclusions about the nature of Old English Christian verse. His conclusions echo those of earlier critics who have dealt with the transformation of Old English heroic verse to Christian subject matter, and his theoretical basis for such conclusions is much more secure than theirs.[49] The Christian themes chosen by the poets are usually stories involving exciting adventures and martial actions; themes for which formulas already existed. Strange proper names were readily assimilated to existing formulaic patterns, often by changing their original accents. Pre-Christian words and compounds used to express the idea of 'ruler' were adapted to serve as synonyms for the word 'God', and other pre-Christian words similarly acquired Christian connotations. Poets avoid expressing ideas of Christian theology, doctrine and dogma for the simple reason that they lack the formulas with which to express them.

---

[47] Chambers, p. 60.
[48] Lord, p. 133.
[49] See, e.g., Skemp, "Transformation".

The preceding discussion tells us why concepts and motifs from pre-Christian heroic tradition should persist in Old English Christian poetry. When studied in conjunction with the somewhat older discussions, such as Skemp's, of how Christian subjects are treated in Old English verse, this theory can, though only in a general way, help to explain how oral poets adapted their Christian subjects. The primary shortcoming of previous scholarship on Old English Christian verse is that scholars when writing about this verse, no matter whether or not they make use of oral-formulaic theory, treat it as a single, homogeneous body of work. Were it not for occasional distinctions, of a rather vague nature, between 'Caedmonian' and 'Cynewulfian' poetry, one might suspect that there is prevalent some unstated assumption of unitary authorship for the entire corpus of religious verse. I intend in the following pages to demonstrate that these poems can and should be differentiated, and that a useful and significant means of differentiation is provided by a close examination of the way in which certain key pre-Christian, traditional ideas are employed in individual poems.

The major problem which confronts us, once we have established theoretically how and why pre-Christian heroic concepts would persist in Old English Christian poetry, is the thorny practical one of distinguishing between Christian and pre-Christian concepts which might agree in their general outlines. Obviously, if certain Christian and pre-Christian concepts appear on the surface to be identical, internal evidence alone is not sufficient to determine which is which. Pre-Christian concepts are here defined as those concepts which antedate the Christian materials in Anglo-Saxon poetry and may therefore be assumed to have been present in the older, heroic oral tradition, but this definition limits these concepts only chronologically and, in the absence of secure chronological data about the poems, is by itself not very helpful. Indeed, since we have no poems in Old English which can be proved to antedate the establishment of Latin Christianity in England, we must assume that, in one way or another, all of the poems extant could have been affected by Christianity.

A survey of modern scholarly opinion concerning Old English

heroic verse indicates that it has become increasingly difficult to determine whether or to what extent any given poem's purpose is Christian or secular. The opinions concerning the Christian content of *Beowulf*, easily the most discussed poem in the language, might well serve as a microcosm of the scholarly opinion which has manifested itself in the macrocosm of Old English poetry in general. We will have occasion later to consider the various positions taken toward the Christian elements in *Beowulf* at some length;[50] it should suffice here to notice that the spectrum of scholarly opinion ranges from interpretations which deny *Beowulf* all but the vaguest relevance to Christianity to those which are rigidly doctrinal, based on patristic and classical literary precedents. This diversity of opinion has extended itself into scholarship on almost every Old English poem which is not overtly Christian in its meaning, with *The Wanderer* and *The Seafarer* receiving the greatest amount of speculation concerning Christian versus 'pagan' elements. No poem, it seems, even though it may contain no overtly Christian references or sentiments, is entirely safe from Christian interpretation.

In spite of this general lack of agreement over the question of the pervasiveness of the Christian spirit in various Old English poems, most scholars agree that pre-Christian, heroic elements are present in these same poems. Indeed, the presence of pre-Christian elements in the poems with which we shall be concerned has never, to my knowledge been seriously questioned. When, however, we turn to particular elements in these poems, agreement as to whether or not they are pre-Christian in origin is quite often less than universal. It is possible to prove by written and archaeological evidence that customs like ship-burial and cremation, to cite two obvious examples from *Beowulf*, antedate Christianity in England, but the genesis of an idea, even one which was pervasive before written records, is a more elusive matter. At the beginning of his study, Skemp defines the problem:

... it must be noticed that very frequently the difference between the early Teutonic and Christian conceptions lay, not in the elements

---

[50]   See Chapter VI.

present in the conceptions, but in their proportion; and the transformation [i.e., from Christian to Teutonic] consisted in change of proportion, bringing into dominance elements previously subordinated. Warrior motives, for example, occurring only incidentally in the Vulgate, are habitually developed by the Anglo-Saxon poets, and a material change of effect is thus produced.[51]

Skemp fails to note, however, that while it is fairly easy to define a "motive" which has been expanded from a hint in the Christian source, the identification of the Germanic "conception" with which it was originally associated is often much more difficult.

It is not my purpose in this study to present a comprehensive survey of Teutonic antiquities in Old English Christian poetry, nor do I intend to unearth every pre-Christian heroic idea in the poems under consideration. On the contrary, only a small group of concepts, closely related to one another, central to secular Germanic heroic thought and, it is hoped, readily identifiable as being pre-Christian, will be examined. These concepts will be treated as literary conventions, preserved by the oral-formulaic tradition and reflecting either the real or the ideal conditions of an earlier, heroic age; their relevance to contemporary conditions in Anglo-Saxon England will be intentionally ignored. The persistence of these concepts as literary conventions, as ideals preserved by a poetic tradition which, as we have seen, clings tenaciously to old, established concepts, strengthens the argument that they are pre-Christian; proof that they were employed in the conduct of contemporary Anglo-Saxon society tells us nothing of their previous history.

There are several ways in which we may verify that the concepts with which we shall deal do indeed antedate Christianity and are remnants of Germanic tradition. The most obvious of these is by citing the testimony of the earliest historian to present a detailed account of Germanic life and customs, Tacitus. In the *Germania* (ca. 98 ad.), Tacitus describes the Germanic tribes north of the Rhine, and therefore free of Roman influence, about two centuries before the 'Heroic Age' and, of course, before these

---

[51]   Skemp, 436.

tribes had come under the influence of Christianity. Some of these tribes, principally the *Anglii,* settled in England (ca. 449) and, presumably, brought with them an oral-formulaic poetic tradition. Tacitus' account of the Germanic peoples is clearly idealized in order to shame his fellow Romans, whom he considers degenerate, and consequently his objectivity is at times suspect. Nevertheless, when we find information from the *Germania* corroborated in Old English poems of the seventh or eighth century, we may be reasonably certain that Tacitus has accurately portrayed an aspect of Germanic culture which has been preserved intact, at least in the heroic verse tradition, in Anglo-Saxon England.

All of the extant Old English poems are chronologically late enough to have been produced in an England which was more or less thoroughly converted to Roman Christianity. Concepts and ideals in these poems which run directly counter to contemporary medieval Christian ideals are very likely to have pre-Christian, Germanic origins, especially if the ideals which they contradict are basic to Christian morality or sentiment. Anglo-Saxon society appears to have nourished a system of secular heroic values alongside of its Christian values, often without recognizing any essential contradiction between the two, but this does not alter the obvious fact that the secular, non-Christian or anti-Christian values must have some sort of ideological origin. If a particular value cannot have arisen from Christian ideology, one may reasonably assume that it comes from pre-Christian Germanic ideology. For example, medieval Christianity, at least in theory, cherished ideals of poverty, modesty and humility. If one finds that wealth, boastfulness and pride appear consistently as positive ideals in a number of poems, he cannot look to Christianity to explain their existence. Germanic heroic tradition offers a propable source for such ideals and the concepts and motifs related to them.

The close and obvious interdependence of the concepts forming the group to be studied strengthens the arguments for their pre-Christian origin when they are examined inidividually. It is virtually impossible to discuss one of these concepts without refer-

ence to the others, and so an argument for the Germanic origin
of one becomes an argument for the Germanic origin of all of
them. Further, motifs associated with and subordinate to a particular concept may also be found in association with other
related concepts. The motif of the joys of the hall, for example,
is intimately related to the concept of loyalty as well as that of
exile. Hence this motif appears when poets treat either of these
themes. If, then, one can state with some assurance that one
concept originates in heroic tradition, and he finds that many
of the motifs associated with it are also associated with a second,
less-certainly pre-Christian concept, this discovery of reciprocity
should strengthen the case for the pre-Christian origin of the
second concept.

Finally, the discussion of the concepts, which must precede
the examination of their use in the selected Christian poems, will
be based upon examples from the least overtly Christian poems
in the Old English corpus. While only *Finnsburh,* among the
poems dealing with heroic subject matter, is wholly free of
Christian references and sentiments, there are several poems which
are sufficiently secular and heroic in subject matter to serve our
purposes. *Beowulf,* whatever the degree to which it has been
Christianized, is a heroic story and contains a wealth of unam-
biguously Germanic passages. The *Waldere* fragment is part of
a similarly Christianized heroic poem, while *Widsith* and *Deor,*
as well as the late battle poems *Brunanburh* and *Maldon,* are
primarily heroic in tone and spirit. *The Wife's Lament* and *The
Husband's Message* appear to be wholly secular poems. It is from
this group of poems, and specifically from certain unambiguous
passages in these poems, that we shall draw our illustrations of
heroic concepts.

Before moving on to a discussion of the heroic concepts with
which we shall be concerned, I must make it perfectly clear that
these basic concepts, their attendant motifs, and the values which
they embody are without exception secular in nature. We shall
not be concerned at all here with 'paganism'. Indeed, those who
seek information about pagan Germanic religion in Old English
poetry find it rather barren ground. The concepts which I am

about to describe embody essentially secular moral values. They have nothing apparent to do with Germanic religion, even though they have their roots in an originally pagan tradition and even though they constitute the social morality which informs that tradition. The adjectives 'pre-Christian', 'Germanic', and 'heroic' are appropriate to these concepts; 'pagan' and 'heathen' are not. The opposition which I intend to investigate in this study is not that of Christian and pagan, but that of Christian and heroic, concepts and values.

II

LOYALTY:
THE FOUNDATION OF GERMANIC HEROIC SOCIETY

Loyalty, the principle of personal allegiance between individual warriors, is the primary concept upon which the ideal society depicted in Germanic heroic poetry is built. Indeed, the word 'loyalty' and the abstract qualities and values which that word implies even today, implies as well the entire system of *comitatus* relationships which inheres in the values put forth by Old English heroic poetry. The importance of personal loyalty to the structure of Germanic society is unmistakably suggested in Tacitus' *Germania,* and is explicitly stated in Old English poetry from *Beowulf* and *Widsith* to the last great example of heroic verse, *The Battle of Maldon.* It is with this concept that any discussion of the central assumptions of Old English heroic poetry must begin.

In Old English poetry, and in Germanic heroic literature in general, we find two primary manifestations of the concept of loyalty. On the one hand there is the bond which may be established between warriors of approximately equal rank in the society, and on the other hand there is the bond between warriors and their social 'betters', specifically between retainers and their lords. The bond established between equals, between warriors who have become friends (in a literature in which the word 'friendship' means considerably more than it does to us today), or between kinsmen of about the same age, requires duties and services of both parties which are, predictably, the same for each of them. 'Wretched is the man who fails his friend' – *earm se him his frynd geswicað* – says the maxim.[1] The bond between a Germanic lord

---

[1] *Maxims I,* l. 37, in *The Exeter Book,* ed. G. P. Krapp and E. V. K. Dobbie (New York, 1936), p. 158.

and his retainer, in a hierarchical society, places specific, clearly differentiated, though nevertheless similar, responsibilities and privileges upon social superior and inferior, leader and follower. These two aspects of the concept of loyalty are not, of course, mutually exclusive, for lord and retainer may be, and often are, kinsmen as well. At his first interview with Hrothgar, Beowulf immediately makes clear his relationship to Hygelac. *Wæs þu, Hroðgar hal! Ic eom Higelaces / mæg ond magoðegn* (407-408). Speaking of the death of Byrthnoth, Ælfwine says, *Me is þæt hearma mæst; / he wæs ægðer min mæg and min hlaford* (*Maldon,* 223-224).[2] In situations where the bond between the two men is both social and familial, it is doubly strong, although the social relationship takes precedence in terms of privileges and obligations.

One indication of the importance of the role which the concept of loyalty plays in Germanic heroic literature is the frequently noted fact that situations in which a hero is faced with a conflict of loyalties are the most common tragic situations in what remains of this body of literature. Thus Hildebrand, in the Old High German *Hildebrandslied,* does not want to fight his own son, Hadubrand (who does not know him), but because of Hadubrand's insistence, and his duty as leader of the Hunnish army, he is ultimately forced into the battle. Hagen, in the *Waltharius* (a Latin version of a lost German poem of which the Old English *Waldere* fragments are part of still another version), is torn between his loyalty to his childhood comrade, Walter, and the command of his lord, Gunther, that he attack Walter. In the Finn episode in *Beowulf,* Hengest is forced by circumstances to pledge his loyalty to Finn, the slayer of his lord, Hnæf, but Hengest is unable to divest himself of his sense of loyalty to his dead lord (1085ff). Likewise, in the Ingeld episode, the loyalty of a young Heathobard warrior to his dead father will, one assumes, cause him to violate the peace treaty between the Heathobards and the Danes, one of whom had slain his father in battle (2009 ff). In

---

[2]   The text of *The Battle of Maldon* used in this study is that found in *The Anglo-Saxon Minor Poems*, ed. E. V. K. Dobbie (New York, 1942), pp. 7-16.

the *Nibelungenlied,* Rudiger finds himself in a dilemma which cannot be resolved because he has sworn loyalty to both the Hunnish king, Etzel, and the leaders of the Burgundian forces with whom the Huns are at war. In each of these instances, the central character becomes a tragic figure because circumstances which he cannot control force him into the dishonorable position of having to shed the blood of someone to whom he owes his allegiance.

Although the bond of loyalty between kinsmen is less prominent in Old English poetry than the bond between lord and retainer, we shall consider the former first, as it probably furnished the historical origin of the later system of personal allegiance. It seems a reasonable conjecture that the Germanic family preceded the tribe as the principal social unit, and that within the family the father held the principal position of respect and loyal obedience. By the time the Heroic Age arrived, the tribe had replaced the family as the unit of Germanic social life, and the chieftain occupied a tribal position analogous to that of the *paterfamilias.* We hear often of boys of noble lineage who have left their immediate families to be raised in the households of either the chiefs of their own tribes, like Beowulf in the household of Hrethel, or the chiefs of other tribes, like Walter in the household of Etzel. Tacitus gives some indications that he is writing not long after the time when the lord-retainer bond had become more important than the earlier familial bonds. Though he emphasizes tribal loyalties, Tacitus still pays considerable attention to Germanic family life. The custom of grouping the army in battle according to family and kinship (*familiæ et propinquitates*) with women and children close at hand, which one does not find in later heroic poetry, may well be a vestige of earlier family-oriented Germanic life.[3]

By the foregoing speculations, I do not mean to suggest that the bond of loyalty between kinsmen is of no importance in Old English verse, but rather to place the importance of that bond in its proper perspective. The loyalty of a warrior to his kinsmen

---

[3] Tacitus, *Germania,* ed. M. Hutton (*The Loeb Classical Library*) (Cambridge, Mass., 1914), ch. 7.

is important in the society depicted in this poetry, so important that the poets usually take it for granted. In the course of answering Unferth's slanderous remarks, Beowulf attacks his character with a not altogether relevant reference to the enormity of an earlier fratricide committed by the Danish warrior:

> ... ðu þinum broðrum   to banan wurde,
> heafodmægum;   þæs þu in helle scealt
> werhðo dreogan,   þeah þin wit duge.   (587–589)

Later, at the first victory banquet, Unferth is again present:

>   Swylce þær Unferþ þyle
> æt fotum sæt frean Scyldinga;   gehwylc hiora his
>   ferhþe treowde,
> þæt he hæfde mod micel,   þeah þe he his magum nære
> arfæst æt ecga gelacum.   (1165–1168)

The point of the poet's reference to Unferth's fratricide is that it is extremely unusual that a warrior who has betrayed his kinsman (*magum*) can still hold a position of honor and trust in his tribe. When Wiglaf enters the action in *Beowulf,* the poet, describing Wiglaf's reaction to the plight of his kinsman, Beowulf, makes a general observation about the loyalty of a good warrior to his kinsmen:

>   Hiora in anum weoll
> sefa wið sorgum;   sibb' æfre ne mæg
> wiht onwendan   þam ðe wel þenceð.   (2599–2601).

The first, and in the context of Old English heroic poetry the only, responsibility to one's kinsman which the concept of loyalty imposes upon a Germanic warrior is that of supporting his feuds and, if necessary, avenging his violent death. Tacitus' description of this practice leaves little to be added by later commentators:

Suscipere tam inimicitias seu patris seu propinqui quam amicitias necesse est; nec implacabiles durant; luitur enim etiam homicidium certo armentorum ac pecorum numero recipitque satisfactionem universa domus, utiliter in publicum, quia periculosiores sunt inimicitiae iuxta libertatem.[4]

---

[4] *Germania*, ch. 21.

Thus, in the Ingeld episode of *Beowulf,* the young warrior's sense of loyalty to his dead father causes him to violate the treaty between the Heathobards and Danes and to avenge his dead kinsman by slaying the son of his slayer (2029-2069). When describing Wiglaf's war-gear, the poet says that Weohstan took the helmet, byrnie and sword from Eanmund after slaying him:

> þæt him Onela forgeaf,
> his gædelinges   guðgewædu,
> fyrdsearo fuslic,—   no ymbe ða fæhðe spræc,
> þeah ðe he his broðor bearn   abredwade.   (2616–19)

That Onela did not attempt to avenge the death of his nephew is a circumstance unusual enough to warrant the especial attention of the poet.

Finally, by way of summary, we may glance briefly at H. M. Chadwick's discussion of the bond of kinship in the Heroic Age:

The chief forces which governed the social system of that age were the bonds of kinship and allegiance. The influence of the former extended not merely, as with us, to rights of succession and duties of guardianship over children and women. It was also the power by which the security of the property and person of each member of the community was guaranteed.[5]

The duty of each kinsman to obtain redress for offenses committed against members of his family assured the security of which Chadwick speaks. He goes on, however, to point out that the bond of kinship was losing its force in the Heroic Age, while the principle of personal allegiance was becoming dominant. That this principle of personal allegiance dominates the society presented in Old English heroic poetry is beyond dispute. Nothing, for example, exists in Old English to parallel the subject matter of the feuds common in the 'family sagas' of Old Norse literature. The relationship between lord and retainer is the central one in Old English verse, and it is to this manifestation of the heroic concept of loyalty that we must now turn.

W. P. Ker, in his discussion of society in the Heroic Age,

---

[5] Chadwick, *The Heroic Age,* p. 344.

finds a useful analogy to the relationship of lord and retainer in the relationship of a sea-captain and his crew:

A gentleman adventurer on board his own ship, following out his own ideas, carrying his men with him by his own power of mind and temper, and not by means of any system of naval discipline to which he as well as they must be subordinate; surpassing his men in skill, knowledge and ambition, but taking part with them and allowing them to take part in the enterprise, is a good representative of the heroic age. This relation between captain and men may be found, accidentally and exceptionally, in later and more sophisticated forms of society. In the heroic age a relation between a great man and his followers similar to that between an Elizabethan captain and his crew is found to be the most important and fundamental relation in society.[6]

Like Ker's captain and crew, the Germanic lord and his retainers share a common goal, personal glory (unlike the goal of personal wealth which motivates the Elizabethan seafarers), and depend upon the loyalty of one another to achieve this goal. The lord is loyal and devoted to his followers, just as they are to him, but the situation is not one of fraternity and equality as it is in the relationship between kinsmen or friends of approximately the same social position in the society. The lord is, in a broad sense, the ruler, and the thane his subject, and each exhibits his loyalty to the other in ways appropriate to his position in this hierarchy.

The desire for personal glory is the motivating force in the life of a Germanic warrior, be he lord or thane. *Dom biþ selast,* 'glory is best,'[7] says the maxim, and, a bit later, this sentiment is repeated:

> Ræd sceal mon secgan, rune writan,
> leoþ gesingan, lofes gearnean,
> dom areccan, dæges onettan.[8]

'A man should ... earn praise, raise up his glory ....' Glory in Old English verse is an abstract concept, and the Old English words which we translate today as 'glory' are all abstract nouns.

---

[6] Ker, *Epic and Romance*, pp. 7-8.
[7] *Maxims I*, l. 80.
[8] *Maxims I*, ll. 138-140.

Dom may mean 'glory' or, depending on the context, 'judgment'; *blæd* means 'glory', 'honor', or 'prosperity', *mærðu* 'glory', 'fame', or 'a glorious or famous action', *tir* 'glory' or 'honor', and *þrymm* 'glory', 'power' or 'might'. *Lof* means 'praise', the instrument by which a hero's glory is made known among men.[9] None of these words carry necessarily Christian connotations and, in fact, Tolkien has written at some length to show that the most common of them, *dom* and *lof*, carry, in *Beowulf* at least, wholly secular meanings.[10] A Germanic warrior's 'glory' is his reputation for greatness, his fame on this earth during and after his own lifetime.

The individual warrior, whether king or thane, wins glory primarily by doing brave deeds. Indeed, the customary way in which an ordinary thane can earn glory is by emerging victorious from a martial encounter. The usual alternatives which a brave warrior faces when he enters a battle are victory, and the glory which victory brings with it, or death. Thus, before diving into Grendel's pond, Beowulf says, *ic me mid Hruntinge / dom gewyrce, oþðe mec dead nimeð* (1490-91), and Hyldegyth tells Waldere before he takes up his arms against Guthhere that the time has come *þæt ðu scealt aninga   oðer twega, / lif forleosan oððe l[an]gne dom / agan mid eldum . . .* (9–11).[11] When Beowulf throws away his useless sword and trusts to the might of his hand against Grendel's mother, the poet restates this either-or principle in general terms:

Swa sceal man don,
þonne he æt guðe   gegan þenceð
longsumne lof;   na ymb his lif cearað.   (1534-1536)

When Beowulf takes up the fight with Grendel's mother, he waxes philosophical over his task, and recites a maxim by which all Germanic warriors should live:

---

[9] Definitions are those of J. Bosworth and T. N. Toller, *An Anglo-Saxon Dictionary* (Oxford, 1882-1920).

[10] J. R. R. Tolkien, *"Beowulf*: The Monsters and the Critics", *Nicholson*, pp. 51-103; appendix, pp. 91ff. Originally published in *Proceedings of the British Academy* XXII (1936), 245-295.

[11] The text of *Waldere* used in this study is that found in *The Anglo-Saxon Minor Poems*, ed. E. V. K. Dobbie (New York, 1942), pp. 4-6.

> Ure æghwylc sceal ende gebidan
> worolde lifes; wyrce se þe mote
> domes ær deaþe; þæt bið drihtguman
> unlifgendum æfter selest. (1386–1389)

Like any ordinary warrior, the Germanic lord wins glory primarily through his personal deeds of valor. In this respect, Beowulf's becoming lord of the Geats does not alter his desire to win glory; he vows *mærðu fremman* (2514) against the dragon, just as he had won glory against Grendel in his youth. There are, however, other ways in which a lord may bring glory and fame to himself. He can, like Scyld, lead his army to victory and subsequently force the defeated tribe to yield tribute to his people (1-11). It is, of course, assumed that as leader of the army, Scyld (or any other lord), would do heroic deeds in battle himself, but his having led his troops to a collective victory further enhances his reputation. The lord gains additional glory for each heroic exploit which is performed by one of his retainers, since each of these exploits increases the reputation of the tribe as a whole; the greater the reputation of the tribe, the greater the glory of the lord who is its foremost member. When Beowulf tells Hygelac that through his exploits in Denmark he brought honor to Hygelac's people – *þær ic, peoden min, þine leode / weorðode weorcum* (2095-2096) – he might well add that in so doing he brought honor to Hygelac also.

Because victory in battle and the deeds of his retainers brings glory to a lord, it follows that the mere possession of a large retinue of proven warriors is in itself a measure of his glory. Tacitus says that there is great rivalry among Germanic chieftains as to who can gain the largest and bravest retinue (*plurimi et acerrimi comites*), and that such a retinue is a measure of a chieftain's stature:

haec dignitas, hae vires, magno semper electorum iuvenum globo circumdari, in pace decus, in bello praesidium. nec solum in sua gente cuique, sed apud finitimas quoque civitates id nomen, ea gloria est, si numero ac virtute comitatus emineat . . .[12]

---

[12] *Germania*, ch. 13.

Hrothgar's glory is reflected in the poet's admiration of the size of his retinue: *Ne gefrægen ic þa mægþe   maran weorode / ymb hira sincgyfan   sel gebæran* (1011-12). For a lord to lose retainers is a disaster, for with them he loses personal glory. Thus, Hrothgar describes his plight to Beowulf at the beginning of their first interview:

> Sorh is me to secganne   on sefan minum
> gumena ængum,   hwæt me Grendel hafað
> hynðo on Heorote   mid his heteþancum,
> færniða gefremed;   is min fletwerod,
> wigheap gewanod;   hie wyrd forsweop
> on Grendles gryre.   (473–478)

Grendel has humiliated Hrothgar personally (*me . . . hynðo*) by decreasing the size of his retinue.

I have been speaking of Beowulf as both a lord and an ordinary (or extra-ordinary) warrior. While in the latter one-third of the poem, Beowulf appears primarily as lord of the Geats, in the earlier two-thirds he is at the same time both *Higelaces þegn* (194, 1574), and the leader of a troop of lesser warriors who are themselves *Higelaces heorðgeneatas* (261). In the same manner, in *The Battle of Maldon,* Byrhtnoth is both lord of the English troops and *Æþelredes þegn* (151). The social structure presented in Old English heroic poetry is such that an individual may at the same time be both a lord and a retainer. Like a modern army, the heroic tribal unit contains (potentially, if not in fact) smaller units whose leaders owe their allegiance to the supreme commander. A secondary leader like Beowulf (in the earlier part of *Beowulf)* has duties as a retainer (to Hygelac) and as a lord (to his own *handscolu*). Moreover, in spite of the historical distinction between obligatory service in the general army and voluntary service under foreign princes, all warriors in Old English heroic poetry seem to serve their lords voluntarily. This ignoring, if not suppressing, of the obligatory aspects of military service suggests the idealized quality of the principal characters in this poetry. A good lord like Hrothgar is presented as an ideal lord, and an outstanding warrior like Beowulf appears as an ideal retainer. In order to fully understand the bond of loyalty between lord and retainer, it is necessary to examine in some detail the idealized functions of each in the heroic world of the poetry.

The ideal Germanic lord is the embodiment and representative of the entire *comitatus* which serves under him. It is instructive to compare the number of names of warriors who serve under Hrothgar, Hygelac or Beowulf, which we are actually given in *Beowulf* with the number of names of Greeks or Trojans which we learn from the *Iliad* or the *Odyssey*. In the Germanic poem, lesser warriors are scarcely individualized at all, so that to speak of the Danes, the poet needs only speak of their lord, Hrothgar, himself. For example, he speaks of the early military successes of the Danes under Hrothgar as Hrothgar's victories:

> þa wæs Hroðgare   heresped gyfen,
> wiges weorðmynd,   þæt him his winemagas
> georne hyrdon,   oðð þæt seo geogoð geweox,
> magodriht micel.   (64–67)

Again, as representative of the tribe, the lord speaks for all of its members. In response to the demand of the Danes for tribute, Byrhtnoth begins his reply with the words, *Gehyrst þu, sælida, hwæt þis folc segeð?* (45). The words of defiance are Byrhtnoth's, but the sentiment is ostensibly that of his followers as well.

The primary duty of a Germanic lord is to lead his followers in battle. He is usually, though not always, the foremost and best warrior in the army which he leads. *Cum ventum in aciem, turpe principi virtute vinci, turpe comitatui virtutem principis non adæquare.*[13] When Hrothgar leaves Beowulf to await Grendel, he says:

> Næfre ic ænegum men   ær alyfde,
> siþðan ic hond ond rond   hebban mihte,
> ðryþærn Dena   buton þe nu ða.   (655–657)

Hrothgar here implies that he has always fought his own battles, and never before needed to find among his retainers a warrior of greater prowess than himself. After Beowulf has defeated Grendel, his victory is praised by the Danish host:

---

[13] *Germania*, ch. 14.

> þær wæs Beowulfes
> mærðo mæned;   manig oft gecwæð,
> þætte suð ne norð   be sæm tweonum
> ofer eormengrund   oþer nænig
> under swegles begong   selra nære
> rondhæbbendra,   rices wyrðra.   (856–861)

Beowulf is worthy of a realm because he is the best warrior in the world; a warrior of such preeminence should be a lord. Although Beowulf proves himself, in Hrothgar's service, to be a better warrior than the Danish lord and is proclaimed by the Danes to be 'worthy of a realm', he nevertheless does not take precedence over Hrothgar in the minds of the Danish retainers. *Ne hie huru winedryhten wiht ne logon / glædne Hroðgar, ac þæt wæs god cyning* (862-863). Hrothgar may not be the best warrior, but he remains 'the best king in the world' (1684-1686). That a lord should not be a warrior, and a good one, is, in this heroic world, unthinkable. Every lord or king in *Beowulf* is described as being fierce in battle, a victorious lord. It is the lord who leads his retinue into battle and provides them with inspiration ... *duces exemplo potius quam imperio, si prompti, si conspicui, si ante aciem agant, admiratione præsunt.*[14] Indeed, actual combat in the poetry is usually preceded by a speech in which the lord exhorts his followers to fight well, as do Hnæf in *Finnsburh* (2-12),[15] and Bryhtnoth in *The Battle of Maldon* (17-21).

The spoils of war, gifts, and credit which his followers receive for brave exploits belong to the lord. Beowulf says that against Grendel he will not use sword or shield:

> ic þæt þonne forhicge,   swa me Higelac sie,
> min mondrihten   modes bliðe,
> þæt ic sweord bere   oþðe sidne scyld,
> geolorand to guþe ....   (435–438)

Hygelac will be happy to learn of his retainer's courageous refusal to bear arms against Grendel because such bravery brings

---

[14] *Germania*, ch. 7. Tacitus distinguishes between the Germanic king (*Rex*) and the general (*dux*), but Anglo-Saxon poets do not clearly separate the two with respect to person or function.

[15] The text of *Finnsburh* used in this study is that found in *The Anglo-Saxon Minor Poems*, ed. E. V. K. Dobbie (New York, 1942), pp. 3-4.

honor to the lord of the Geats. Before he fights Grendel (452-455), and again before he dives into the pond (1452-1457), Beowulf asks Hrothgar to send his weapons and treasures to Hygelac if he should be killed. The Lord embodies the glory of the entire *comitatus,* and whatever glory his retainers win in battle, along with the items of plunder which betoken that glory, are properly his. Because the tribal treasures are his to protect and preserve, the lord often receives the epithet 'hordweard'. [16] All of the treasures and favors which the retainers receive come directly from their lord, even though they have originally won these treasures in battle themselves. Beowulf gives all of the rich gifts which he has received from Hrothgar to his lord, Hygelac, saying, *Gen is eall æt ðe / lissa gelong; ic lyt hafo / heafodmaga nefne, Hygelac, ðec.* (2149-2151). Likewise, after the battle at Ravenswood and the subsequent battles between the Geats and Swedes, Hygelac's retainers bring him the plunder, which he then redistributes along with other rich gifts (2985-2998).

Generosity toward his retainers is, along with prowess in battle, the most important virtue which a lord can possess, and is the quality most often praised in Germanic heroic poetry. Beowulf praises Hrothgar for giving him gifts munificently and, in so doing, living 'according to custom':

> Swa se ðeodkyning þeawum lyfde;
> nealles ic ðam leanum forloren hæfde,
> mægnes mede, ac he me maðmas geaf,
> sunu Healfdenes on minne sylfes dom .... (2144–2147)

We observed earlier that good kings in *Widsith* are highly praised for their generosity, and regal generosity is prescribed in both sets of Anglo-Saxon *Maxims:*

> Cyning sceal mid ceape cwene gebicgan,
> bunum ond beagum; bu sceolon ærest
> geofum god wesan. (I, 81–83)
>
> Cyning sceal on healle
> beagas dælan. (II, 28–29) [17]

[16] See e.g., *Beowulf*, 1047, 1852.
[17] *Maxims II, The Anglo-Saxon Minor Poems*, ed. E. V. K. Dobbie (New York, 1942), pp. 55-57.

A Germanic lord cannot hope to keep his retinue if he is unable or unwilling to distribute gifts freely among his retainers:

... magnumque comitatum non nisi vi belloque tueare: exigunt enim a principis sui liberalitate illum bellatorem equum, illam cruentam victricemque frameam; nam epulae et quamquam incompti, large tamen apparatus pro stipendio cedunt. materia munficentiae per bella et raptus.[18]

Similarly, at the beginning of *Beowulf* the poet makes a general observation about generosity, in connection with the line of Scylding kings:

> Swa sceal geong guma   gode gewyrcean
> fromum feohgiftum   on fæder bearme,
> þæt hine on ylde   eft gewunigen
> wilgesiþas,   þonne wig cume,
> leode gelæsten ....   (20–24)

Hrothgar, the model of everything a Germanic lord should be, gives gifts so freely that no man can ever reproach him (1046-1049). The traditional and imperative quality of the lord as a giver of gifts is reflected in the word commonly used to designate his high seat in the hall, *gifstol*. From the *gifstol* the lord distributes to his followers gold rings, armor and weapons, horses and land from his own personal property and from the communal plunder which comes to him as *hordweard*. Hrothgar's generous impulses are so powerful that he builds Heorot that he may have a hall in which he can give away everything he possesses, except the common-land and the lives of his people:

>   eall gedælan
> geongum ond ealdum,   swylc him God sealde
> buton folcscare   ond feorum gumena.   (71–73)[19]

The lord is expected to be devoted to the welfare of his followers. Grendel's raids cause Hrothgar great personal anguish; he suffers *þegnsorge* 'sorrow for [his] thanes', because he is powerless to

---

[18] *Germania*, ch. 14.

[19] Bosworth-Toller defines *folc-scearu* as 'nation', 'host of people', while noting that 'common land' has also been suggested; Klaeber accepts 'common land' without comment. Klaeber's choice seems justified in view of the fact that 'host of people and the lives of warriors' is rather redundant.

prevent their slaughter (129-154). Upon Beowulf's return home, Hygelac expresses the apprehension which he felt for the safety of his thane when he embarked upon his adventure, and the joy which he feels to see him safe once again:

Ic þæs modceare
sorhwylmum seað   siðe ne truwode
leofes mannes;   ic ðe lange bæd,
þæt ðu þone wælgæst   wihte ne grette,
lete Suð-Dene   sylfe geweorðan
guðe wið Grendel.   Gode ic þanc secge,
þæs ðe ic ðe gesundne   geseon moste.   (1992–1998)

Before diving into Grendel's pond, Beowulf takes especial pains to ensure that Hrothgar will care for his followers if he should be killed – *Wes þu mundbora*   *minum magoþegnum, / hondgesellum,*   *gif mec hild nime* (1480-1481) – and he finally surrenders his life in order to win the dragon's hoard for his people:

Ic ðara frætwa   Frean ealles ðanc,
Wuldurcyninge   wordum secge,
ecum Dryhtne,   þe ic her on starie,
þæs ðe ic moste   minum leodum
ær swyltdæge   swylc gestrynan.
Nu ic on maðma hord   mine behohte
frode feorhlege,   fremmað gena
leoda þearfe;   ne mæg ic her leng wesan.
(2794–2801)

The loss of a retainer through death or departure on a journey gives a lord cause for great sorrow. The death of Hrothgar's beloved companion, Æschere, throws the Danish king into a veritable orgy of despair, while the poet comments upon his loss with characteristic understatement: *Ne wæs þæt gewrixle til, / þæt hie on ba healfa bicgan scoldon / freonda feorum!* (1304–1306).

The lord's devotion is returned by his retainers, who love him dearly. One of the most common epithets used to describe a lord or king is 'wine', 'friend', or its compounds.[20] Scyld and Hrothgar

[20] See L. L. Schucking, "The Ideal of Kingship in *Beowulf*", *Nicholson*, pp. 35-49; p. 41. Originally published in *MHRA Bulletin* III (1929), 143-154.

are both *wine Scyldinga* (30, 170); Hrothgar is Wulfgar's *wine-drihtne* (360), the *freowine folca* (430), *goldwine gumena* (1476, 1602). A good lord is a consolation to his people, one to whom they can look for aid and comfort in times of tribulation. God sends Scyld to the Danes *folce to frofre* (14), and Hrothgar predicts of Beowulf: *þu scealt to frofre weorþan / eal langtwidig leodum þinum, / hæleðum to helpe* (1707-1709). At his funeral, Beowulf's retainers praise him specifically for his mildness and kindness to his people:

> Swa begnornodon Geata leode
> hlafordes hryre, heorðgeneatas;
> cwædon þæt he wære wyruldcyning[a]
> manna mildust ond monðwærust,
> leodum liðost ond lofgeornost. (3178–3182)

The devotion of the lord to his followers, and the love of the followers for their lord, are at least partially the result of the role which the lord plays as protector of his people. The lord's first duty toward the *comitatus* is to protect his followers from whatever harm might befall them were he not present. Beowulf explicitly tells his retainers that protecting the Geats from the dragon is his duty, and his alone:

> Nis þæt eower sið,
> ne gemet mannes, nefne min anes,
> þæt he wið aglæcean eofoðo dæle,
> eorlscype efne. (2532–2535)

Earlier, before diving into the pond after Grendel's mother, he is careful to arrange that his followers will have a protector (*mundbora* – 1480) even if he is killed. Epithets meaning 'protector' are very commonly applied to Hrothgar – *leodgebyrgean* (269), *helm* (371, 456), *eodor* (428, 663), *wigendra hleo* (429), *folces hyrde* (610), *eorla hleo* (1035) – to Beowulf – *eorla hleo* (791), *wigendra hleo* (1972, 2337), *eald eþelweard* (2210), *folces weard* (2513) – and somewhat less frequently to Hygelac – *eorla hleow* (1967) – to Sigemund – *wigendra hleow* (899) – and, in *Maldon,* to Byrhtnoth – *hæleða hleo* (74).

The lord protects his people primarily by means of his prowess in battle. The direct manifestation of this active, martial form of protection consists in the lord's actually taking up arms against an enemy who threatens his tribe, as does Beowulf against the dragon. Indirectly, the mere presence of a lord who has won great renown in battle acts as a deterrent to enemies who would otherwise readily attack his people. As Beowulf himself says, his fifty-year reign was a peaceful one because no one dared attack the Geats:

> Ic ðas leode heold
> fiftig wintra; næs se folccyning,
> ymbesittendra ænig ðara,
> þe mec guðwinum gretan dorste,
> egesan ðeon. (2732–2736)

After Beowulf's death, a series of wars is predicted for the Geats. As the Geatish messenger makes clear, these wars are inevitable because, with their lord dead, the Geats will have to deal directly with the long-standing hostility of the Franks, Frisians, and Swedes (2999-3007).

In addition to protecting his people by means of his martial prowess, the lord protects them by forming alliances with other tribes. Chadwick says that alliances in the Heroic Age are personal rather than national in character,[21] but, because of the nature of lordship in the idealized Germanic society with which we are dealing, it seems misleading to make such a distinction. The lord and his *comitatus* are ideally one in thought and action; an alliance between two lords is in effect an alliance between their two tribes. Beowulf's services to Hrothgar create a firm bond of friendship between the two men, and their positions as lord of the Danes and representative of the Geats give the personal bond national significance. Hrothgar's statement makes this phenomenon quite explicit:

> Me þin modsefa
> licað leng swa wel, leofa Beowulf.
> Hafast þu gefered, þæt þam folcum sceal,
> Geata leodum ond Gar-Denum
> sib gemæne, ond sacu restan,

---

[21] Chadwick, *The Heroic Age*, ch. XVII.

> inwitniþas,   þe hie ær drugon,
> wesan, þenden ic wealde   widan rices,
> maþmas gemæne,   manig oþerne
> godum gegrettan   ofer ganotes bæð;
> sceal hringnaca   ofer heafu bringan
> lac ond luftacen.   (1853–1863)

One should note that the *maþmas* of which Hrothgar speaks are *gemæne,* 'shared', and are, unlike the *gomban,* 'tribute', which Scyld commands from his neighbors (4-11) or the *gafole* which the Danes in *Maldon* demand (29 ff), tokens of amity (*luftacen*) between the two tribes. In this instance, personal service leads directly to tribal friendship. This same national aspect of personal alliances is evident in the practice of forming inter-tribal bonds through the marrige of a lord to one of the female members of the family of a rival lord. Hrothgar intends the marriage of his daughter, Freawaru, to Froda, the son of the lord of the Heathobards, to end the strife between that tribe and the Danes. If sons and daughters are unavailable for intermarriage, a lord may cement an alliance by taking a lord or warrior of another tribe as a sort of adopted son. Thus Hrothgar takes Beowulf *for sunu* (947), and this arrangement justifies Wealtheow's plea that the famous Geat should have a sense of responsibility toward her sons (1168 ff).

Alliances, be they personal, national, or both, are made by verbal agreement, and in this connection we should pause briefly to emphasize the importance attached to the lord's word. Should a lord say that he will do something, his words, once they have been actually spoken, bind him to do precisely as he says, lest he dishonor himself; the words are taken as his vow, his *biot.* Of course, the *biot* of an ordinary Germanic warrior is no less binding than that of his lord,[22] but it is less important by just so much as the ordinary retainer is a less important member of the *comitatus* than is his lord. If a lord makes an alliance with the lord of another tribe, and one of his retainers violates the terms

---

[22] For a cogent discussion of the heroic oath, see Alain Renoir, "The Heroic Oath in *Beowulf*, the *Chanson de Roland*, and the *Nibelungenlied*", in *Studies in Honor of Arthur G. Brodeur,* ed. S. B. Greenfield (Eugene, Ore., 1963), 237-266, hereafter cited as *Brodeur Studies.*

of that alliance, the violation brings dishonor to the lord and to his entire *comitatus* as well. Moreover, if a lord should once break his word, then the members of his *comitatus* would have reason to place less than absolute trust in him, and the bond of loyalty, which depends upon mutual trust and which holds the *comitatus* together, would disintegrate. Hrothgar, like any worthy lord, swears that he will give gifts in his hall, and so he does. *He beot ne aleh, beagas dælde / sync æt symle* (80-81). When Beowulf returns from Grendel's pond with tokens of his victory, Hrothgar remembers his earlier promises. *Ic þe sceal mine gelæstan / freode, swa wit furðum spræcon* (1706-1707), says he to Beowulf, and proceeds to fulfill his promises. Beowulf always carries out his vows so that at his death he points with pride to the fact that he did not swear *fela / aða on unriht* (2738-2739), certainly an essential quality in a worthy lord.

Lords in Old English heroic poetry are often praised for their wisdom, but it is not always clear what precisely the words which we translate as 'wise' or 'wisdom' meant to the poet and his audience. At times words meaning 'wise' (*wis, snotor*) seems to be no more than conventional, formulaic epithets, while at other times the statement that a lord is 'wise' seems to mean specifically that he lives and acts in accordance with the ideals of lordly behavior which we have been considering. Hrothgar is called 'wise' by the poet, no matter what circumstances of his life are being discussed. In a passage in which the poet points out his failure to discover a means of dealing with Grendel, Hrothgar remains a *snotor haleð* (189-193). Elsewhere he is *se snotera* (1313), *snottra fengel* (1475), *se wisa* (1698), *wisa fengel* (1400), where no particular respect for the context is shown by the poet. Beowulf calls Hrothgar *snotor guma* when, after the attack by Grendel's mother, he advises the Dane to behave differently and, presumably, more wisely (1383 ff). The brief description of Offa's reign seems almost to equate wisdom with success in battle and generosity:

> forðam Offa wæs
> geofum and guðum,   garcene man,
> wide geweorðod,   wisdome heold
> eðel sinne . . . .   (1957–1960)

Wisdom is commonly equated with old age. The maxims state unequivocally that 'old men are wisest',[23] and Hrothgar praises Beowulf for words which are exceptionally wise for so young a man; Beowulf, says he, is *on mode frod* (1840-1845), where *frod* means either 'old' or 'wise' or both. In addition to its relationship to wisdom, age is often associated with military prowess and leadership in battle. Hrothgar is called *gamolfeax and guðrof* (608), which is no doubt a formulaic phrase. Hrothgar says that Heregar was his *yldra mæg* and, as if by that fact alone, his *betera*, 'better', in a general sense (467-469). Beowulf is *se yldesta* of his troop and its *wisa*, 'leader' (258-259), but *yldesta*, 'eldest', must be synonymous with 'leader' when, in line 363, Wulfgar uses this word to describe Beowulf to Hrothgar. The formula *snotor and swyðferhð*, applied to Beowulf (826), relates wisdom and courage. While there is not sufficient evidence to deny that Old English words meaning 'wise' and 'wisdom' have the same denotations as our modern words 'wise' and 'wisdom', the interrelationship between the qualities of wisdom, courage, leadership and old age which I have attempted to demonstrate suggests that the words *wis* and *snotor* carry somewhat broader connotations than our modern equivalent words. One gets the distinct impression that, when a poet calls his heroes *wis* or *snotor*, he often means 'wise in the conduct of warfare' or 'wise in that he lives in a way which is appropriate to his station in his society'. If this is the case, then a lord who performs the duties and services expected of a good Germanic lord is by definition a 'wise ruler'.

Obviously a lord cannot exist as such without a retinue; he must, after all, be lord over someone. In Old English heroic poetry, we hear almost nothing about any members of the tribe who are not retainers; slaves, women (with the exception of an occasional queen or princess), children, and other unimportant members of the society, are ignored by the heroic poet. The subject matter of Germanic heroic poetry is martial combat and so, for the purposes of the heroic poet, a tribe consists almost exclusively of retainers who live for such combat. Predictably,

---

[23] *Maxims II*, 11-12.

the principal duty of the retainer is that of supporting his lord in battle:

illum (i.e., the lord) defendere, tueri, sua quoque fortia facta gloriæ eius adsignare praecipuum sacramentum est; principes pro victoria pugnant, comites pro principe.[24]

The *comitatus* is ever ready to fight for its lord, and its weapons are never far from its hands. When the Danes go to sleep with their weapons in readiness, the *Beowulf*-poet praises their zeal and fidelity to Hrothgar:

> Wæs þeaw hyra,
> þæt hie oft wæron   an wig gearwe,
> ge æt ham ge on herge,   ge gehwæþer þara
> efne swylce mæla,   swylce hira mandryhtne
> þearf gesælde;   wæs sio þeod tilu.   (1246–1250)

Before Beowulf himself became lord of the Geats, he was as nearly perfect a retainer as Hygelac could desire. As he recalls his youthful service before his last battle, Beowulf says that he repaid Hygelac's favors by always preceding him in battle and fighting so well that Hygelac never needed to seek elsewhere for fighting men to support him:

> Ic him þa maðmas,   þe he me sealde,
> geald æt guðe,   swa me gifeðe wæs,
> leohtan sweorde;   he me lond forgeaf,
> eard eðelwyn.   Næs him ænig þearf,
> þæt he to Gifðum   oððe to Gar-Denum
> oððe in Swiorice   secan þurfe
> wyrsan wigfrecan,   weorðe gecypan;
> symle ic him on feðan   beforan wolde,
> ana on orde....   (2490–2498)

This duty to serve one's lord in battle is liksewise apparent in *The Battle of Maldon*. Byrhtnoth tells the Viking messenger that he will defend the people and property of his lord, Æthelred, against the invaders:

> ...sege þinum leodum   miccle laþre spell,
> þæt her stynt unforcuð   eorl mid his werode,
> þe wile gealgean   eþel þysne,

[24] *Germania*, ch. 14.

> Æþelredes eard,   ealdres mines,
> folc and foldan.   (50–54)

Just as the lord vows to give gifts and to protect his people, so do his retainers publicly swear to fight for him should the need arise. When Beowulf begins his battle with the dragon, Wiglaf recalls that he and the other retainers have promised (*geheton* – 2634) in the hall to support their lord; Wiglaf fulfills his vow and is praised in gnomic fashion by the poet for conducting himself properly – *swylc sceolde secg wesan, / þegn æt ðearfe!* (2708–2709). Hrothgar tells the newly-arrived Beowulf that Danish retainers swore (*gebeotedon* – 480) to meet Grendel in combat and died doing so. As a result of Grendel's strife, he now has fewer loyal men (*holdra þy læs* – 487) to serve him. In like manner Eadric fulfills his vow to defend his lord, Byrhtnoth: . . . *beot he gelæste / þa he ætforan his frean   feohtan sceolde* (*Maldon*, 15-16).

To fail one's lord in battle through cowardice, to violate one's oath of service, results in the permanent disgrace of the offending retainer. Since the entire heroic social system is founded upon loyalty and mutual dependence, disloyalty in so basic a social activity as battle would, if permitted to go uncensored, ultimately subvert the entire *comitatus* structure, and consequently disloyalty in a retainer is never tolerated. Tacitus comments upon the fate of warriors who show cowardice in battle:

scutum reliquisse praecipuum flagitium, nec aut sacris adesse aut concilium inire ignominioso fas; multique superstites bellorum infamiam laqueo finierunt.[25]

Wiglaf readily enters the fight against the dragon and helps Beowulf to slay that beast, after which he bitterly rebukes the rest of Beowulf's troop for failing to join him:

> þæt, la, mæg secgan   se ðe wyle soð specan,
> þæt se mondryhten,   se eow ða maðmas geaf,
> eoredgeatwe,   þe ge þær on standað –
> þonne he on ealubence   oft gesealde
> healsittendum   helm ond byrnan,

> þeoden his þegnum,   swylce he þrydlicost
> ower feor oððe neah   findan meahte –
> þæt he genunga   guðgewædu
> wraðe forwurpe,   ða hyne wig beget.
> ....   Wergendra to lyt
> þrong ymbe þeoden,   þa hyne sio þrag
>   becwom (2864–2883)

The greatest honor which a lord may bestow upon one of his retainers is to choose him to serve in the vanguard of his army, for this means that the lord considers that retainer to be one of the fiercest, most valiant, loyal and steadfast warriors in the entire *comitatus*. A warrior must be tried in battle and proven worthy in order to merit a place at the front of the host, where the lord himself fights:

gradus quin etiam ipse comitatus habet, iudicio eius quem sectantur; magnaque et comitum aemulatio, quibus primus apud principem suum locus . . . . [26]

In the speech quoted above, Wiglaf observes that the troop which accompanied Beowulf to meet the dragon is composed of those warriors who were 'the mightiest that he could find, far or near', and this makes their cowardice all the more disgraceful. When preparing for his trip to Denmark, Beowulf chose warriors for his *handscole* whom he *cenoste / findan mihte* (206-207), among the Geats, and in *The Battle of Maldon* Byrhtnoth fights at the front of his army, where his men are most loyal:

> þa he hæfde þæt folc   fægere getrymmed,
> he lihte þa mid leodon   þær him leofost wæs,
> þær he his heorðwerod   holdost wiste.   (22–24)

In return for fidelity and service to his lord, the retainer receives, in addition to a share of the plunder which the tribe has won in battle, rich gifts from his lord. Thus, Hrothgar is said to 'repay the battle-rush', *heaþorǣsas geald* (1047), by giving magnificent gifts to Beowulf. A lord may also give such gifts before the retainer actually earns them, in expectation of future service and continuing loyalty. Beowulf says that he 'repaid at war', *geald æt guðe* (2491), the gifts given him by Hygelac, and a bit of gnomic

[26] *Germania*, ch. 13.

wisdom early in *Beowulf* (20-25) advises a young prince to give gifts so that when war comes his retainers will remain loyal. Wiglaf's conduct when he sees Beowulf in distress illustrates the wisdom of this precept; he remembers the gifts which his lord has given him, and rushes to his defense:

> ... geseah his mondryhten
> under heregriman   hat þrowian.
> Gemunde ða ða are,   þe he him ær forgeaf,
> wicstede weligne   Wægmundinga,
> folcrihta gehwylc,   swa his fæder ahte;
> ne mihte ða forhabban,   hond rond gefeng,
> geolwe lind,   gomel swyrd geteah .... (2604–2610)

Retainers not only receive gifts, they sometimes give them as well:

mos est civitatibus ultro ac viritim conferre principibus vel armentorum vel frugum, quod pro honore acceptum etiam necessitatibus subvenit. gaudent praecipue finitimarum gentium donis, quae non modo a singulis, sed et publice mittuntur, electi equi, magna arma, phalerae torquesque; iam et pecuniam accipere docuimus.[27]

That retainers give gifts to their lords which are comparable to those gifts which they receive suggests that the exchange of treasures is not a system of payment for mercenary soldiers, but rather one of the ways in which lords and retainers demonstrate their affection and loyalty to one another. The gifts which a retainer gives to his lord are *luftacen;* they are *pro honore acceptum* by the lord. Thus, when Beowulf returns to his own tribe, he gives the gifts which he has acquired from Hrothgar to Hygelac, and the poet remarks that such gestures are proper for a retainer who is loyal (*hold*) to his lord:

> Hyrde ic þæt þæm frætwum   feower mearas
> lungre, gelice   last weardode,
> æppelfealuwe;   he him est geteah
> meara ond maðma. – Swa sceal mæg don,
> nealles inwitnet   oðrum bregdon
> dyrnum cræfte,   deað renian
> hondgesteallan.   Hygelace wæs
> niða heardum   nefa swyðe hold,
> ond gehwæðer oðrum   hroþra gemyndig. (2163–2171)

Hygelac responds to Beowulf's open-handed loyalty by bestowing Hrethel's sword and a large estate upon his retainer (2190-2199). One warrior may exchange gifts with another warrior, or he may give the other warrior a gift outright if he wishes to do so. Beowulf, before diving after Grendel's mother with Unferth's sword, Hrunting, requests that Hrothgar give his sword to Unferth if he should fail to return (1488-1490). Beowulf is obligated to either return or replace the valuable weapon which Unferth has generously lent him. So long as the exchange is equal, neither warrior will remain in the debt of the other. When he is ready to leave Denmark Beowulf gives the shore-guard another valuable sword (1900-1903). The guard has done him a service by watching his ship, and Beowulf scrupulously discharges this debt. No lord-retainer relationship is implied in either of these instances of gift-giving; the gifts are given to one warrior by another as tokens of gratitude and mutual obligation.

Wisdom is a quality desirable in retainers as well as lords. Just as wisdom in a lord seems to be related to his proper lordly conduct, so a retainer's wisdom seems to be associated with proper conduct in his primary sphere of activity, in the defense and succor which he gives his lord in battle. Beowulf's successful battle against Grendel earns him the epithet 'wise and courageous':

> Hæfde þa gefælsod   se þe ær feorran com,
> snotor ond swyðferhð,   sele Hroðgares,
> genered wið niðe.   (825–827)

When Hrothgar laments the death of Æschere, he remembers the dead man as a wise councillor who supported his lord in battle (1323-1329). The shore-guard also raises the subject of a warrior's good judgment in matters of martial importance:

>   Æghwæþres sceal
> scearp scyldwiga   gescad witan,
> worda ond worca,   se þe wel þenecð.
> Ic þæt gehyre,   þæt þis is hold weorod
> frean Scyldinga.   (287–291)

Good judgment (*gescad*) here consists of the warrior's being able to distinguish the potential enemies of one's lord from those heroes who sincerely intend to offer loyal service to him. The wise warrior is courageous and loyal to his lord, and performs his functions and duties well. It is apparently possible for the retainer of one lord to give a sort of secondary allegiance to another lord. This secondary allegiance binds the warrior to perform the same services and to maintain the same steadfast loyalty to his new lord as he does for his original lord, so long as this new allegiance does not interfere with the older one. In Denmark, Beowulf occupies the position of a retainer in Hrothgar's *comitatus*, performing services for, and receiving benefits from the Danish lord while, at the same time, he remains Hygelac's *mæg and magoðegn* (408). When Beowulf takes leave of Hrothgar, he tells the Dane that he will gladly offer his services in the future should they be needed, and will bring a thousand thanes to protect Hrothgar from his enemies. It is clear from Beowulf's very next statement, however, that Hygelac's consent is necessary to any such undertaking:

> Wæron her tela,
> willum bewenede;   þu us wel dohtest.
> Gif ic þonne on eorþan   owihte mæg
> þinre modlufan   maran tilian,
> gumena dryhten,   ðonne ic gyt dyde,
> guðgeweorca,   ic beo gearo sona.
> Gif ic þæt gefricge   ofer floda begang,
> þæt þec ymbstittend   egesan þywað,
> swa þec hetende   hwilum dydon,
> ic ðe þusenda   þegna bringe,
> hæleþa to helpe.   Ic on Higelace wat,
> Geata dryhten,   þeah ðe he geong sy,
> folces hyrde,   þæt he mec fremman wile
> wordum ond weorcum,   þæt ic þe wel herige
> ond þe to geoce   garholt bere,
> mægenes fultum,   þær ðe bið manna þearf.
>   (1820–1835)

Beowulf's first loyalty is to Hygelac, and so any commitment which he makes to Hrothgar is contingent upon the consent of the lord of the Geats. No such dual loyalty can exist, however, where there is a conflict between the lords to whom one owes allegiance. In such cases one's loyalty always belongs to his ear-

lier, principal lord. Thus Hengest's loyalty is first and foremost
to Hnæf, even though he has sworn oaths to Hnæf's slayer, Finn
(1063 ff), and likewise the young Heathobard warrior remains
loyal to his dead father, in spite of the alliance which his tribe
has made with the Danes (2029 ff).

The ideal society in Old English heroic poetry consists of an
ideal lord and retainers, as we have described them above, living
in close daily contact with one another and conducting themselves
as is proper to their respective positions within the *comitatus*. The
Danish court at Heorot, the most fully-drawn heroic social unit
in Old English verse, is presented as an ideal society whose well-
being and tranquility is broken only by the external forces which
Beowulf must subdue. Wealtheow, in the act of giving gifts and
praising the deeds of Beowulf, describes this perfect social order
over which Hrothgar presides:

> Her is æghwylc eorl   oþrum getrywe,
> modes milde,   mandrihtne hol[d],
> þegnas syndon geþwære,   þeod ealgearo,
> druncne dryhtguman   doð swa ic bidde.   (1228–1231)

Hrothgar has led his followers to military pre-eminence, and has
built the greatest of buildings, Heorot, in which at magnificent
feasts he gives generous gifts to his loyal retainers (64-85). For
fifty years no enemy dared to wage war against so mighty a tribe
(1769-1773). Beowulf, describing the communal life at Heorot
even during the dark days of Grendel's terror, says that he has
never seen such magnificence:

> Weorod wæs on wynne;   ne seah ic widan feorh
> under heofones hwealf   healsittendra
> medudream maran.   (2014–2016)

In descriptions of ideal societies like the one at Heorot, heavy
stress is placed upon unity and harmony; lords are powerful, but
always kind and generous, retainers fierce in battle, but always
loyal. The necessity of loyalty and courage among the members
of a prosperous *comitatus* receives additional emphasis from a
negative point of view by the predictions of continual warfare
and social disorder which are expected to follow the defection of

Beowulf's retainers and subsequent death of their lord. Wiglaf's words sum up the situation admirably:

> Nu sceal sincþego   ond swyrdgifu,
> eall eðelwyn   eowrum cynne,
> lufen alicgean;   londrihtes mot
> þære mægburge   monna æghwylc
> idel hweorfan,   syððan æðelingas
> feorran gefricgean   fleam eowerne
> domleasan dæd.   (2884–2890)

The Germanic society in which all of the duties and standards of conduct appropriate to its members are observed, which, in short, is an ideally ordered society, is often described as living 'by custom', 'according to the old ways'. It is significant of the kind of court which Beowulf finds at Heorot that Wulfgar, the warrior who first receives him there, 'knew the custom of the retainers' – *cuþe he duguðe þeaw* (359). Beowulf describes Hrothgar's generosity and general demeanor as living 'by custom' – *Swa se ðeodkyning þeawum lyfde* (2144). When Hrothgar proposes to Beowulf that a period of amity will ensue between Geats and Danes, he knows that any gifts which he sends to the Geats will be well received and that the Geats will reciprocate, because they live according to traditional Germanic customs just as the Danes do:

> Ic þa leode wat
> ge wið feond ge wið freond   fæste geworhte,
> æghwæs untæle   ealde wisan.   (1863–1865)

In *Widsith,* we are told that a lord who desires a prosperous reign should conduct himself 'according to custom':

> Sceal þeodna gehwylc   þeawum lifgan,
> eorl æfter oþrum   eðel rædan,
> se þe his þeodenstol   geþeon wile.   (11–13).

The well-being of an ideal heroic society, a society which lives 'by custom', is reflected in the abundance of 'hall-joys' of which the *comitatus* partakes. The words *dream* and *wynn,* appearing alone or in compounds with words which refer to the great hall and the activities which take place there, usually mean in a general sense the pleasures of which happy warriors are able to partake.[28] Eating and drinking (though, it seems, primarily drinking), the songs of the *scop,* the giving and receiving of gifts, and the swearing of oaths are the major activities with which in times of peace, Germanic warriors fill their waking hours. The greater the tribe, the more abundant these pleasures are. The banquets at Heorot seem lavish affairs indeed (489 ff, 1008 ff) and, as we have seen, Beowulf is not at all reticent in describing their magnificence to Hygelac. It is not surprising that Grendel, a solitary creature and a hater of men, should detest the sounds of communal joy which he hears coming from Heorot (86-90).

Grendel's repeated attacks severely undermine the social order of the Danes by inducing the retainers to forsake the joys of the hall and avoid the communal center of heroic life:

> þa wæs eaðfynde þe him elles hwær
> gerumlicor ræste [sohte],
> bed æfter burum, ða him gebeacnod wæs,
> gesægd soðlice sweotolan tacne
> healðegnes hete; heold hyne syðþan
> fyr ond fæstor se þæm feonde ætwand.
>
> (138–143)

When the great hall ceases to be a place of joy for the lord and his retainers, the dissolution of the society becomes imminent, for the ritual of gift giving and the vows of loyalty and service may no longer be properly performed.

Loyalty is the bond which ties the members of the heroic *comitatus* together in a harmonious union. Retainers loyally serve their lord, and the lord loyally cares for his retainers. As a concept, an abstract ideal, loyalty is the foundation upon which the other concepts which we shall examine are built; without the concept of loyalty, these other concepts are almost meaningless. In a passage cited earlier, Beowulf delivers to Hygelac the gifts which he has received from Hrothgar, and the poet's comment, along with the action of mutual giving and receiving, emphasizes the reciprocal quality of the loyalty between lord and retainer. 'His nephew, brave in battle, was exceedingly loyal to Hygelac,

[28] E.g., *gleo-dream, medu-dream, sele-dream, symbel-wyn, eðel-wyn.*

and each was mindful of the comfort of the other' (2169-2171). The closeness of the relationship between lord and retainer is reflected in the terms of endearment which appear regularly in the formulas. Retainers are *swæse gesiþas,* their lords *leof land fruma, leofne þeoden, leof leod-cyning.* Service to a lord, whether actually performed or merely promised, is *prima facie* proof of a warrior's loyalty. Thus, having heard from Beowulf that the Geats have come to offer aid to Hrothgar, the shore-guard concludes that 'this is a troop loyal (*hold*) to the Scylding lord' (290-291). By the same token, the mere acceptance of the proffered services of a warrior entails the loyalty of the lord to that warrior. Hrothgar, upon learning of Beowulf's arrival, concludes that he has come seeking a 'loyal friend' (*holdne wine* – 376), and promises to give him gifts for his courage – *Ic þæm godan sceal / for his modþræce madmas beodan* (384-385) – well in advance of any actual service which he might perform.

The bond of loyalty, even though it is a personal bond formed by the lord and each of his retainers on an individual, man-to-man basis, may nevertheless be inherited. Retainers usually remain loyal to the heirs of their lords, as do lords, presumably (though there is no evidence in the poetry to verify this assumption), to the sons of their retainers. Though such hereditary loyalty does not seem to be imperative, retainers often remain loyal to their dead lord's sons out of a sense of responsibility and gratitude for the benefits which they received from the lord while he lived. Thus Wealtheow assumes that Hrothulf will repay Hrothgar's kindness to him by maintaining his loyalty to her sons (1180-1187). Upon Hygelac's death, Beowulf refuses the rule of the Geats which is offered by Hygd, and serves as regent to Heardred until Hygelac's son grows old enough to rule by himself:

> No ðy ær feasceafte   findan meahton
> æt ðam æðelinge   ænige ðinga,
> þæt he Heardrede   hlaford wære,
> oððe þone cynedom   ciosan wolde;
> hwæðre he hine on folce   freondlarum heold,
> estum mid are,   oð ðæt he yldra wearð,
> Weder-Geatum weold.   (2373–2379)

A few lines later we learn that Beowulf's devotion to Hygelac arises, in part, from the kindness which Hrethel showed to Beowulf when he was a child (2428-2434). Beowulf had been loyal to three generations of Geatish lords before he himself became lord of that tribe.

From the foregoing, it should be apparent that one cannot speak of the functions of a lord, in the society portrayed in Old English heroic poetry, without also speaking of the functions of the retainers, and vice versa. Lord and retainer share the same goal in life, the acquisition of personal glory, and pursue this goal by much the same means. Both lord and retainer are fundamental parts of a unified, harmonious social organism in which service given and loyalty received, whether by lord or thane, are functions of one another, and therefore are inseparable in actual practice. The relationship of a lord and his retainer, or of kinsmen or friends of equal rank, depends upon an ideal conception of loyalty which forms the backbone of the society; it is reciprocal in operation and absolutely inflexible in its demands. The lord must be devoted to his retainers, and the retainers to their lord, if the heroic society is to function at all. In cases of warriors of equal rank, the duties and benefits which each owes the other are identical in form, and consist primarily in mutual protection and the exchanging of gifts. In cases of lord and thane, the duties and benefits which each owes the other are complementary. The lord is the embodiment of the entire tribe, and it is he who holds it together as a unit. He leads his retainers in battle, and receives both the credit for victory, and the titular possession of any wealth acquired thereby. Retainers support and defend their lord, and in return receive gifts from him in proportion to the quality of their service. The lord is the devoted and loving protector of his people; his people in return love and honor him. In Old English heroic poetry, no hero exists in isolation; he is part of a society and, as such, is either a lord or a retainer or both. If a warrior is neither lord nor retainer, then he is by definition an exile, a special category of heroic life with which we must deal separately.

III

VENGEANCE:
THE DEMONSTRATION OF LOYALTY IN ACTION

The concept of heroic vengeance is essentially that aspect of the concept of loyalty which manifests itself in action in the principal activity of heroic life, physical combat. The zeal with which the heroes of Germanic heroic literature perform the duties of vengeance which are placed upon them reflects their devotion to those warriors whom they avenge. Acts of vengeance emphasize the intensity and seriousness of the heroic vows of loyalty, loyalty which survives even the death of the party to whom it has been sworn. Beowulf states the heroic code of vengeance quite succinctly in his words to Hrothgar upon learning of the murder of Æschere by Grendel's mother:

> Ne sorga, snotor guma!   Selre bið æghwæm,
> þæt he his freond wrece,   þonne he fela murne.
> (1384–1385)

In this particular instance, Beowulf is speaking of a dead retainer, but his words would be no less significant were he speaking of a lord who had been slain. The principle does not vary; all offenses must be avenged by those warriors who have sworn their loyalty to the offended party.

The violent death of a warrior is, in Old English heroic poetry, the primary motive for most campaigns of vengeance, but homicide is only the most serious of what must have been a number of offenses serious enough to call for prompt retaliation. In general, we must assume that any insult or injury to a man's honor or his person demands repayment in kind by the offended party and by those closest to him. When, for example, Unferth

casts aspersions upon Beowulf's physical prowess, in a speech
calculated to reduce the stature of the newcomer in the eyes of
the Danish *comitatus* (... *forþon þe he ne uþe,   þæt ænig
oðer man / æfre mærða þon ma   middangeardes / gehede
under heofenum   þonne he sylfa*...), Beowulf not only re-
futes the charges against him, but repays Unferth in kind by
charging the *þyle* with cowardice and fratricide (499-606). The
dragon, though he is scarcely a warrior, reacts precisely as a
human warrior would and should to the most heinous offense
which anyone can commit against a dragon – the theft of part
of his treasure-hoard:

> wæs ðe gebolgen   beorges hyrde,
> wolde se laða   lige forgyldan
> drincfæt dyre.   (2304–2306)

While we must condemn the dragon for the ferocity and indis-
criminate nature of the vengeance which he takes upon the Geats,
we cannot, in the light of the heroic code of vengeance, deny the
justice of his desire to repay the culprit for the theft of his 'dear
cup'.

Whether the principals be men or monsters or both, it is
imperative that the offended party, unless he wishes to lose
stature in the eyes of his peers, repay the offender for his trespass.
The use of the word 'repay' in connection with acts of vengeance
reflects, in its positive sense (*gyldan*), the reciprocal quality of
the loyalty of lord and thane; the avenger 'repays' the offended
lord or thane for his generosity or service. In its negative sense
(*forgyldan*) the word reflects the 'eye for an eye' morality of
Germanic heroic life; the avenger 'repays' the offender in kind.

The origins of this heroic code of vengeance are certainly
rooted in pre-Christian Germanic tradition. Tacitus mentions that
it is imperative for a Germanic warrior to take up his family's
feuds, and that the family insists upon satisfaction (*satisfactionem*)
for offenses against its members. In noting that even homicide
may be atoned for by the payment of a fixed number of cattle,
Tacitus implies by his silence on the subject the alternative
method of gaining 'satisfaction', that of repaying blood with

blood.[1] Christian doctrine contains no possible justification for a code of vengeance like the one embodied in the previously quoted words of Beowulf. The 'eye for an eye' morality of much of the Old Testament had, long before the composition of Christian Old English poetry, given way to the 'vengeance is mine' 'turn the other cheek' doctrines of the Gospels, in theory if not in fact. Even if *Beowulf* is a thoroughly Christian poem, as some critics have argued, the code of vengeance by which all of the characters in the poem live cannot be accounted for by Christian sources, since, as we shall see, vengeance is given positive value throughout the poem.

The duty of a retainer to avenge his lord, should the lord be slain in battle, is an essential stipulation of the heroic oath of loyalty. Retainers vow to protect their lord, to support him in battle, and to avenge his death. The importance of the oath in Germanic heroic society was mentioned earlier, but bears repeated emphasis. An examination of the Unferth episode in *Beowulf* (499-606) reveals the pervasive quality of the notion that one must fulfill all of his vows, no matter what they may be. Unferth begins his challenge of Beowulf by remarking that the contest with Breca was the result of 'pride' and 'foolish boasting':

> ... git for wlence   wada cunnedon
> ond for dolgilpe   on deop wæter
> aldrum neþdon.   (508–510)

He further claims that Breca fulfilled his boast by defeating Beowulf in the contest. *Beot eal wið þe / sunu Beanstanes soðe gelæste* (523-524). If Breca succeeded then, by the nature of the boast, Beowulf must have failed to fulfill his vow to win the contest. Beowulf tacitly admits the justice of Unferth's first assertion by excusing the whole affair as the contest of two rash young boys:

> Wit þæt gecwædon   cnihtwesende
> ond gebeotedon – wæron begen þa git
> on geogoðfeore – þæt wit on garsecg ut
> aldrum neðdon,   ond þæt geæfndon swa.   (535–538)

---

[1] *Germania*, ch. 21.

In spite of this admission, Beowulf proceeds to recount the entire contest in order to prove that he did indeed fulfill his vow, foolish though it was, by defeating Breca. The fulfillment of a vow, no matter what it may be, is more important than its content, and Beowulf would rather bear the onus of having sworn a rash vow than bear the dishonor of having failed to accomplish it. All oaths are important in heroic society, but most important and most binding is the oath of loyalty to one's lord. This oath takes precedence over any oath which may conflict with it. Thus, though Hengest must out of necessity swear to keep peace with Finn and his Frisians, he and his Danes ultimately attack the Frisians and so avenge their dead lord, Hnæf (1095 ff).

The oath of loyalty, together with its implications of promised vengeance, occurs under a variety of circumstances in Old English heroic poetry. The general oath, unconnected with any specific act of vengeance, is ususally sworn in the great hall during the banquets with which the *comitatus* fills its days in times of peace. Wiglaf, at the beginning of his first speech, refers to these general vows of loyalty:

> Ic ðæt mæl geman,   þær we medu þegun,
> þonne we geheton   ussum hlaforde
> in biorsele,   ðe us ðas beagas geaf,
> þæt we him ða guðgetawa   gyldan woldon,
> gif him þyslicu   þearf gelumpe,
> helmas ond heard sweord.   (2633–2638)

Although Wiglaf appears here to be referring to a specific banquet (*ðæt mæl*), the situation he describes is typical, and the promises of aid clearly were not for a particular battle, but rather for any future battle in which the lord stood in 'such need' as he now does.

A retainer may also swear, in the hall or elsewhere, to perform a specific deed of vengeance. Hrothgar's retainers had sworn in the hall to await the visits of Grendel:

> Ful oft gebeotedon   beore druncne
> ofer ealowæge   oretmecgas,
> þæt hie in beorsele   bidan woldon
> Grendles guþe   mid gryrum ecga.   (480–483)

Indeed, many Danish warriors died attempting to avenge their dead comrades. Beowulf vows specifically before the Danish *comitatus* to meet Grendel (601-606) and, later, Grendel's mother (1386-1389). A retainer may swear to perform a specific deed at the scene of a battle which is about to begin, as does Beowulf just prior to calling the dragon forth from his barrow (2524-2537) and, finally, the retainer may, and if he is truly loyal usually does, swear in the heat of battle to avenge his fallen lord or comrades, almost as soon as he is aware of their deaths. In *Maldon,* all of Byrhtnoth's loyal followers swear to avenge him; Leofsunu's oath is typical:

> Is þæt gehate,   þæt ic heonon nelle
> fleon fotes trym,   ac wille furðor gan,
> wrecan on gewinne   minne winedryhten.
> Ne þurfon me embe Sturmere   stedefæste hælæð
> wordum ætwitan,   nu min wine gecranc,
> þæt ic hlafordleas   ham siðie,
> wende fram wige,   ac me sceal wæpen niman,
> ord and iren.   (246–253)

The substance of these words are echoed in the poet's report, a few lines later, of the words and deeds of Eadweard the Long who, after vowing vengeance, *feaht, / oðþæt he his sincgyfan on þam sæmannum / wurðlice wrec,   ær he on wæle læge* (273-279).

The oaths of vengeance which we find scattered through *Beowulf* and *The Battle of Maldon* share certain common elements which, we may assume, are typical of such oaths.[2] Indeed, the oath of vengeance appears to be a theme, in Lord's sense of the term, in Germanic heroic poetry. Often the offense which has prompted the intended retaliation is specifically mentioned. The hero may boast of his own prowess, which he has proved by his earlier deeds, and may also add that he will not now act in a manner which could bring the reproach of other warriors down upon him. In almost every instance, the avenger specifically states what act he intends to perform, since such a statement is after

---

[2]   See e.g., *Beowulf,* 405-455, 601-606, 677-687, 1384-1396, 1474-1491, 2510-2537; *Maldon,* 211-224, 244-253, 255-259, 273-279, 309-319.

all the core of his vow. The avenger includes in his vow any and all special stipulations connected with his intended deed, such as forswearing or justifying the use of weapons, refusing aid, or rejecting the possibility of even a foot-step's retreat. The possibility of death is always prominent in the mind of a hero as he goes into battle, and so every oath includes either a reference to this eventuality, or to the battle's outcome being in the hands of God or *wyrd*. In some cases, the hero may make some last requests of those who will survive him should he fail.

I have been speaking of acts of vengeance which are brought about primarily by offenses against various lords, but the code, the oaths and the procedures are essentially the same when a warrior avenges an offense to another warrior or to a kinsman. Loyalty and vengeance go hand-in-hand in Old English poetry, and a warrior's loyalty to, for example, a kinsman, includes a duty to avenge any wrong done to him. Even Grendel's mother reveals her familial devotion in her desire to avenge her son. Although she is more monster than mother, she nevertheless follows the dictates of the human code of vengeance after her kinsman has been mortally wounded by Beowulf:

>   þæt gesyne wearþ,
> widcuþ werum,   þætte wrecend þa gyt
> lifde æfter laþum,   lange þrage,
> æfter guðceare;   Grendles modor,
> ides aglæcwif   yrmþe gemunde,
> . . . .
> . . . .
> . . . .
> . . . . his modor þa gyt
> gifre ond galgmod   gegan wolde
> sorhfulne sið,   sunu deoð wrecan.   (1255–1278)

Just as the death of a kinsman demands retaliation by his surviving family, so the death of a retainer demands vengeance of his lord and his friends. Beowulf's formulation of the code of vengeance, that it is better to avenge one's friend than to mourn much (1384-1385), comes as a prelude to an oath in which he swears to avenge the death of Hrothgar's retainer, Æschere. It is even possible, though no doubt unusual, for a warrior to avenge his own death. Beowulf, as Wiglaf says, avenged himself before he died, by slaying the dragon:

> Nealles folccyning fyrdgesteallum
> gylpan þorfte; hwæðre him God uðe,
> sigora Waldend, þæt he hyne sylfne gewræc
> ana mid ecge, þa him wæs elnes þearf. (2873–2876)

So long as the offender is slain, the vengeance demanded for Beowulf's death has been accomplished.

We have observed in the previous chapter that, because of the threat of reprisal which they pose, a mighty lord and his valiant retinue are, by their very existence, a deterrent to the strife which contentious neighbors might raise against their tribe. Thus, Beowulf tells Unferth that Grendel would not have dared to wreak such havoc in Heorot had he not scorned the threat of vengeance posed by Hrothgar's retainers (590-601) and, after his last battle, he says that during his long reign no neighboring lord dared raise strife with the Geats (2732-2736). The threat of vengeance deters acts of aggression in heroic society, precisely because every offense requires that the offended party, his followers, his kinsmen or his lord repay the offense in kind. It is worth noticing that, in all of the Old English heroic poetry extant, the heroes fight only in retaliation to acts of overt aggression and therefore are, in every instance, avengers. Each of Beowulf's three great battles is fought to gain vengeance for crimes which the monsters have perpetrated against the Geat or his allies or friends. Grendel killed numerous retainers of Hrothgar, to whom Beowulf has temporarily attached himself, and immediately before coming to grips with the Geat, he kills and eats one of Beowulf's own retainers, thus giving Beowulf an added justification for slaying him. Likewise, Grendel's mother deserves death not only because she is a monster, but also because she has carried off and decapitated one of Hrothgar's thanes. Finally, although the poet mentions no specific deaths, the dragons' fiery rampage must have been as deadly as it was destructive, and the destruction of his own home (2325-2326) is by itself, reason enough for Beowulf to seek revenge.

While it is no doubt true that, in Anglo-Saxon society, relatively minor offenses like the theft of one's cattle or one's daughter often erupted into bloody feuds, in the heroic poetry acts of vengeance are confined almost exclusively to retaliation for violent deaths. To be heroic at all, heroic poetry cannot concern itself with trivial or mundane events. Vengeance in heroic poetry must have a sufficient motive and, of the transgressions important enough to demand retaliation, the death of one's lord is the most common. The latter portion of Wiglaf's first speech reveals his (and the poet's) preoccupation with his duty to avenge his lord, and suggests the importance attached to this duty:

> God wat on mec,
> þæt me is micle leofre,   þæt minne lichaman
> mid minne goldgyfan   gled fæðmie.
> Ne þynceð me gerysne,   þæt we rondas beren
> eft to earde,   nemne we æror mægen
> fane gefyllan,   feorh ealgian
> Wedra ðeodnes.   Ic wat geare,
> þæt næron ealdgewyrht,   þæt he ana scyle
> Geata duguðe   gnorn þrowian,
> gesigan æt sæcce;   urum sceal sweord ond helm,
> byrne and beaduscrud   bam gemæne.   (2650–2660)

The same sense of duty to one's fallen lord and desire for vengeance appears in the last great Old English heroic poem, *The Battle of Maldon,* in the speech of Ælfwine (212-224). Both Wiglaf and Ælfwine place vengeance above life itself; it is unworthy, and so cause for reproach and dishonor, that a warrior should fail to carry out his oath of vengeance. As we have seen, it is unusual for a warrior who is worthy of respect not to avenge the death of a loyal friend or kinsman, and the *Beowulf*-poet takes special note of such a situation when he tells us that Onela forgave Weohstan *no ymbe ða fæhðe spræc, / þeah ðe he his broðor bearn abredwade* (2618-2619).

Very often in the course of making an oath of vengeance, an Old English hero swears that he will 'win glory or die in the attempt'. The possibility of losing his life in battle is never far from a hero's consciousness, but the alternatives of glory or death are the only honorable ones open to him. Beowulf, before

each of his three great battles, swears to fight his adversary to
the death:

<pre>
                        ... ic mid grape sceal
fon wið feonde   ond ymb feorh sacan,
lað wið laþum;   ðær gelyfan sceal
Dryhtnes dome   se þe hine deað nimeð.   (438–441)

                        .... ic me mid Hruntinge
dom gewyrce,   oþðe me deað nimeð!   (1490–1491)

                        Ic mid elne sceall
gold gegangan,   oððe guð nimeð,
feorhbealu frence,   frean eowerne!   (2535–2537)
</pre>

In his last battle, war does take Beowulf, even though he wins
the gold as he had promised. Indeed, warriors choose death rather
than lives of reproach for having failed to carry out acts of
vengeance which they are duty-bound to perform. In *Maldon,*
after Byrhtnoth is killed and the English forces are consequently
thrown into confusion, those retainers who flee are excoriated by
the poet and by the loyal retainers who remain to avenge their
lord in battle:

<pre>
þa ðær wendon forð   wlance þegenas,
unearge men   efston georne;
hi woldon þa ealle   oðer twega,
lif forlætan   oððe leofne gewrecan.   (205–208)
</pre>

The loyal retainers scorn flight and, regardless of their personal
safety, go forth to slay as many of the enemy as they can. Each
warrior fights furiously *þa hwile ðe he wæpna wealdan moste*
(272) and, one by one, the English heroes are slain. Byrhtwold's
justly famous speech, near the end of the poem, epitomizes the
single-minded spirit of all the heroes of Old English poetry who
have acts of vengeance which they are obligated to perform:

<pre>
"Hige sceal þe heardra,   heorte þe cenre,
mod sceal þe mare,   þe ure mægen lytlað.
Her lyð ure ealdor   eall forheawen,
god on greote.   A mæg gnornian
se ðe nu fram þis wigplegan   wendan þenceð.
Ic eom frod feores;   fram ic ne wille,
</pre>

> ac ic me be healfe   minum hlaforde,
> be swa leofan men,   licgan þence."   (312–319)

Even if a warrior fails to accomplish the act of vengeance which he has set out to perform, he earns the praise of his fellows and dies a worthy hero so long as he is killed in the attempt. Hrothgar's retainers vowed to confront Grendel in Heorot at night, died attempting to avenge the murders which that monster committed, and remain a *deorre duguðe* in the memory of their lord (480-487). Likewise Hæthcyn, the second of Beowulf's beloved lords, is killed while trying to avenge the strife begun by the Swedes after the death of his father, Hrethel (2472-2483). In *Maldon,* the youths Ælfnoth and Wulfmær are the first of the English to surrender their lives as they fight alongside of the body of their newly-slain lord (181-184), and Offa is praised for dying as a thane should (*ðegenlice*) near his lord (288-294). Victory is always worthy of praise in Old English heroic poetry, but honorable defeat in battle can be equally admirable.

Imperative though it is that vengeance be sought for all offenses, an honorable Germanic warrior nevertheless takes scrupulous care that he should have no unfair advantage over his adversary. In the heroic world, a victory obtained through superiority in number, armament or other circumstances of the battle itself is considered unworthy of warriors whose fame depends upon their individual prowess. Thus, Beowulf, knowing that Grendel scorns the use of weapons, himself forswears the use of sword and shield, and places his trust in the might of his handgrip. To use weapons against an unarmed adversary would cost him self-esteem, if not the esteem of his peers, even if he should successfully avenge the Danes. His own words make his concern for his reputation clear:

> "No ic me an herewæsmun   hnagran talige
> guþgeweorca,   þonne Grendel hine;
> forþan ic hine sweorde   swebban nelle,
> aldre beneotan,   þeah ic eal mæge . . . .".   (677–680)

When Beowulf decides to use sword and shield in his battle with the dragon, he carefully justifies himself by pointing out that the dragon, too, is 'armed' – with his fiery breath:

Nolde ic sweord beran,
wæpen to wyrme,   gif ic wiste hu
wið ðam aglæcean   elles meahte
gylpe wiðgripan,   swa ic gio wið Grendle dyde;
ac ic ðær heaðufyres   hates wene,
[o]reðes ond attres;   forðon ic me on hafu
bord ond byrnan.   (2518–2524)

He does, however, specify that he intends to fight alone, without the aid of his retainers (2345-2354, 2529-2535) and, rejecting the opportunity to take his foe by surprise, he calls the dragon forth from the barrow to do battle with him (2550-2553). In all of his battles, Beowulf abides by the same heroic code which underlies Byrhtnoth's decision in *Maldon* to permit the invaders to cross unopposed over the causeway (89-99). An honorable hero will never take any undue advantage of an enemy in battle.[3]

A successful campaign of vengeance wins high praise for a warrior from his fellows and from the poet who is chronicling his deeds. In general, we may observe that the accomplishment of revenge is accompanied by joyous exultation on the part of those who are sympathetic to the avenger's cause and, more important, by a sense of justice and propriety which attaches itself to the abstract idea of vengeance itself. This attitude toward vengeance as a positive value is best seen in the main events in the life of the foremost hero in Old English poetry, Beowulf. Beowulf's victory over Grendel is, as might be expected, cause for rejoicing among the Danes. He has, after all, succeeded where they had failed:

---

[3] Although J. R. R. Tolkien claims that Byrhtnoth is guilty of the Christian sin of Pride in permitting passage over the causeway, Rosemary Woolf is more probably correct in stating that Beowulf's rejection of weapons and Byrhtnoth's decision "both spring from an unwillingness to profit from an advantage over the enemy gained by fortunate circumstances, not by personal achievements". Taylor Culbert echoes Miss Woolf when discussing Beowulf and Grendel, and Ralph W. V. Elliott shares her view concerning Byrhtnoth's decision. J. R. R. Tolkien, "The Homecoming of Beorhtnoth Beorthelm's Son", *E&S*, n.s. IV (1953), 1-18. Rosemary E. Woolf, "The Devil in Old English Poetry", *RES*, n.s. IV (1953), 1-12. Taylor Culbert, "The Narrative Functions of Beowulf's Swords", *JEGP* LIX (1960), 13-20. Ralph W. V. Elliott, "Bryhtnoth and Hildebrand: A Study in Heroic Technique", *CL* XIV (1962), 53-70.

> Hæfde þa gefælsod   se þe ær feorran com,
> snotor ond swyðferhð,   sele Hroðgares,
> genered wið niðe.   Nihtweorce gefeh,
> ellenmærþum.   Hæfde East-Denum
> Geatmecga leod   gilp gelæsted,
> swylce oncyþðe   ealle gebette,
> inwidsorge,   þe hie ær drugon
> ond for þreanydum   þolian scoldon,
> torn unlytel.   (825–833)

The primary emphasis in this passage is upon the relief from suffering which Beowulf has brought to the Danes, but when he completes his task by cutting off Grendel's head, the reiteration of Grendel's cowardly crimes brings the justice of Beowulf's deed, together with the idea of 'repayment', to the forefront:

>   næs seo ecg fracod
> hilderince,   ac he hraþe wolde
> Grendle forgyldan   guðræsa fela
> ðara þe he geworhte   to West-Denum
> oftor micle   ðonne on ænne sið,
> þonne he Hroðgares   heorðgeneatas
> sloh on sweofote,   slæpende fræt
> folces Denigea   fyftyne men,
> ond oðer swylc   ut offerede
> laðlicu lac.   He him þæs lean forgeald.... (1575–1584)

When he presents the magic sword-hilt to Hrothgar, Beowulf notes that vengeance for crimes as heinous as Grendel's is 'fitting':

>   Ic þæt hilt þanan
> feondum ætferede;   fyrendæda wræc,
> deaðcwealm Denigea,   swa hit gedefe wæs.
> (1668–1670)

When the poet, at the point in the narrative at which Beowulf is about to enter his last battle, wishes to re-emphasize the greatness and worth of his hero, he does so by telling us that Beowulf avenged the deaths of his two lords, Hygelac and Heardred (2354-2400). Finally, Beowulf's last act, the culmination of his long and distinguished career, is to give his life while avenging the deaths of his people. *Feond gefyldon – ferh ellen wræc* (2706).

Because of the importance attached to the expiation of offenses

against one's tribe or family in the heroic world, and because of
the dishonor which failure to gain satisfaction brings to the offended party, the duty of vengeance is often inherited by the heirs
of those upon whom the offense was originally perpetrated.
Furthermore, the vengeance which is required can be taken upon
the heirs of the offender. In the Heathobard digression in
Beowulf (2032-2069), the son of a Heathobard warrior killed in a
battle against the Danes is urged by an *eald æscwiga* to renew the
old war by taking vengeance upon the son of his father's slayer.
Such unavenged deaths create unrest among the Danes as well
as the Heathobards until new battles break out:

> ... ðæt sæl cymeð,
> þæt se fæmnan þegn   fore fæder dædum
> æfter billes bite   blodfag swefeð,
> ealdres scyldig ....   (2058-2061)

The Heathobard prince whose marriage was intended to end the
strife between the two tribes is slain in the renewed war, not
because of any offense which he has committed against the Danes,
but 'for his father's deeds'.

Because of the zeal with which warriors, tribes and families in
heroic society pursue vengeance for offenses against their honor,
the commission of a single violent act might well lead to a series
of reprisals and counterreprisals which would end only with the
extermination of one or the other of the participating groups.
Such situations would be intolerable insofar as they would keep
the society in a constant state of turmoil and would ultimately
destroy it, and so the system of *wergild,* literally 'payment for a
man', was devised at some early date in the history of Germanic
society. By Tacitus' time, payment of a *wergild* was accepted
instead of the life of the offending person:

> Suscipere tam inimicitias seu patris seu propinqui
> quam amicitias necesse est; nec inplacabiles durant;
> luitur enim etiam homicidium certo armentorum ac
> pecorum numero recipitque satisfactionem universa
> domus, utiliter in publicum, quia periculosiores
> sunt inimicitiae iuxta libertatem. [4]

[4] *Germania,* ch. 21.

In the Heroic Age, the amount of payment for particular crimes had apparently been set in monetary terms, with a graduated scale of values placed upon the members of the *comitatus* according to their ranks in the society. Should a thane, for example, slay another thane in a quarrel, he might avoid reprisals, and thus avert a bloody feud, by paying the amount of *wergild* specified by law for a thane's life to the dead man's family. In *Beowulf*, the attitude behind the *wergild* system is given voice by the poet as he describes the raid made by Grendel's mother on Heorot. The she-monster has avenged her son (*Heo þa fæhðe wræc* – 1333) by carrying off Hrothgar's retainer, Æschere:

> Ne wæs þæt gewrixle til,
> þæt hie on ba healfa   bicgan scoldon
> freonda feorum!   (1304–1306)

It is a 'poor exchange' when one life is traded for another; this kind of vengeance can, among civilized people, be averted by the payment of a *wergild*. Thus, Hrothgar tells Beowulf that, when Ecgtheow killed Heatholaf and then fled from the avenging Wylfings, he settled the feud by paying the *wergild* of the dead man for Ecgtheow:

> Siððan þa fæhðe   feo þingode;
> sende ic Wylfingum   ofer wæteres hrycg
> ealde madmas;   he me aþas swor.   (470–472)

The Wylfings were apparently satisfied with this restitution and so gave up their intention to take Ecgtheow's life in return for that of Heatholaf.

A warrior who fails to gain satisfaction for an offense to his friends or family, and does not die attempting to gain this necessary satisfaction, suffers the scorn of the society in which he lives. He loses stature in the eyes of his peers and is ultimately consigned to a life of disgrace. For this reason, it is often said of the family or friends of a warrior who has died in combat and remains unavenged, that they 'have no cause to boast'; that is, they have no cause to boast of having gained satisfaction for their loss, and have cause to be ashamed of their failure. Thus,

Beowulf tells Hygelac that he avenged the Danes by slaying Grendel:

> ic ðæt eall gewræc,
> swa begylpan [ne] þearf   Grendeles maga
> ænig ofer eorðan   uhthlem þone,
> se ðe lengest leofað   laðan cynnes,
> facne bifongen.   (2005–2009)

Grendel's kinsmen must suffer shame because their relative has been slain and the slayer lives on. Wiglaf bitterly observes that, because the Geats failed to support their lord and he had to 'avenge himself', Beowulf 'had no cause to boast of his retinue' – *Nealles folccyning   fyrdgesteallum / gylpan þorfte* (2873–2874). In general the survivors of the losing side in any battle are dishonored, not because they have lost the fight, but because of necessity they have left their dead comrades unavenged. We are told that, after Beowulf by himself avenged the death of Hygelac in battle against the Hetware, they 'did not need to exult in the battle' because 'few came home from the fight' (2353-2356), while Beowulf returned safely to his own tribe. In *Brunanburh,* Constantinus leaves his kinsmen and his own son lying unavenged on the battlefield:

> Swilce þær eac se froda   mid fleame com
> on his cyþþe norð,   Costontinus,
> har hilderinc,   hreman ne þorfte
> mæca gemanan;   he wæs his mæga sceard,
> freonda gefylled   on folcstede,
> beslagen æt sæcce,   and his sunu forlet
> on wælstowe   wundun forgruden,
> giungne æt guðe.   (37–44)[5]

Like Constantinus, the other Scots and Vikings who survive the battle 'have no cause to boast' (44) as they flee in disgrace to seek their homes *æwiscmode* (56).

In *Maldon,* the cowardly retainers who, after Byrhtnoth's death, flee from the battle in order to save their own lives are treated

---

[5] The text of *The Battle of Brunanburh* used in this study is that of E. V. K. Dobbie, ed., *The Anglo-Saxon Minor Poems* (New York, 1942), pp. 16-20.

with contempt by both the poet and the loyal retainers who remain behind to die while avenging their fallen lord. In his description of the cowards' flight, the poet emphasizes the unrighteousness and impropriety of this deed, the lack of gratitude which they show for their lord's generosity, and their failure to fulfill their vows of service:

Hi bugon þa fram beaduwe   þe þær beon noldon.
þær wearð Oddan bearn   ærest on fleame,
Godric fram guþe,   and þone godan forlet
þe him mænigne oft   mear gesealde;
he gehleop þone eoh   þe ahte his hlaford,
on þam gerædum   þe hit riht ne wæs,
and his broðru mid him   begen ærndon,
Godrine and Godwig,   guþe ne gymdon,
ac wendon fram þam wige   and þone wudu sohton,
flugon on þæt fæsten   and hyra feore burgon,
and manna ma   þonne hit ænig maeð wære,
gyf hi þa geearnunga   ealle gemundon
þe he him to duguþe   gedon hæfde.
Swa him Offa on dæg   ær asæde
on þam meþelstede,   þa he gemot hæfde,
þæt þær modiglice   manega spræcon
þe eft æt þearfe   þolian noldon.   (185–201)

Offa reiterates the poet's judgment; he excoriates Godric for his cowardice, for betraying his comrades, and for causing disorder within the English ranks, and concludes by cursing him (237–243). The loyal retainers remain on the field to die avenging Byrhtnoth, while the cowards, we must assume, save their own lives at the cost of their honor, and must henceforth live a life of shame for their failure.

A Germanic tribe or family can usually obtain satisfaction for a serious offense against its honor either by a violent act of vengeance or by claiming a *wergild* from the offender. Sometimes, however, a violent death by the nature of its circumstances precludes all possibility that the dead man's family or friends can obtain honorable satisfaction. When neither revenge nor monetary restitution is attainable, the dead man's survivors are left with their grief which is, in heroic terms, inconsolable. In *Beowulf,* one such unhappy situation is averted by the generosity of Hrothgar.

Although he is in no way obligated to do so, Hrothgar pays a *wergild* for the Geat, Hondscioh, whom Grendel killed in Heorot (1050-1055). Presumably, the gold given by Hrothgar will help to ease the grief that Hondscioh's family must suffer for a loss which they did not and could not have avenged. In this case, the peculiar nature of the offender would have hindered any ordinary means of obtaining satisfaction. A slaying which results from a quarrel within a family or tribe cannot result in any really honorable resolution because the bonds of loyalty within the social unit have been severed. A *wergild* would serve no purpose since the tribe's or family's wealth could not be augmented from its own stores, while killing the offender would further lessen the communal strength, and might lead to further reprisals. Thus, internecine strife must necessarily lead to the dishonor of the group so engaged. In Denmark, the usurpation by Hrothulf of the throne from Hrothgar's sons must, judging by the frequency and subtlety of the allusions to it,[6] have resulted in a civil war terrible enough in its reputation to have become a famous event in oral heroic literature. Likewise, an oblique reference to the war between Hrothgar and his son-in-law, Froda, is used by the poet to emphasize by contrast the magnificence and prosperity of Heorot in times of peace:

>   Sele hlifade
> heah ond horngeap;   heaðowylma bad,
> laðan liges;   ne wæs hit lenge þa gen,
> þæt se ecghete   aþumsweoran
> æfter wælniðe   wæcnan scolde.   (81–85)

In connection with this problem of offences which cannot be expiated, the passage in *Beowulf* dealing with Herebeald's death (2435-2467), is worth considering in some detail. Hæthcyn, we learn, killed his elder brother, Herebeald, by accident when his arrow missed its intended mark. Beowulf says Herebeald was slain 'unfittingly' (*ungedefelice* – 2435), perhaps because he was not slain, as befits a hero, in battle, but more probably, as the juxtaposition of *mæges dædum* in the next half-line (2436) sug-

---

[6] *Beowulf*, 1018f, 1164f, 1178ff, 1228ff.

gests, because it is never 'fitting' for one kinsman to kill another. The killing is *feohleas* (2441), not to be expiated by payment of a *wergild,* because the slayer is himself one of the kinsmen to whom such payment would ordinarily be made. Herebeald must die unavenged – *æðeling unwrecen   ealdres linnan* (2443) – even though, as Klaeber points out,[7] accidental homicide might be punishable, since his father, Hrethel, cannot take vengeance upon his own son. The intolerable grief and helplessness from which Hrethel suffers as a result of this fratricide is emphasized by a simile, certainly the most Homeric one in the poem, in which the grieving father is compared to a man whose son has been hanged (2443-2471). Whitelock has pointed out that "no vengeance could be taken for an executed criminal";[8] Hrethel and the hypothetical hanged man's father are alike in that neither man can take vengeance or claim a *wergild* to alleviate the grief from which he suffers. Each man is desolated by the loss of his son, and neither can do anything to relieve his suffering; the criminal's father ... *him helpe ne mæg / eald ond infrod   ænige ge- fremman* (2448-2449) and Hrethel *wihte ne meahte / on ðam feorhbonan   fæghðe gebetan* (2464-2465). Both men finally retire from the world of the joys of men, the former to his lonely bedchamber (2460-2462), the latter to the kingdom of the dead (2468-2471).

The final effect of this passage is to render vividly and movingly the tragic quality of the unappeasable suffering which results from a violent death whose circumstances preclude vengeance and monetary restitution. The importance of vengeance in the lives of the heroes of Old English poetry depends upon the central position of the idea of loyalty in the world in which these heroes live. The zeal and determination with which they seek to avenge the deaths of their lords, kinsmen and friends, and the disgrace which they suffer should they fail in their duty, suggest that they place great value upon the lives of those whom they have lost. Yet one might argue that a society which can accept monetary restitution for a homicide cannot value human life or human

---

[7]   Klaeber, *Beowulf,* p. 213.
[8]   Dorothy Whitelock, *The Audience of Beowulf* (Oxford, 1951), p. 18.

affection very highly. The answer to this argument lies in a proper understanding of the role which money, and treasure in general, plays in the heroic world of Old English poetry. It is this aspect of the pre-Christian world-view to which we must now turn our attention.

IV

TREASURE:
THE MATERIAL SYMBOL OF HUMAN WORTH

The modern reader may easily overlook or misunderstand the role played by treasure in the system of values which informs Old English heroic poetry. While no one could deny that fabulous wealth holds a prominent place in *Beowulf* and, to a lesser extent, in the other surviving Germanic heroic poems, one is likely to assume that 'treasure' or 'riches' is synonymous with 'money'. Indeed, material wealth has for so many centuries of English life and literature been understood simply as a means of exchange, that it is difficult for a reader to recognize that the heroic world has a quite different conception of the function of treasure and that a hero's treasure hoard represents more than just his financial solvency. Nevertheless, a careful examination of the function of treasure in Old English heroic poetry should reveal not only that treasure plays a central role in the conceptual world which we are discussing, but also that this role is not what it seems at first glance.

Before taking up the problem of treasure in Old English poetry, we must indicate more precisely what we mean by that rather vague term. For the present purpose, we may assume that any object which appears to have material value in the poetry is 'treasure'. The words *feoh, sinc, gestreon, wela,* and *frætwe* all can mean treasure or wealth, and are employed either to describe objects or as synonyms for valuable objects which are unnamed. *Gold, seolfor, gimmas, sigel, mene,* and *beagas* are always 'treasure', while swords, helmets, shields and other battle implements are often designated as 'treasures'. The common characteristic of all these words is that they denote objects or materials whose possession seems desirable within the context of the poetry.

Scholarly opinion has varied considerably as to the role of treasure in early Germanic poetry. Gummere, one of the first important investigators of early Germanic life and customs, describes the heroic love of treasure as "a franker and more childish love of gold than our modern and tempered affection, in days when we have so many people to tell us the vanity of riches". He thus attempts to excuse Germanic acquisitiveness while assuming that it corresponds, more or less, to modern avarice.[1] R. W. Chambers takes less of a paternally indulgent view of the custom of gift-giving which, he says, "is not so much an exchange as a recognition of mutual dependence. The winnings of the retainer fall to the chief; the chief values wealth only as he may share it with his retainers".[2] Dorothy Whitelock may have Chambers' observation in mind when she says that "the giving of arms and treasure, which was ceremoniously performed, had a symbolic significance", though she does not mention just what this "symbolic significance" is.[3] These scholars see treasure as having positive value in Old English heroic poetry, but H. L. Rogers, one of the many Christian interpreters of *Beowulf*, would have us believe that weapons, treasure, and heroic society itself represent the forces of evil in that poem.[4] Likewise, Kemp Malone says that the dragon's hoard in *Beowulf* symbolizes "the vanity of worldly goods", even though Beowulf, whom Malone describes as "an ideal hero", seems rather fond of it.[5] E. G. Stanley carries Christian interpretation of *Beowulf* to its logical limit by accusing the hero of "avarice" because he wants to see the hoard before he dies, a conclusion which might well raise the hackles of anyone

---

[1]   Francis B. Gummere, *Founders of England*, with supplementary notes by Francis P. Magoun, Jr. (New York, 1930), p. 37. Originally published as *Germanic Origins* (1892).

[2]   Chambers, *Widsith*, pp. 24-25.

[3]   Dorothy Whitelock, *The Beginnings of English Society* (Baltimore, 1952), pp. 30-31.

[4]   H. L. Rogers, "Beowulf's Three Great Fights", *Nicholson*, 233-256. Originally published in *RES*, n.s., IV (1955), 339-355.

[5]   Kemp Malone, "Symbolism in *Beowulf*: Some Suggestions", *English Studies Today*, second series, ed. G. A. Bonnard (Bern, 1961), 81-91.

who believes that the tone and texture of poetry has some relevance to its meaning.[6] In the midst of all this confusion concerning the significance of treasure in *Beowulf* (and consequently, in the other heroic poems as well), the most sensible and convincing solution to the problem, an article by Ernst Leisi, "Gold und Manneswert im *Beowulf*",[7] has received little attention. Leisi recognizes that treasure in *Beowulf* is conceived of in positive terms, but is not equivalent to money:

> Es sind also Dinge, die gewissermassen mit Prestige geladen sind und dieses auch ihrem Besitzer verleihen ... Die Wörterbücher geben deshalb für *weorðian* auch die Bedeutungen „beschenken", „schmücken" an, was aber insofern unpräzis ist, als dadurch gerade der wichtigste Inhalt des Begriffes, nämlich die Erhöhung des persönlichen Wertes verwischt wird. Darin lieget jedoch offenbar der Sinn des Reichtums. Er dient nicht in erster Linie dazu, dem Besitzer einen ästhetischen Genuss zu verschaffen: Beowulf kann unmöglich alle die geschenkten Ringe tragen, und man hört auch nie von reich geschmückten Männern. Der Reiche fürht auch kein komfortableres Leben als der Arme; er kann seinen Reichtum auch nicht beliebig konvertieren, da es noch keinen Kauf gibt, und endlich verbindet sich mit dem Empfang von Schätzen sogar die Verpflichtung zum Weiterschenken .... [8]

The views to be expressed here correspond in their general outlines with those of Leisi. The primary assumption which this discussion will attempt to prove about the objects and materials which we have designated as 'treasure' is that they give moral value to their possessors; that they are, in fact, the material manifestations or representations of the proven or inherent worthiness of whoever possesses them. We may define the function of treasure as that of a tangible, material symbol of the intangible, abstract qualities of virtue in a warrior.[9]

[6] E. G. Stanley, "*Hæthenra Hyht* in *Beowulf*", *Brodeur Studies*, 136-151.
[7] *Anglia* LXXI (1953), 259-273. Some of the general observations and specific examples in this chapter echo those of Leisi, but since the bulk of this discussion was formulated prior to my reading of his article, and since many of my conclusions differ from his, I have elected to follow my own exposition of the topic and to footnote him when it seems appropriate.
[8] Leisi, p. 262.
[9] M. I. Finley, in *The World of Odysseus (Compass Books)* (New York,

Treasure is the material manifestation of the honor to which a warrior is entitled for worthy deeds which he has performed or for virtues which he possesses. A few examples should make this function more readily apparent. Before Beowulf departs from Denmark, after his successful campaign against the Grendel family, he gives the Danish shore-guard a 'sword bound with gold', and the poet tells us that the guard *syþðan wæs / on meodubence maþme þy weorþra, / yrfelafe* (1901-1903). He is more honored by his companions because he has more treasure than he had formerly; the sword brings him more honor, more personal glory. This interdependence of treasure and individual merit can again be observed in the scene when, after Beowulf has concluded his account of his exploits at Heorot, Hygelac gives him Hrethel's sword and a large estate. The poet interjects a few words concerning the low esteem in which the Geats had formerly held Beowulf (2183-2189), and immediately thereafter describes Hygelac's gifts to him (2190-2196). The juxtaposition of these two passages emphasizes the fact that Beowulf has established his worth as a warrior, and that Hygelac acknowledges this newly-discovered worthiness in his kinsman by giving him more of the visible symbols of that worthiness, more 'medals of honor'. Beowulf and Hygelac exchange gifts as an expression of mutual respect but, of course, neither man impoverishes himself, nor has the social hierarchy been altered; the lord remains wealthier than his thane:

> Him wæs bam samod
> on ðam leodscipe   lond gecynde,
> eard eðelriht,   oðrum swiðor
> side rice,   þæm ðær selra wæs.   (2196–2199)

In the heroic social structure of *Beowulf*, the 'better' man is the richer one, and vice versa. Because the lord is 'better' in a general, abstract sense than any of his followers, he necessarily is also wealthier than they are.

Beowulf contains by far the greatest store of examples of this

---

1965), pp. 58-59, suggests a similar function for treasure in the Homeric poems.

heroic function of treasure, but one can find suggestions of it in other Old English heroic poems as well. In *The Battle of Maldon*, Byrhtnoth's refusal to yield tribute to the Danish invaders reflects the intimate relationship between treasure and honor. He thinks it 'too shameful' (*to heanlic* – 55) that he and his companions should surrender a portion of their wealth without a fight (*unbefohtene* – 57). The invaders should not be able to gain treasure, and therefore honor, so easily: *Ne sceole ge swa softe sinc gegangan* (59). The central situation in *Waldere*, as we know from the Latin *Waltharius*, is similar to that in *Maldon*. Guthhere, not satisfied with the treasure which Waldere has offered him, greedily demands all of the hero's wealth. The suggestion at the end of the first *Waldere*-fragment is that, having refused the treasure he was offered, Guthhere will gain no honor at all in the coming battle:

> Forsoc he ðam swurde   and ðam sincfatum,
> beaga mænigo,   nu sceal bega leas
> hworfan from ðisse hilde,   hlafurd secan
> ealdne [eðel]   oððe her ær swefan ... (I, 28–31)

In the second *Waldere*-fragment, we learn that Waldere's sword is one of a number of treasures (*sinc micel, maðma, golde* – II, 5-7) which Theodric once sent to Widia in recognition of the merit of the heroic exploit which the latter performed against a 'monster' (*fifela* – II, 10). Finally, compound words in which treasure and honor or merit are equated, such as *sincweorðunge, hordweorðunge,* and *breostweorðunge,* are common in Old English poetry, and further suggest this identity of wealth and abstract virtue. [10]

The ultimate goal of the Germanic hero is to ensure that his glory (*dom*) will live on after his death by performing deeds worthy of praise (*lof*). The hero's treasure serves as a measure of this glory. Thus, in *Beowulf,* Hrothgar promises Beowulf that

---

[10] See, e.g., *sincweorðunga* (*Andreas* 272, 477; *Elene* 1218); *breostweorðunge* (*Beowulf* 2504); *hringweorðunge* (*Beowulf* 3017); *hordweorþunge* (*Beowulf* 952). One might also note phrases like *since gewurþad* (*Beowulf* 1038): *welum weorðode* (*Andreas* 755); *æt feohgyftum ... Dene weorþode* (*Beowulf* 1089-1090).

he will give the young Geat treasure commensurate with the
honor which he deserves for defeating so formidable a monster
as Grendel:

> Ne bið þe [n]ænigre gad
> worolde wilna,   þe ic geweald hæbbe.
> Ful oft ic for læssan   lean teohhode,
> hordweorþunge   hnahran rince,
> sæmran æt sæcce.   þu þe self hafast
> dædum gefremed,   þæt þin [dom] lyfað
> awa to aldre.   (949–955)

The relationship between treasure, great deeds, and that same
dom which survives its possessor's death could scarcely be more
clearly stated. Treasure (*hordweorþunge*) is due to the warrior
who, by deeds in battle (*æt sæcce*) has won eternal glory (*dom*).
Even Grendel's hand is a kind of treasure in so far as it is the
material symbol of a great martial victory. When Grendel's
mother reclaims this trophy, the juxtaposition of statements makes
its importance apparent: *Hream wearð in Heorote; heo under
heolfre genam / cuþe folme* (1302-1303). To the heroes of Old
English verse, treasure and the trophies of one's victories are
virtually identical, as the description of Beowulf's plundering of
Grendel's grotto makes clear:

> Ne nom he in þæm wicum,   Weder-Geata leod,
> maðmæhta ma,   þeh he þær monige geseah,
> buton þone hafelan   ond þa hilt somod
> since fage . . . .   (1612–1615)

When he arrives back at Heorot, he describes his 'booty' (*sælac* –
1652) as the 'tokens of victory' (*tires to tacne* – 1654).

If we assume that human worth is represented in Old English
heroic poetry in material terms, then the existence of regulations,
in the society portrayed in that poetry, concerning the *wergild,*
seems much less inhumane. We know that amounts of money paid
by the slayer of a man were graduated according to the position
of the slain man in the society, so that the family of a slain churl
could be placated much less expensively than that of a king or
a nobleman. One may guess that, at least in the society of the
Heroic Age and in the poetry of that age, the payment of a

wergild was not thought of as the replacement of a human life with material goods, but rather the acknowledgement by the slayer before the entire society of the intangible, unmeasurable worth of the man whom he slew. Also, as Leisi point out, when the slayer surrenders a part of his material wealth, he surrenders at the same time a part of his own reputation (*Ansehen*).[11] Since a lord holds the position of highest honor in the heroic society, it is entirely fitting, according to the relationship between wealth and individual merit which we are considering, that his life should command the highest *wergild* when other more violent forms of vengeance are deferred by the loyal followers who survive him.

The use of treasure in the burial rites in *Beowulf* (and, as the discoveries at Sutton-Hoo have proved, in pre-Christian and early Christian society) constitutes a further indication of the symbolic function performed by material wealth. In the description of the burial at sea of Scyld (26-52), we are told that the burial ship is laden with treasures of all sorts. Presumably, these are the same treasures which Scyld had won during his reign as a "good king". The poet stresses the fact that Scyld leaves the world much wealthier than he entered it:

> Nalæs hi hine læssan   lacum teodan,
> þeodgestreonum,   þon þa dydon,
> þe hine æt frumsceafte   forð onsendon
> ænne ofer yðe   umborwesende.   (43–46).

The implication here is that the mysterious orphan who entered the world destitute leaves it with high honor and the veneration which such well-earned honor commands. Similarly, Beowulf's funeral pyre (3137-3142) and his burial mound (3163-3168), are laden with the treasures which he has won during his lifetime. There is no indication in the poem that the treasures which are interred with the dead are ever expected to be of use to them, or to anyone else. These treasures function as symbols of the honor and veneration which the warriors have achieved in life, and since the virtues of these warriors have died with them (except, of course, in the minds of the living), the outward symbols of these virtues must also 'die' and be buried.

[11] Leisi, 272.

Because the possession of treasure reflects a warrior's worthiness, the unrightful possession of treasure is severely dealt with in Old English heroic poetry. The question of whether or not one is worthy of possessing treasure is particularly important to a full understanding of the events in that portion of *Beowulf* which deals with the dragon and his hoard. Before discussing this section of *Beowulf*, however, we must briefly discuss the nature of the dragon himself. Since the appearance of Tolkien's article in 1936, a lively controversy has raged over whether, as Tolkien claims, Grendel and the dragon are "creatures, *feond mancynnes*, of a similar order and a kindred significance",[12] and whether that significance is indeed symbolic. T. M. Gang, in an article which raises some pertinent questions concerning Tolkien's symbolic reading of *Beowulf*, agrees that Grendel may be symbolic, but denies that the dragon is clearly symbolic of the same kind of evil as Grendel:

The fact is that the dragon is altogether a different sort of creature from the Grendel – tribe. For he is nowhere called God's enemy, or a fiend, or joyless; in fact, no words of moral disapprobation are applied to him; his wrath is not aroused by any unreasonable jealousy of human happiness, but by a very definite outrage.[13]

Adrien Bonjour defends Tolkien's symbolic approach to *Beowulf* in general terms, but fails to invalidate Gang's well-founded distinction between the two monsters,[14] and J. C. Van Meurs, reviewing the various critical approaches to the poem, sides with Gang, and against Tolkien and Bonjour.[15] Dorothy Whitelock avoids the question, making the quite reasonable observation that it is "not necessary to give mythological or allegorical significance to the monsters", since the members of the Anglo-Saxon audience would believe in their actual existence.[16] That the medieval poet and his audience believed in dragons and trolls, that they did

---

[12]   Tolkien, "Monsters", p. 86.
[13]   T. M. Gang, "Approaches to *Beowulf*", *RES*, n.s., III (1952), 6.
[14]   Adrien Bonjour, "Monsters Crouching and Critics Rampant: or The *Beowulf* Dragon Debated", *PMLA* LXVIII (1953), 304-312.
[15]   J. C. Van Meurs, "*Beowulf* and Literary Criticism", *Neophil.* XXXIX (1955), 114-130.
[16]   Whitelock, *Audience*, pp. 71-72.

not conceive of them as fictions, as we do today, is I think indisputable, and the important point for our purposes is that they conceived of these monsters which they had never seen to some extent anthropomorphically. This is not to say that the *Beowulf*-poet assumes that his monsters look like men, or that they think and act as men do consistently, but that when these monsters behave monstrously, they deviate from accepted human behavior. Moreover, there is in the actions and motives of the monsters a recognizable basis of human thought and behavior, and when they do in fact act and think like men, they act and think like the men in *Beowulf*, that is, like men who live in Germanic heroic society.

The dragon arrives soon after the burial of the hoard to protect it from robbers. As we know from Germanic legends like that of Fafnir, and from the Old English maxims, this is the natural function of Germanic dragons. The maxim, *Draca sceal on hlæwe / frod, frætwum wlanc (Maxims II,* 26-27) almost exactly parallels the remark of the *Beowulf*-poet concerning his dragon: *He gesecean sceall / hord on hrusan, þær he hæðen gold / warað wintrum frod* (2275-2277). Gummere and Chadwick both allude to an early pagan belief that dragons are the reincarnations of the warriors whose burial mounds they inhabit and are, therefore, protecting their own treasures.[17] We cannot know whether the Beowulf-poet was even aware of this belief, but this much, I think, is clear: the treasure represents the dragon's honor. Further, the function of the dragon in *Beowulf* is, at least in part, to force any potential owner of the hoard to establish his worthiness to possess this great treasure by defeating him, the dragon, in open combat. A warrior should not be able to gain the honor which riches represent simply by stumbling across them. The dragon's honor is like that of any Germanic warrior in that it is earned by the proper performance of his duty (as guardian of the treasure) and is represented materially (by that treasure).

---

[17] Gummere, p. 317; Chadwick, p. 127. G. V. Smithers, *The Making of Beowulf* (Durham, Eng., 1961), pp. 11-12, argues from this pagan belief that the dragon is in fact the 'last survivor' who buried the hoard, though the poet is no longer aware of this identity.

The original rifling of the dragon's hoard is an unrighteous deed. The dragon loses a portion of his wealth, not to a hero who wins it in open combat, but to a nameless, insignificant person (*niðða nathwylc* – 2215) who steals it while the dragon sleeps. The thief "deceives" the sleeping dragon through *þeofes cræfte* (2218-2219), and violates the hoard "without authority" (*Nealles mid gewealdum* – 2221).[18] The robbery by stealth is an offense against the honor of the dragon and against the honor of men. The dragon is therefore justified in seeking to humiliate those people whom he believes to be responsible for dishonoring him. The thief has decreased the dragon's honor and augmented his own, but his newly-acquired honor is unearned because he has not won it properly. Of course, the dragon's vengeance is misdirected and excessive, and Beowulf's retaliation is both justified and neccessary, but the fact remains that the dragon has been unjustly offended. Indeed, Beowulf recognizes the dragon's wrath to be punishment for a crime – *wende se wisa,   þæt he Wealdende / ofer ealde riht, ecean Dryhtne / bitre gebulge* (2329-2331) – and he later discovers the true nature of that crime:

> hæfde þa gefrunen,   hwanan sio fæhð aras,
> bealoni∂ biorna;   him to bearme cwom
> ma∂þumfæt mære   þurh ∂æs meldan hond. (2403–2405)

Ultimately, the thief receives no honor from Beowulf, in spite of his stolen treasure, and is taken as a captive (*hæft* – 2408) to show the lord of the Geats the location of the barrow. Obviously a coward, the thief goes 'lowly' (*hean* – 2408), 'against his will' (*ofer willan* – 2409), back to the scene of the crime. He is unworthy of the protection and respect which is usually due to one who possessess wealth, and he disappears from the narrative.[19]

---

[18] Klaeber translated the phrase *mid gewealdum* as 'of his own accord' assuming, I would guess, a parallel with *sylfes willum* in the following line (2222a), in spite of the fact that *geweald* usually means 'power', 'rule', or 'authority'.

[19] Klaeber's reconstruction of the events preceding the dragon-fight is unnecessarily complicated and not altogether justified by the text of the poem: "A slave, a fugitive from justice, stole a costly vessel from the dragon's hoard, and upon presenting it to his master – one of Beowulf's

The heroic antipathy toward the unrighteous possession of wealth, which is reflected in the poet's portrayal of the hoard-robber, is central to an understanding of the dragon-fight and its aftermath. In contrast to the thief's secretive approach to the barrow Beowulf, who will prove himself worthy of the hoard, calls the dragon forth to battle in a heroic manner (2550ff.). Beowulf, like Sigemund (884 ff.), will earn his treasure, and the honor which it represents, by winning a great martial victory. Beowulf's retainers, with the single exception of Wiglaf, fail to support their lord when he has need of them, and consequently earn no share in the victory or the hoard. Wiglaf, in his first speech to the retainers (2631-2660), emphasizes the gifts which they have already received from their lord, and says that it is not 'fitting' (*gerysne* – 2653) that they should carry shields (which are treasures, and therefore symbolic of the merit of those who bear them) to the place of battle, and then fail to use them in support of their lord. A display of cowardice, he implies, will mark them as being unworthy of the treasures which they possess and of the complement which Beowulf paid them by selecting them from the entire Geatish *comitatus* (*he usic on herge geceas* – 2638) to accompany him on this exploit.

After the battle, the retainers return 'ashamed' (*scamiende* – 2850) with the shields and arms whose significance their conduct has belied, and they are severely reproached by Wiglaf (2860-2891). Again Wiglaf emphasizes the fact that they received

---

men – obtained his pardon, 2288ff. The vessel was then sent to Beowulf himself (2404f.). In the meantime the dragon had commenced his reign of terror." (p. 208) In fact, the social rank of the thief is not clear; *þeow* in line 2223 is a conjectural reading, and *þegn* is equally possible. That the thief's 'master' is one of Beowulf's men is only a guess, and it is unnecessary to assume an intermediary owner between the thief and Beowulf; the *hlaford* in 2281ff. could be Beowulf himself, and the *meldan* in 2405, the thief. My own reconstruction is as follows: The thief, an exile (hence *wræcsið* – 2292) from an unnamed tribe which may or may not be Geatish, stole the cup and took it to Beowulf, who accepted it as a token of the man's loyalty and became the man's *hlaford* (or, re-received him into the *comitatus*). When he discovered the source of the gift, however, Beowulf realized that the giver had not come by it honorably and, having been attacked by its rightful owner, the dragon, he made the thief a captive and forced him to lead the way to the barrow.

maðmas (2865) because their lord considered them the *þrydlicost*
(2869) warriors in his retinue. He predicts evil days to come for
the Geats because their symbols of valor no longer have any
meaning. The messenger who carries the news of the battle back
to the tribal dwelling place, after his account of the dangers
which will beset the Geats in the near future, likewise predicts a
period of misery and exile for them, and says that, contrary to
Beowulf's intentions, the tribe will not possess the treasure-
hoard:

> . . . þa sceall brond fretan,
> æled þeccean – nalles eorl wegan
> maððum to gemyndum,   ne mægð scyne
> habban on healse   hringweorðunge. . . .   (3014–3017)

The implication here, apparently, is that since the best of the
tribe's warriors have shown themselves to be unworthy, no honor
will be wrongfully gained by any member of the tribe. The honor
of the hoard belongs to Beowulf and Wiglaf alone.

A similar instance of the failure of retainers to serve their lord
properly appears in *Maldon,* and the element of unworthily-held
treasure accompanies this failure also. The cowardly followers of
Byrhtnoth flee the scene of the battle (185-190), and take with
them the steed and trappings of their lord. The crime of cowardice
in battle is especially reprehensible here because the cowards take
with them treasure to which they are not entitled. Godric *gehleop*
þone eoh   þe ahte his hlaford, / on þam gerædum   þe hit
riht ne wæs (189-190). It 'was not right' to acquire a symbol of
honor while performing a dishonorable deed. Godric and the
other cowards have no legitimate claim to the treasure because
they have not avenged their slain lord; they stand in direct
opposition to Wiglaf who, in *Beowulf,* receives his lord's personal
possessions (2809-2812) because he has served him well.[20]
Wiglaf is the only member of Beowulf's *comitatus* who is worthy

[20]   Leisi, 271, speculates that the strict Germanic laws against thievery
spring directly from the equation of treasure with human worth: "Der Ger-
manische Dieb nimmt mit dem fremden Reichtum nicht nur eine Sache in
Besitz, sondern er schmückt sich mit fremder Tugend, Ehre, Macht, all-
gemein mit menschlichem Wert, der ihm nicht zukommt . . .".

of possessing the dragon's hoard, for he alone has assisted Beowulf in the slaying of the dragon. In spite of Beowulf's injunction that his followers refrain from entering the fight (2529-2537), it is clear from the text that Wiglaf has acted properly. He justifies his entry into the battle on the basis of Beowulf's need for help (2642-2650), and the poet emphasizes the propriety of his intervention – *swylc sceolde secg wesan, / þegn æt ðearfe!* (2708-2709). Thus, Wiglaf has the authority of heroic custom when, at Beowulf's request (2747 ff.), he enters the dragon's barrow and plunders the hoard. In the heroic system of values, the plundering of enemies slain in battle is an integral part of worthy conduct. Wiglaf receives no reproach for entering the barrow after he has aided in the slaying of the monster who *ðara maðma   mundbora wæs / longe hwile* (2779-2780). Earlier in the poem we learn that Sigemund won 'great glory' (*dom unlytel* – 885) because he was able to plunder the hoard of the dragon he killed and carry off *selfes dome . . . beorhte frætwa* (895-896). Wiglaf has joined the illustrious company of monster-slayers to which Sigemund and Beowulf belong, and he likewise carries treasure out of the hoard *sylfes dome* (2776).

After Beowulf's death, we learn of a 'curse' (*galdre* – 3052) upon the hoard (3047-3075). This curse has caused commentators much discomfort because it is not at all clear from the text who placed the curse on the hoard, or how long it has been in effect, or precisely what it has to do with the subsequent cremation of both the hoard and Beowulf. The description of the curse does not necessarily contradict the earlier description of the burial of the hoard (2231 ff.), although we are not told specifically that the 'last survivor' cursed his treasure, nor is it inconsistent with the foregoing explanation of the Geat's failure to carry out Beowulf's wishes by distributing the treasure among the members of the *comitatus*. Rather than assume that the curse is the direct cause of the burial of the treasure with the dead hero, one might just as easily view the failure of the retainers as the manifestation of the curse in the normal course of human events. More important for this discussion however, is the wording of the curse as it is reported by the poet. All the curse says is that no one might *hrinan* (3053), literally 'touch', but by implication 'possess', the hoard, except that warrior whom God considered *gemet* 'fit' or 'worthy' to do so. Beowulf (were he ambulatory) and Wiglaf, because they have defeated the dragon in open combat, have certainly proved themselves 'fit' to possess the treasure, and Wiglaf does indeed possess it briefly (2752 ff.).[21]

Wiglaf is worthy of the treasure, but he does not retain possession of it; rather, he commands that it be placed upon Beowulf's funeral pyre (3010 ff.). The motives for this sacrifice are reasonably clear. Whatever the actual facts of the battle are, Wiglaf takes almost no credit for slaying the dragon. He tells the cowardly retainers that he could offer Beowulf little support in the fight, and that he was the *sæmra* of the two. Wiglaf's modesty and his desire to glorify his dead lord and kinsman is admirable by any standard. Furthermore, having relinquished his claim to a large share of the honor for defeating the dragon, he cannot legitimately retain the hoard, even if he desired to do so. The glory of the victory, and the treasure which represents that glory, now belongs to Beowulf alone.[22]

In the foregoing discussion I have suggested that, in the heroic system of values, the plundering of enemies slain in battle is an integral part of worthy conduct. The treasure which a warrior gains by plundering is the concrete representation of the honor which he has won in battle and is, indeed, the only tangible proof of the honor and esteem to which his deeds entitle him. When a warrior is slain in battle, the honor which he has won by his former deeds passes with his war-implements to his slayer, who holds both the treasure and the veneration until he, in turn, is

---

[21] One might profitably compare the implied necessity that the dragon's hoard have a fitting possessor with the description of the sword with which Beowulf kills Grendel's mother (1557-1562). While we are not told that there is a 'curse' on this sword, we are told that no man but Beowulf is able to 'bear it to battle'. In each case there is an explicit relationship between the quality of the treasure and the martial virtue of the warrior who is able to gain possession of it.

[22] It should be noted, however, that Wiglaf has augmented his store of treasure-honor by his valor, for he has received the necklace worn formerly by Beowulf (2809-2812).

vanquished. Thus, in *Beowulf*, Wiglaf receives no reproach for entering the dragon's barrow and Sigemund is praised for the 'great glory' he won because he was able to plunder the hoard of the dragon he killed. In *Maldon*, the first act of the unnamed warrior who reaches the dying Byrhtnoth is to attempt to take his *reaf and hringas and gerenod swurd* (161); such plundering is quite customary and draws no adverse judgments from the narrator.

An integral part of the honor which treasure brings to a hero is the concomitant duty which he has to give portions of his wealth to his followers and, if he should have one, to his leader. *Maþþum oþres weorð, / gold mon sceal gifan*, says the *Exeter Book* maxim (154-155). The highest mark of a warrior's worth is an award of treasure *selfes dom*. In *Beowulf*, Sigemund's great victory over the dragon entitles him to the dragon's hoard *selfes dom* (895), and when Beowulf is recounting to Hygelac the honors which he received at Heorot, he says that Hrothgar gave him treasure *on mynne sylfes dom* (2147). This phrase is customarily translated 'according to my (his, one's) own judgment', in which case Beowulf is exaggerating his rewards at Heorot, for he did not get permission from Hrothgar to choose them himself. If, however, we adopt the alternate meaning of *dom* 'glory', then this phrase means 'according to my (his, one's) own glory', that is, commensurate with one's proven worth, a speculative translation which fits in very well with our assumption about the function of treasure. A leader, whether he is a king or a thane, is measured by his readiness to acknowledge the worthiness of his followers (or leader) by giving them tokens of their worthiness in the form of rings, horses, or other treasures. Hence, Hrothgar's gifts to Beowulf reflect not only the honor due to the warrior, but the honor due to the old king as well. Heremod was a bad king because he did not give treasure to his followers according to their merit (*nallas beagas geaf / Denum æfter dome* – 1719-1720), thereby depriving them of the symbols of their human worth. In his long 'sermon' (1724-1784), Hrothgar describes the crime of avarice in a king as the failure to give rings to his followers, and, indeed, the contrast to Hrothgar himself is striking, for he is highly praised throughout the poem for his great generosity.

When he is ready to depart from Denmark, Beowulf gives a valuable sword to the boat-guard. This gesture reflects Beowulf's worthiness as a leader in the same way that Hrothgar's gifts reflected that leader's worthiness. A hero who can afford to magnanimously give away the symbols of honor which he possesses must, after all, have accumulated so much honor that it seems no great loss for him to part with some of it and, as Leisi points out, he gains more honor by the very act of giving.[23] And when he is reunited with Hygelac, Beowulf transfers all of the honor which he has won to his lord with the words, *Gen is eall æt ðe / lissa gelong;   ic lyt hafo / heafodmaga   nefne, Hygelac, ðec* (2149-2151). The loyalty of Beowulf to his lord is here expressed by the gifts which he gives Hygelac and, similarly, the loyalty of Hygelac to Beowulf is expressed in the gifts which Hygelac gives in return.[24]

The primarily symbolic, ethical function of treasure in Old English heroic poetry should be evident by now, but since 'treasure' and 'honor' seem almost interchangeable terms in this poetry, another problem must be dealt with. In none of the foregoing examples is it altogether clear whether virtue entitles a warrior to treasure, of whether treasure makes him worthy of respect for some hidden virtue. Stated another way, are we to assume that a man is a hero because he is rich, or rich because he is a hero? As a corollary problem, we may ask whether the possessor gives intrinsic value to his treasure or the treasure gives value to its possessor. These problems may be satisfactorily disposed of by showing that the bestowing of value works both ways; that is, from the man to his treasure and from the treasure to the man. As we have seen, inequities between the merit of a man and the value of his possessions are usually either set right in the course of the narrative, (as in the case of the hoard-robber in *Beowulf*),

---

[23] Leisi, 265-266. Leisi goes a bit far, I think, when he asserts that in the course of exchanging gifts the parties involved attempt to outdo one another in a kind of contest to determine who is more open-handed.
[24] Compare *Widsith*, 88-98.

or severely censured by the narrator (as in the case of the cowards in *Maldon*). Let us now turn to two examples from *Beowulf* of the reciprocal nature of human worth and rightfully-held material wealth.

Beowulf receives, among the gifts given him by Hrothgar, an extremely valuable necklace. In order to emphasize the value of this necklace, the poet tells us that he never heard of a greater necklace on earth, and he compares it to the famous Brosing necklace (1192-1214). The favorable comparison of Beowulf's necklace with the *brosinga mene* (1199) of Hama raises Beowulf to the level of esteem of that legendary hero. Thus the necklace brings honor to its new owner. The poet continues, however, to tell us that this same necklace was worn by Hygelac when he embarked upon his last exploit, and here an illustrious owner increases the apparent value of the treasure by his association with it. Later, the necklace is mentioned again as bestowing honor upon its possessor, when it is given to Hygd, whose *breost* it *geweorðod* (2176).

This rather roundabout method by which the poet establishes the value of Beowulf's necklace suggests that the lineage of a treasure is somehow important in Old English heroic thought. Before moving on to our second example of the reciprocity of wealth and virtue, a few words upon the subject of lineage and genealogy are therefore necessary. Walter Hart attributes the genealogies in *Beowulf* to "the delight of the Anglo-Saxon poet in sonorous names" and says that the relationships which these genealogies enumerate are "of no moment to the action",[25] but surely he has missed the point. Tacitus suggests the real importance of genealogy in his observations concerning the young men of the *comitatus: Insignis nobilitas aut magna patrum merita principis dignationem etiam adulescentulis adsignant: ceteris robustioribus ac iam pridem probatis adgregantur, nec rubor inter comites adspici.*[26] If a warrior has noble, heroic ancestors, he is entitled to the respect of his peers. Likewise, a warrior who has won a place of honor in the retinue of a famous lord is worthy

[25] Walter M. Hart, *Ballad and Epic* (Boston, 1907), p. 163.
[26] *Germania*, ch. 13.

of respect. When a warrior identifies himself by stating the names of his lord and of his father, he is at the same time stating his stature as a man. Thus, in *Beowulf,* the hero introduces himself to the shore-guard by stating first his tribe and lord, then his father's name, and finally his reason for coming to Denmark (260-285). Hrothgar identifies Beowulf first by his father, then by his reputation (372-389). Wulfgar introduces himself to the newly-arrived Geats not by his name, but by his relationship to Hrothgar, his lord (335-336). In *Maldon,* Ælfwine declares his lineage as a prelude to his vow of loyalty (216-219), and the poet follows the same pattern in introducing the Northumbrian *gysel* (265-267). This association of virtue with noble ancestry is reflected in *Brunanburh* by the poet's comment upon the quality of the fighting done by 'Edward's heirs':

	Bordweal clufan,
heowan heaþolinde	hamora lafan,
afaran Eadweardes,	swa him geæþele wæs
from cneomægum,	þæt hi æt campe oft
wiþ laþra gehwæne	land ealgodon,
hord and hamas.	(5–10).

In like manner, the worth of an object, especially an implement of war, may be established by a statement of its 'genealogy', the names of the heroes who have owned and used it. Beowulf's corselet is *Hrædlan laf, / Welandes geweorc* (454-455), and the horse and saddle which he is given are the very ones which Hrothgar himself is accustomed to ride to battle (1035-1042). In *Waldere,* Waldere's sword is one which Theodric sent to Widia, as a reward for his victory over a 'monster' (*fifela* – II, 4-10) and his corselet is *Ælfheres laf* (II – 18-22).

The genealogy of Wiglaf's old sword serves to establish both the value of the sword itself, and the merit of its young owner. Wiglaf enters the poem rather abruptly; we know nothing about him, and it is therefore necessary that the poet establish his character for us before proceeding with the battle. Since this will be Wiglaf's first battle (2625-2627), the poet cannot recount his earlier exploits, and so he establishes the young man's worthiness by means of his possessions. He tells us the history of the sword.

helmet and byrnie which Wiglaf wears – we are expected to recognize the value of these implements by the account of their former owners, Eanmund and Weohstan, and in turn to recognize the worth of one who can possess such valuable treasures at present. Only a worthy and heroic warrior could conceivably own and use this venerable sword, helmet, and byrnie. Hence, the treasure is here given value by its previous owners and, at the same time, it gives stature to its new owner. We may further assume that the heroic deed which Wiglaf is about to accomplish against the dragon will add another name to the list of heroes who have owned these treasures, and thus give them even more value. The process of giving and receiving honor will become completely circular; from owners to treasure to owner to treasure again.

Treasure in Old English heroic poetry, as might be expected, serves the same function on a collective level that it does on an individual level. The honor and merit of a tribe is made manifest by its collective wealth, just as the honor and merit of an individual warrior is represented by his personal wealth. Many of the epithets which are applied to individuals are often applied to groups as well. Beowulf's troop at Heorot, for example is *wæpnum gewurþad* (331) just as Beowulf himself, as described by the shore-guard, is *wæpnum geweorðad* (250). The dragon's treasure-hoard is an example of collective wealth; it is *eormenlafe æðelan cynnes, / . . . deore maðmas* (2234-2236). The warrior who buried the treasure was the last survivor of this 'noble race', and was therefore the only guardian of the collective honor of the tribe. Though death in battle had taken all but this last member of the race, the tribal honor, represented by the treasure, was still intact; it was buried and 'died' with its last owner just as Beowulf's treasure-honor 'dies' with him. So long as one representative of the tribe can hold the symbols of its glory until a natural death takes him (2267-2270), there is no reason why that glory should pass to another tribe after that last survivor has disappeared. The final fate of the treasure-hoard on Beowulf's funeral pyre likewise marks the end of the Geat's honor and, subsequently, the end of the Geat race itself. In the case of the

Geats, the tribe's failure to support its lord costs it its symbols of collective honor and merit; the members of the tribe have earned no collective share in the treasure, and it is clear that the loss of the treasure will soon be followed by the disappearance of the race.

In *Maldon* we see again that a tribe's sense of its own worthiness depends heavily upon the treasure which it holds. Byrhtnoth's refusal to yield tribute to the Danes (42-61) is in essence the refusal of a tribal spokesman to give up any portion of the collective honor in a disgraceful manner. It seems 'too shameful' *(to heanlic* – 55) for the tribe to give up its treasure without a fight; the English must fight in order to preserve their treasure-honor. Such forced tribute would demean the English, just as the bribes which Scyld extracts from his neighbors are a measure of their subservience to him *(Beowulf,* 9-11). It is entirely different from the *maþmas gemæne,* the 'shared treasures', which Hrothgar predicts will flow between the Geats and the Danes in *Beowulf* (1855-1865). Just as a lord and his retainer exchange gifts on an individual basis, so on a collective basis will each tribe send treasures to the other as tokens of mutual esteem and loyalty, thereby increasing the honor of both tribes.

On the basis of the previous discussion of the duty of a wealthy, virtuous hero to give away portions of his wealth, the relationship of treasure to good government in Old English heroic poetry should be obvious. The well-ordered heroic society is one in which the bond between lord and thanes is maintained by a continuous flow of gifts from lord to thanes and from thanes to lord. These gifts reflect the loyalty and veneration between the members of the *comitatus;* without the tokens of acknowledged respect the communal structure would probably break down. In *Beowulf,* good kings like Hrothgar, Hygelac, and Beowulf maintain the social bonds by giving treasure as a token of their esteem for their followers, while a bad ruler like Heremod fails to give treasure, and thus subverts the social structure of his *comitatus.* The uneasy truce under which, in the Finn digression, the Danes and Frisians live together during the winter is based upon Finn's promise to give gifts equally to the warriors of both tribes:

                          ac hig him geþingo budon,
þæt hie him oðer flet   eal gerymdon,
healle ond heahsetl,   þæt hie healfre geweald
wið Eotena bearn   agan moston,
ond æt feohgyftum   Folcwaldan sunu
dogra gehwylce   Dene weorþode,
Hengestes heap   hringum wenede
efne swa swiðe   sincgestreonum
fættan goldes,   swa he Fresena cyn
on beorsele   byldan wolde.   (1085–1094).

Whatever unity there is through the winter between the hostile forces must be attributed to the free flow of treasure from Finn. Again, when we first see the Geatish court, the poet at once establishes the quality of Hygelac's government by describing the generous conduct of Queen Hygd (1925-1931), and at our first sight of Hygelac himself, he is discovered 'dealing rings' (1966-1970).

The plundering of one army by another is, in Old English heroic poetry, simply a multiplication of the plundering of one warrior by another. So long as the battle has been won honorably, there is no stigma attached to the robbing of a fallen army of its weapons and gold. Indeed, the plundering which follows a battle provides the victorious tribe with its only source of communal treasure, and therefore is its only source of the symbols of its glory. Thus, the plundering of Finn's home is the natural consequence of the Danes' final victory over the Frisians. The victors take everything they can carry off:

                          þa wæs heal roden
feonda feorum,   swilce Fin slægen,
cyning on corþre,   ond seo cwen numen.
Sceotend Scyldinga   to scypon feredon
eal ingesteald   eorðcyninges,
swylce hie æt Finnes ham   findan meahton
sigla searogimma.   Hie on sælade
drihtlice wif   to Denum feredon,
læddon to leodum.   (1151–1159)

There can be little doubt that this heroic concept of treasure as the symbol of merit and virtue is pre-Christian. The evidence in

Tacitus is inconclusive, perhaps because Tacitus himself did not fully understand the implications of gift-giving among the Germanic peoples. He says that the tribes which he admires are scarcely affected by the love of gold and silver – *possessione et usu haud perinde adficiuntur*[27] – but he does indicate that the gifts which warriors receive from their lords are not exactly a salary,[28] and that the members of these tribes bestow gifts upon their lords *pro honore*.[29] From our discussion, it should be clear that there is a close relationship between treasure as the symbol of one's personal honor, and the pre-Christian concept of loyalty. The gifts which a warrior receives from his lord are commensurate with the quality of his deeds and services. Much of a warrior's honor and reputation depends upon his unfaltering loyalty to his lord, and this loyalty is symbolized by the treasure which he possesses. Finally, this veneration of riches, at least in literature, runs directly counter to Christian tradition. According to the Gospels, poverty is a most desirable condition for the faithful, and no medieval saint, so far as I know, ever died wealthy. Chaucer's most religious pilgrims, the Knight, the Parson and the Plowman, are all poor, and are praised for their lack of concern for earthly possessions, but in Old English heroic poetry earthly possessions, un-Christian though they may be, are always presented in positive terms, as things indicative of moral qualities to be desired and sought after by worthy warriors.

In light of the foregoing arguments, we may reasonably conclude that treasure or wealth is, in Old English heroic poetry, the material manifestation of the proven or inherent worthiness of whoever possesses it. It is a positive indication of the physical and moral virtue of an individual or a society. The methods of gaining and keeping treasure are regulated by a strict ethical code, and violations of this code result in dishonor and the loss of the transgressor's material symbols of virtue. For the Old English poet, therefore, wealth is a useful and convenient device for presenting abstract qualities of moral 'goodness' in a concrete

---

[27]   *Germania*, ch. 5.
[28]   *Germania*, ch. 14.
[29]   *Germania*, ch. 15.

and external form in his characters. If the reader of this poetry makes the mistake of taking treasure at its face value, he will miss many of the more subtle implications in the poems.

V

EXILE:
THE EPITOME OF MISFORTUNE IN HEROIC LIFE

Many, if not all, of the qualities and conditions which have positive value in the heroic poetry of the Anglo-Saxons are reflected in the concepts of loyalty, vengeance and treasure. The bond of personal loyalty holds the heroic society together, and so makes it possible for a loyal retainer to enjoy the pleasures of the mead-hall in the company of his lord and his fellows. The promise of vengeance for offenses against the person or property of a warrior gives him a sense of personal security in a world of danger and sudden violence. The possession of treasure, and the possibility of having his treasure-hoard increased through the generosity of his lord provides the warrior with tangible symbols of his own worth and status in his society. Loyalty, vengeance and treasure thus give coherence and meaning to the life of a warrior in the Heroic Age; exile, as it is conceived of in the poetry which we are considering, deprives the warrior of these benefits, and thus represents the greatest evil which can befall him.

Within the framework of heroic concepts and values, exile may be defined most simply as the state of being alone, without a lord, without retainers, and usually without human companionship of any kind. An exile is a warrior who has no social bonds and is therefore cut off from the social intercourse, protection, and recognition to which an honorable position in a great tribe would entitle him. He is loyal to no man, and no man is loyal to him; he is bound to avenge no offenses against friends and kinsmen, and no one will avenge offenses against him; he gives no treasure to men whom he would honor, and no man gives him gifts in recognition of his value as a warrior and a human being. He is, in short, deprived of the pleasures and values of heroic life. Thus, the heroic concept of exile is somewhat different from the modern one. Today we tend to think of exile in terms of geography; for us an exile is one who has been forced to leave his native place of habitation, be it his nation, his city, or his house. The warriors in the poems which we are considering, however, do not properly have nations, cities or houses; they have only tribal groups which may upon occasion migrate all the way across the European continent. The warrior who is exiled from his tribe has thus not lost a dwelling place, but, rather, he has lost a way of life. It is not at all extravagant, under such circumstances, to think of heroic exile as a spiritual, as well as a physical, condition.[1]

A retainer might become an exile either because he has lost the favor of his lord, or because his lord has died. It should be rather obvious that, since the primary way in which a warrior gains the favor of a lord is by demonstrating his loyalty in combat, the quickest way for him to lose that favor is for him to show himself to be a coward in the face of his lord's enemies. According to Tacitus, the warrior who has abandoned his shield in battle is so disgraced that he cannot take part in the religious or civil assemblies of his tribe. He is spiritually, if not literally, an outcast, who not infrequently turns to suicide to end his misery.[2] In the limited corpus of Old English heroic poetry, we have no instance of a lord driving a cowardly retainer from his retinue, but this absence of examples is in itself significant. In the idealized tribes which our poets depict, it is unthinkable that cowardly retainers would be permitted to remain; when hitherto loyal retainers reveal cowardice in the extant poems, it is always too late for their lords to do anything about them.

It is also possible that a warrior might lose his lord's favor and be forced into exile because he has rebelled unsuccessfully against his lord's authority, or because another warrior has maliciously slandered him before his lord, or because of the fickle, unjustified

---

[1]   Frank Bessai has discussed some of the social implications of exile in his article, "Comitatus and Exile in Old English Poetry", *Culture* XXV (1964), 130-144.

[2]   *Germania*, ch. 6.

whim of the lord himself. While such situations must have been common in the real life of the Heroic Age, rebellion and covert malice are rare, and royal capriciousness nonexistent, in the idealized world of heroic poetry. A rather special case is recorded in *Deor*, where the speaker tells us that his position as *scop* of the *Heodeningas* has been taken by another man, while he has been forced into exile:

þæt ic bi me sylfum	secgan wille,
þæt ic hwile wæs	Heodeninga scop,
dryhtne dyre.	Me wæs Deor noma.
Ahte ic fela wintra	folgað tilne,
holdne hlaford,	oþþaet Heorrenda nu,
leoðcræftig monn	londryht geþah,
þæt me eorla hleo	ær gesealde. (35–41)[3]

There is, it seems, room for but one *scop* among the *Heodeningas,* and Deor has lost his place, his lord, the retinue of which he had been a part, and his personal wealth, because of a change in his lord's aesthetic taste.

The death of a lord may, at least temporarily, plunge all of his retainers into exile if he has no immediate heir and no arragements have been made for another lord to succeed him. It is for this reason that Beowulf makes a point of securing a new lord for his followers before he dives into Grendel's pond. He says to Hrothgar, *Wes þu mundbora   minum magoþegnum, / hondgesellum,   gif mec hild nime* (1480- 1481). Because of the circumstances of the expected battle, his men cannot accompany him or die fighting in his defense, and he does not wish them to become lordless exiles, should he lose his life. The 'lone survivor' of the vanished race whose treasure the dragon has come to protect has outlived his lord, as well as his fellow retainers and, after burying the treasure, he must live the life of an exile until death takes him:

Swa giomormod	giohðo mænde
an æfter eallum,	unbliðe hwearf
dæges ond nihtes,	oð ðæt deaðes wylm
hran æt heortan.	(2267–2270)

[3]   The text of *Deor* used in this study is that of G. P. Krapp and E. V. K. Dobbie, eds., *The Exeter Book* (New York, 1936), pp. 178-179.

Ideally, of course, a lord's retainers are not supposed to survive him in battle unless they avenge his death. When Hrethel dies a natural death (*Beowulf* 2468-2471), there is no stigma placed upon his retainers; his son Hæthcyn succeeds him as lord of the Geats, and all of his retainers, we assume, remain in the *comitatus*. When, however, a lord dies, like Byrhtnoth, in battle, his retainers are expected to carry out their vows to avenge his death or else, like Offa, *on here crincgan, / on wælstowe wundum sweltan; / . . . laeg ðegenlice ðeodne gehende* (Maldon, 292-294). Thus Beowulf's cowardly retainers, after their lord dies, deserve no better than the life of exiles which Wiglaf predicts for them:

> Nu sceal sincþego   ond swyrdgifu,
> eall eðelwyn   eowrum cynne,
> lufen alicgean;   londrihtes mot
> þære mægburge   monna æghwylc
> idel hweorfan,   syððan æðelingas
> feorran gefricgean   fleam eowerne,
> domleasan dæd.   Deað bið sella
> eorla gehwylcum   þonne edwitlif!   (2884–2891).

Under certain circumstances which are rather unusual, at least in heroic poetry, a lord may himself become an exile. He may, like Heremod, perform his duties so negligently and behave in so high-handed a manner that his retainers either abandon him or drive him away. Heremod, who as a lord should have been the protector of his people, instead slew them in anger (*breat bolgenmod beodgeneatas – Beowulf*, 1713), and failed entirely to reward them for their service (*nallas beagas geaf / Denum æfter dome –* 1719-1720). Although it is not entirely clear within the context of the verse whether his men abandoned him or drove him away, his subsequent condition is clearly that of an exile: *. . . he ana hwearf, / mære þeoden   mondreamum from . . .* (1714-1715). If indeed Heremod became an exile because he was abandoned by his followers, he must have gained a thoroughly vile reputation for his conduct, since it would no doubt be unusual for a lord whose honorable reputation, and therefore his wealth, were intact not to attract new retainers even if, for example, he had lost all of his retinue in a battle which he alone had survived. On the other hand, a lord may be driven into exile by a rebellious retinue, as seems to have been the fate of the writer of the *Husband's Message*. Although the details are obscure, the general situation presented in this poem is apparently that a lord had been driven through some sort of treachery from his own tribe – *Hine fæhþo adraf / of sigeþeode* (19-20)[4] – into an exile's journey:

> . . . nyde gebæded,   nacan ut aþrong,
> ond on yþa geong   [ana] sceolde
> faran on flotweg,   forðsiþes georn,
> mengan merestreamas.   (40–43)

He has since become a lord once more, and is writing his wife so that she will rejoin him and they can again share his prosperity:

> . . . ætsomne   siþþan motan
> secgum ond gesiþum   s[ync bryttnian]
> nægelde beagas . . . .   (33–35)[5]

The death of a lord can force not only a small group of retainers but indeed an entire tribe into a life of exile. The lord, as we have seen, holds the tribe together in a cohesive social unit; if he dies and no one is willing or able to succeed him, the unit will break down into its component parts. Thus, in the lines quoted earlier Wiglaf predicts an *edwitlif* (2891) not only for those retainers whose courage has failed them, but for the entire race of the Geats. Although the greater part of the Geatish *comitatus* was not even present at the dragon-fight, the *comitatus* is now without a lord, and it is not likely that a tribe whose best warriors have failed their lord will be able to find a good lord who is willing to replace him. The messenger who brings the news of Beowulf's death to the Geats echoes Wiglaf as he, too, predicts a future of exile and suffering for them:

---

[4] The text of *The Husband's Message* used in this study is that of G. P. Krapp and E. V. K. Dobbie, eds., *The Exeter Book* (New York, 1936), pp. 225-227.

[5] It is not absolutely certain that the husband had been a lord before his exile, but the epithet *sinchroden* (14) is usually reserved for queens, and it is unlikely that a *þeodnes dohtor* (47) should have been married to a common retainer.

> ... nalles eorl wegan
> maððum to gemyndum, ne mægð scyne
> habban on healse hringweorðunge,
> ac sceal geomormod, golde bereafod
> oft nalles æne elland tredan,
> nu se herewisa hleahtor alegde,
> gamen ond gleodream. (3015–3021)

Clearly then, although exile is most commonly conceived of as a condition of single persons, nevertheless a group of warriors may, at least in theory, be collectively considered to be 'exiled' so long as it has no leader to whom it can devote itself and from whom it can receive treasure for its devotion. Number alone does not imply social coherence and unity; a band of warriors may seek service as a group and still be 'exiled'. For this reason Wulfgar, when confronted with a band of unknown warriors, must judge whether they are seeking Hrothgar because they are exiles in need of a protector, or for some other purpose. His judgment does not fail him:

> Ne seah ic elþeodige
> þus manige men modiglicran.
> Wen'ic þæt ge for wlenco, nalles for wræcsiðum,
> ac for higeþrymmum Hroðgar sohton. (336–339)

The principal reason for the wretchedness of the exile's life is the deprivation of the pleasures of the hall which he has enjoyed as a member of a *comitatus*. He can no longer take part in the mead-drinking and gift-giving, nor listen to the music and song of the *scop* in the great hall, and the memory of this communal *dream* and *wynne* of happier times intensifies his present feeling of loneliness and isolation. As Deor tells us, Weland once suffered the woes of exile, with only sorrow and longing as companions:

> Welund him be wurman wræces cunnade,
> anhydig eorl earfoþa dreag,
> hæfde him to gesiþþe sorge ond longaþ,
> wintercealde wræce; wean oft onfond,
> siþþan hine Niðhad on nede legde,
> swoncre seonobende on syllan monn. (1–6)

Weland endures 'sorrow' for the 'wretchedness' of his outcast state, and 'longing' for the joys of the past. The adjective *winter-cealde* (4), which appears often in descriptions of exile, brings to mind the warmth of the fire in the great hall, another of the comforts which the exile is denied. In *Beowulf*, we learn that Cain, another famous exile, was forced to flee the joys of men and live a life of isolation:

>   ... he þa fag gewat,
> morþre gemearcod   mandream fleon,
> westen warode.   (1263–1265)

In *The Wife's Lament*, the speaker utters what is apparently a curse upon a 'young man', who may be her husband,[6] declaring that he should endure the pains of exile:

> A scyle geong mon   wesan geomormod,
> heard heortan geþoht,   swylce habban sceal
> bliþe gebæro,   eac þon breostceare,
> sinsorgna gedreag,   sy æt him sylfum gelong
> eal his worulde wyn,   sy ful wide fah
> feorres folclondes ...   (42–47)[7]

We have already noted that in the ideal heroic society the pleasures and favors which the warrior enjoys come from his lord. One need only recall the words of Beowulf to Hygelac:

>   Gen is eall æt ðe
> lissa gelong;   ic lyt hafo
> heafodmaga   nefne, Hygelac, ðec.   (2149–2151)

The exile from heroic society must, in his isolation, 'depend upon himself for all his wordly joy' – an extremely unpleasant prospect in a world in which all joys are communal.

The exile, lordless and alone, is continually vulnerable to physical danger not only from the forces of nature, but also from other men. A warrior's lord is his sworn protector and no matter where the warrior travels, if he serves a powerful lord, he is secure in the knowledge that any man who might assault him would be subject to the vengeance of his lord, as well as his

---

[6] See, e.g., Stanley B. Greenfield, "*The Wife's Lament* Reconsidered", *PMLA* LXVIII (1953), 907-912.

[7] The text of *The Wife's Lament* used in this study is that of G. P. Krapp and E. V. K. Dobbie, eds., *The Exeter Book* (New York, 1936), pp. 210-211.

kinsmen and friends. The exile, however, is far from his dear
ones and should he be slain for any reason whatever, no man will
avenge him or grieve for his life. He is subject to the whims of
any persons into whose company he may fall or whose paths he
may cross. Thus the *Exeter Book* maxim advises a man to keep
as many friends as he can:

> Wel mon sceal wine healdan   on wega gehwylcum;
> oft mon fereð feor bi tune,   þaer him wat freond
>   unwiotodne.   (144–145)

This maxim goes on to describe the probable fate of the warrior who has no friends, no lord and no *comitatus:*

> Wineleas, wonsælig mon   genimeð him wulfas to
>   geferan,
> felafæcne deor.   Ful oft hine se gefera sliteð;
> gryre sceal for greggum,   græf deadum men;
> hungre heofeð,   nales þæt heafe bewindeð,
> ne huru wæl wepeð   wulf se græga,
> morþorcwealm mæcga,   ac hit a mare wille. (146–151)

The wolf is typical of the dangers to which the exile is exposed
from the world of nature. It is perhaps fanciful, but nevertheless
plausible, to read this passage on a second, non-literal, level as a
metaphorical description of the treatment of the exile at the
hands of wolfish men on alien lands among unknown tribes.

As we might expect, the exile's condition is one of poverty.
If he has been driven from his tribe for disloyalty or cowardice,
then, given the function of treasure in Old English heroic poetry,
his dishonor will be reflected in his lack of the treasure which
betokens value and honor in the heroic world. If he has merely
outlived his lord and companions then, like the warrior who
buried the dragon's hoard in *Beowulf,* he must either divest
himself of the riches in his possession or else run the risk of
protecting them himself from whomever might wish to augment
his own honor at the exile's expense. Because he is lordless, the
exile has no source of new treasure as he did when he was able
to receive rings in the hall. He might, of course, win treasure in
battle, but he has no group of fellow-retainers among whom

he can fight, and to engage in battle independently would be foolish for a lordless man unless he were a great hero. A warrior capable of winning treasure in single combat would not remain poor, nor would he remain an exile, for very long. The writer of *The Husband's Message* had been driven from his *meoduburgum* (17), but managed to recover his former prosperity:

> Nu se mon hafað
> wean oferwunnen;   nis him wilna gad,
> ne meara ne maðma   ne meododreama,
> ænges ofer eorþan   eorlgestreona....   (43–46)

Likewise, as we learn in *Beowulf*, Sigemund was an exile, but so great a warrior as he could win fabulous riches in single combat with a dragon, thus redeeming himself from ignominy:

> Se wæs wreccena   wide mærost
> ofer werþeode,   wigendra hleo,
> ellendædum....   (898–900)

The Geats who survive Beowulf's death, however, are not great heroes, but ordinary exiles who *sceal geomormod, golde bereafod / oft nalles æne   elland tredan* (3018–3019).

An exile, excluded as he is from the centers of heroic civilization and social life, must inhabit the least desirable places in his world, places in which no *comitatus* would choose to dwell. Thus, the exile seeks whatever refuge is offered him by the thick forests and misty moors which border the lands of the various tribes. Here, if he is fortunate, he may find an earthen cave in which he avoids the winter weather as best he can. The wild, inhospitable neighborhood in which Grendel and his mother dwell is quite naturally spoken of as an 'unpleasant place' (*nis þæt heoru stow* – 1372) which is reached by 'exile-paths' (*wræclastas* – 1352):

> Hie dygel lond
> warigeað wulfhleoþu,   windige næssas,
> frecne fengelad   ðær fyrgenstream
> under næssa genipu   niþer gewiteð,
> flod under foldan.   (1357–1361)

A dwelling-place like this one suggests to the poet's audience all of the other unhappy circumstances, about which we have been speaking, which the exile must endure. It is a wasteland (*westen* – 1265), in which a warrior can find no human companionship, much less a lord whom he might serve. One who wanders in such places is exposed to continual physical danger; to the severe cold of the winter, to wolves (hence the substantive *wulfhleoþu* in line 1358 above), and other beasts, to the unknown and to the supernatural. The fens are, in fact, the natural habitat of demons – *þyrs sceal on fenne gewunian / ana innan lande* (*Maxims II*, 42-43). Only an impoverished, dishonored man would live in fens and forests, and he would live there out of necessity, not choice. The exile who must leave the company of men has one alternative to the forests, and it is equally uninviting; he may go on a sea-journey. Thus, the writer of *The Husband's Message* fled his enemies by sailing away *forðsiþes georn, / mengan merestreamas* (42-43). Life at sea is no more pleasant or safe than life in the forests; it is lonely, cold and dangerous. Thus it is that forests, fens and seas are, in Old English heroic poetry, associated primarily with the wretched lives of exiles.

The expression of the 'theme' (in Lord's sense of the term) of exile in Old English poetry has been examined by Stanley B. Greenfield in an article published in 1955.[8] By examining closely the relevant passages in both the heroic and the Christian poetry, Greenfield discovers four primary aspects of the exile state with which Anglo-Saxon poets are concerned. These features are (1) a statement of the status of the exile (e.g., *wineleas wrecca*), (2) references to his deprivation of physical property or abstract comforts and joys or both (e.g., *golde bereafod, dreame bedæled*), (3) some expression of his state-of-mind (e.g., *hean and earm*), and (4) some expression of his movement in or into exile (e.g. *wunode wræc-lastum*). The *Beowulf*-poet, in the passage describing the burial of the dragon's hoard (2231-2270), utilizes these four aspects of the exile-theme

---

[8] "The Formulaic Expression of the Theme of 'Exile' in Anglo-Saxon Poetry", *Speculum* XXX (1955), 200-206.

to describe the 'sole survivor'. As the last living member of a once-great tribe, he is by definition an exile:

Ealle hie deað fornam
ærran mælum,   ond se an ða gen
leoda duguðe,   se ðær lengest hwearf,
weard winegeomor,   wende þæs ylcan,
þæt he lytel fæc   longgestreona
brucan moste.   (2236-2241)

By burying the tribal riches, he completes the process of his deprivation, which began with the loss of his lord and his companions:

Heald þu nu, hruse,   nu hæleð ne mostan,
eorla æhte!   Hwæt, hyt ær on ðe
gode begeaton;   guðdeað fornam,
feorhbealo frecne   fyra gehwylcne
leoda minra   þara ðe þis [lif] ofgeaf,
gesawon seledream.   (2247-2252)

Sad in mind, he laments his loss – *giomormod giohðo mænde* ... (2267) – and turns to wander aimlessly until death overtakes him:

... unbliðe hwearf
dæges ond nihtes,   oð ðæt deaðes wylm
hran æt heortan.   (2268-2270)

Often found in conjunction with the exile theme in Old English poetry are reflective passages written in what has come to be known as the 'elegiac mood'. In these elegiac passages the speaker meditates upon the transitory nature of earthly goods and of human life, contrasting his present misfortunes with the joys of the past, and sometimes making a general statement about the world in which he lives. The warrior who buries the dragon's hoard speaks his monologue in this mood (*Beowulf*, 2247-2266). As he gazes upon the treasures of his tribe, he remembers the warriors who owned and used the gilded cups, shields, and armor, and reflects that without owners these treasures must rust and decay in the earth. The hall-joys which he once shared with his companions are part of a past which can never be restored to him:

>   Næs hearpan wyn,
> gomen gleobeames,   ne god hafoc
> geond sæl swingeð,   ne se swifta mearh
> burhstede beateð.   Bealocwealm hafað
> fela feorhcynna   forð onsended!   (2262–2266)

The reason behind the common juxtaposition of the exile theme
and the elegiac mood should be evident. The exile's unfortunate
circumstances bring him quite naturally to recall more fortunate
days, days when he shared the pleasures and benefits of the
comitatus. His grief over his own loss may, if he is of a philosophical turn of mind, lead him to the realization that his state
is typical, and that all living creatures are subject to the viscis-
situdes of fate and, ultimately, to death.

The immediate goal, whether it is explicitly stated or not, of
most of the exiles which we encounter in Old English heroic
poetry is to find a new lord and a new *comitatus,* and thus to
regain the joys of life in heroic society. Sigeferth, in the *Finnsburh*
fragment, identifies himself as an exile:

> "Sigeferþ is min nama," cwep he,   "ic eom Secgena
>   leod,
> wreccea wide cuð;   fæla ic weana gebad,
> heardra hilda."   (24–26)

It is clear from the context of the poem, however, that, since he
is fighting in the Danish army led by Hnæf, he has found a new
lord to serve. When we consider the deprivation and danger
which the exile must endure, we cannot wonder at his desire to
return to the world of men, but this return is no easy matter.
A lord would probably not be eager to accept a hitherto unknown
warrior into his service without first determining whether that
warrior would be likely to prove an asset or a liability to the
comitatus. The warrior who appears, as it were, out of nowhere
to seek the favor of a powerful lord is one whose prowess in
battle, and hence whose value to the tribe, is not known. As an
exile he may very well be a coward who has been sent in disgrace
from his tribe after having failed to support his former lord
in battle. This seems to be the reason behind Wulfgar's actions
as messenger between Hrothgar and the newly-arrived Geats.

He appraises the Geats' appearance, and concludes that they have come, not because of *wræcsiðum*, but for *higeþrymmum*, and he then recommends that Hrothgar give audience to them:

> no ðu him wearne geteoh
> ðinra gegncwida,   glædman Hroðgar!
> Hy on wiggetawum   wyrðe þinceað
> eorla geæhtlan;   huru se aldor deah,
> se þæm heaðorincum   hider wisade.   (366–370)

One of Wulfgar's functions in the Danish court seems to be that of keeping worthless exiles from wasting his lord's time, while securing for worthy men the audiences they desire.

There are a number of ways in which an exile might be able to obtain a new place in a lord's retinue. He could conceivably be taken in simply on the basis of his lineage and reputation, if these were great enough, but this would necessarily depend upon the circumstances of his exile, since the very fact of his exile would make his worthiness suspect. Thus, in *Beowulf,* the sons of Ohtere are taken in by Heardred; they are exiles (*wræcmæcgas* – 2379) through no fault of their own, but rather because their throne has been usurped by their uncle, Onela (2379-2396). A warrior might win a place by demonstrating to his new lord his loyalty and worth through the performance of a valuable service for him. Beowulf (had he been an exile) would no doubt have been able to secure a permanent place in Hrothgar's retinue after killing Grendel; we observe Sigeferth in the act of fighting for Hnæf; and Widsith, a rather special case since he is described as an exile (cf. 50-56) but is not properly a warrior at all, again and again wins new lords by, we must assume, demonstrating his talent as a *scop*. A warrior might demonstrate his loyalty to, and secure a place from, a lord by offering him a fine gift, as does the robber of the dragon's hoard:

> . . . mandryhtne bær
> fæted wæge,   frioðowære bæd
> hlaford sinne.   (2281–2283)

Such instances are rare in the poetry, since it is unusual for an exile to have any treasure in the first place. Finally, although the evidence is scant, it is possible that a warrior might earn respect and a position by responding properly to the challenge of that lord's retainers. This would help to explain Unferth's unprovoked attempt to assassinate Beowulf's character (499ff). Unferth addresses Beowulf as if he were an exile, in disgrace after being defeated by Breca, and Beowulf responds worthily by denying the charge and offering a counterinsult to his challenger.

That the condition of exile is, within the context of Old English heroic poetry, universally recognized to be the worst fate which may befall a warrior is attested to by the frequency with which aspects of the exile theme appear, and the variety of wretched creatures which these aspects are used to describe. Even death is preferable to the miserable life of the exile: *Deað bið sella / eorla gehwylcum   þonne edwitlif!* (*Beowulf* 2890-2891). The portrayal of Grendel is the most striking example which we have of the versatility of the exile theme, for Grendel is certainly the most wretched and despicable creature in all of Old English heroic poetry. The dragon in *Beowulf* may be unpleasant, but he at least has a few redeeming heroic qualities, while Grendel has none; Grendel is thoroughly unappealing and he is essentially an 'exile'. He is, indeed, one of a long line of exiles, a descendant of Cain, whom *feor forwræc, / Metod for þy mane   mancynne fram* (109-110). In a world in which one's lineage is important, this is a serious handicap. He travels by himself, thus earning the epithet *angenga* (449). Like all exiles, he is 'deprived of joy' (*dreamum bedæled* – 721), he begrudges the Danish *comitatus* the 'dream' it enjoys at Heorot (86-90) and, fittingly, he dies 'joylessly' (*dreama leas* – 850). He is an inhabitant of the borderlands (*mearcstapan* – 1348) whose dwelling and its environs reflects in its dreariness the wretchedness of his own person. Grendel's neighborhood is pre-eminently a place of 'exile-paths' (*wræclastas* – 1352):

> ... se þe moras heold,
> fen ond fæsten ...   (103–104)

> ... sinnihte heold
> mistige moras;   men ne cunnon
> hwyder helrunan   hwyrftum scriþað.   (161–163)

> ... steap stanhliðo,   stige nearwe,
> enge anpaðas,   uncuð gelad,
> neowle næssas,   nicorhusa fela ....   (1409–1411)

Of course, Grendel is not a human being, and is therefore
not really an exile, in so far as he could never actually be a
member of a *comitatus*. There is no question, however, that his
race has been exiled and that, within the framework of the
heroic concepts of conduct which inform *Beowulf,* he himself
deserves the equivalent of an exile's life. He does not meet his
enemies in open combat, like an honorable warrior, but rather
he kills (and eats) them as they sleep (115-125, 728-745). He
has no desire for peace and will not receive tribute (*fea þingian* –
156), as would a victorious lord, in place of human lives. For
all his ferocity, when he is finally confronted by a warrior who
is capable of fighting effectively against him, he immediately
reveals his cowardice and attempts to flee:

> Sona þæt onfunde   fyrena hyrde,
> þæt he ne mette   middangeardes,
> eorþan sceata   on elran men
> mundgripe maran;   he on mode wearð
> forht on ferhðe;   no þy ær fram meahte.
> Hyge wæs him hinfus,   wolde on heolster fleon,
> secan deofla gedræg;   ne wæs his drohtoð þær
> swylce he on ealderdagum   ær gemette.   (750–757)

Grendel dwells outside of heroic society and, unlike those who
serve and protect one another, his life is of no value to anyone
– *ne his lifdagas   leoda ænigum / nytte tealde* (793-794).
Although he does have a mother who will attempt to avenge
him, the expression of his death suggests that of an exile. No
comitatus grieves for Grendel:

> No his lifgedal
> sarlic þuhte   secga ænegum
> þara þe tirleases   trode sceawode,
> hu he werigmod   on weg þanon,
> niða ofercumen,   on nicera mere
> fæge ond geflymed   feorhlastas bær.   (841–846)

Thus, it should be clear that much of the moral revulsion and
ethical disapproval which the audience is expected to feel toward

Grendel results from the poet's use of descriptive elements and character traits most commonly associated with the concept of exile.

Another excellent example of the versatility and usefulness of the various aspects of the expression of the exile theme as vehicles for portraying human wretchedness and suffering is *The Wife's Lament*. The prevailing critical view that this poem is a lament spoken by a woman whose husband had abandoned her has recently been challenged in articles by Rudolph C. Bambas, and Martin Stevens, who argue that it is the lament of an exiled warrior.[9] This reading of the poem has not won favor with critics,[10] but it is easy to see how one might arrive at such a reading, for the poem is the fullest expression of the exile theme which we have in an entirely secular context. Whether we accept the interpretations of Bambas and Stevens or not, a reading of their articles is useful, for it helps one to realize how thoroughly the poet's depiction of a forsaken woman depends upon elements regularly used to depict exiled warriors. One must conclude that the Anglo-Saxon poet who wished to portray a suffering human being vividly and convincingly would quite naturally make use of the themes and formulas of heroic exile, whether his sufferer were male or female.[11] The emotional impact of *The Wife's Lament* depends entirely upon our consciousness of the concept of masculine exile, but it is no less effective for that consciousness. On the contrary, a firm understanding of the implications of the concept of exile makes us more keenly aware of the suffering of any person who can be so described. Let us examine briefly the theme of exile as it appears in *The Wife's Lament*.

We begin with the speaker's own statement that hers is a life

[9] Rudolf C. Bambas, "Another View of the Old English *Wife's Lament*", *JEGP* LXII (1963), 303-309. Martin Stevens, "The Narrator of *The Wife's Lament*", *NM* LXIX (1968), 72-90.

[10] See e.g., Greenfield, *Critical History*, pp. 225-226. Angela M. Lucas, "The Narrator of *The Wife's Lament* Reconsidered", *NM* LXX (1969), 282-297.

[11] For a similar conclusion see Matti Rissanen, "The Theme of 'Exile' in *The Wife's Lament*", *NM* LXX (1969), 90-104.

of exile (*minra wræcsiþa* – 5). She was first separated from her 'lord' (*min hlaford* – 6) when he departed on a sea-journey (*ofer yþa gelac* – 7) which has apparently since become his own life of exile in a distant land:

> ... min freond siteð
> under stanhliþe   storme behrimed,
> wine werigmod,   wætre beflowen
> on dreorsele.   Dreogeð se min wine
> micle modceare;   he gemon to oft
> wynlicran wic.   (47–52)

She has lost her lord's favor because of the veiled malice (*dyrne geþoht* – 12) of his kinsmen (11-14). Her attempt to find a new *comitatus* (*folgað* – 9) to protect her has been unsuccessful, and so she now dwells alone (*ana* – 35), deprived of human intercourse (*ahte ic leofra lyt   on þissum londstede, / holdra freonda* – 16-17), recalling old vows of loyalty (*Bliþe gebæro ful oft wit beotedan / ... eft is þæt onhworfen* – 21-23), and suffering longings (*longaþes* – 41) for the past. She dwells in a cave (*eorðscræfe* – 28) in a wooded barrow (*wuda bearwe* – 27), which is without joy (*wic wynna leas* – 32). Filled with sadness (*ful geomorre* – 1, *hyge geomor* – 17), her only activity is to emerge at dawn from her cave and bewail her wretched state (35-41). There seems at the end of the poem to be little or no hope that she will ever be redeemed from her exile.

Of the four concepts which we have been discussing, exile is, when considered by itself, the least obviously pre-Christian. Judaeo-Christian tradition contains a profusion of exiles, of whom Adam and Moses are but two prominent examples. Christian saints depicted in Saint's Lives which follow the model of Athanasius' *Life of St. Antony* (fourth century) lead lives which are in some respects similar to those of the Germanic exiles of whom we have been speaking. But while Christian exile is conceived of in positive terms as a voluntary rejection of the vanities of the world,[12] Germanic exile is never voluntary and

---

[12]   On the Christian theme of voluntary exile in Old English poetry and culture see Dorothy Whitelock, "The Interpretation of *The Seafarer*", *The*

is always an abhorrent state. In Old English heroic poetry, the concept of exile is expressed in purely heroic, Germanic terms, and when we consider the relationship of heroic exile to the other three heroic concepts which we are examining, there can be little doubt of its pre-Christian origin and character. The concept of heroic exile depends for its efficacy, indeed, for its very meaning, upon the concepts of loyalty, vengeance and treasure. Exile means deprivation; deprivation of the bonds of loyalty, of the protection of an avenger, of the honor symbolized by treasure. It is the greatest misfortune which can befall a Germanic warrior. The concepts of loyalty, vengeance, treasure and exile, inextricably bound to one another and pervasive in Old English heroic poetry, form the conceptual backbone which gives this poetry strength and coherence.

Early Cultures of North-West Europe, ed. Sir Cyril Fox and Bruce Dickens (Cambridge, 1950), pp. 261-272. P. L. Henry, *The Early English and Celtic Lyric* (London, 1966).

VI

HEROIC POETRY AND *BEOWULF*

In the introductory chapter of this book, I outlined in some detail the tradition of heroic poetry which the continental ancestors of the Anglo-Saxons brought to England. In the four succeeding chapters I attempted to describe four key concepts which constituted the ideological framework upon which the heroic poetry of Germania was built. Scholars know a good deal about the probable subject matter of pre-Christian Germanic poetry from various and diverse sources. Tantalizing allusions to the heroes and stories of Germanic history and legend appear in *Deor,* and virtually abound in *Beowulf. Widsith* contains a veritable catalogue of stories which might have been found in the repertory of a Germanic *scop* in the seventh century. A considerable number of these and other stories are preserved in one or another form in the Old Norse eddas and sagas, in Middle High German poems like the *Nibelungenlied* and *Kudrun,* and in ostensibly historical writings like Saxo Grammaticus' *Gesta Danorum.*

In spite of the apparent existence of a Germanic heroic tradition among the early Anglo-Saxons, however, there survive today no poems of substantial length which have not been at least touched by the traditions and ideas of Latin Christianity. This phenomenon is less than surprising, since in order to get themselves written down at all the heroic legends of Germania necessarily had to pass through the minds and hands of scribes trained under the auspices of the Christian Church. What is rather surprising is that there does exist a body of Germanic heroic poetry, written in the Roman alphabet and for the most part free of Christian influence. I am, of course, speaking of the heroic and mythological poems of the Old Norse *Edda*. The reasons why 'pure' Germanic heroic poetry exists in Old Norse and not to any extent in any other Germanic languages we cannot discuss here; it suffices to know that such poetry does exist outside of the imaginations of nostalgic Romantic scholars and antiquarians.

The poems of the *Edda* were written down in the latter half of the thirteenth century, almost three hundred years later than the four major Old English poetic manuscripts. The style of the eddic poems is terse, sometimes to the point of obscurity, and in general not very like that of Old English poetry. The only bit of Germanic heroic poetry which is nearly contemporary with early Old English heroic poetry and composed in a similar style is the Old High German fragment known as the *Hildebrandslied*.[1] This sixty-nine line fragment was copied down around the year 800, two centuries before the Old English poetic manuscripts. Nevertheless, anyone searching for a specimen of 'pure' pre-Christian heroic poetry composed about the time of *Beowulf* will come away disappointed from the *Hildebrandslied*. Even this brief fragment of a poem which in complete form was probably not much more than twice its present length contains what appear to be Christian allusions. The hero, Hildebrand, calls to witness a universal God who lives in heaven[2] and, a few lines later, remarks to this God that his evil fate seems to be sealed.[3] One cannot be absolutely certain that Hildebrand's God is not Wotan, but He at least appears to be the Christian God.

In Old English poetry, only the forty-eight line *Finnsburh* fragment unquestionably deals with subject matter from the Germanic past and is free of Christian references and allusions. In spite of metrical evidence to the contrary, scholars usually date *Finnsburh* as roughly contemporary with *Beowulf* on the basis of its style and subject matter.[4] The story appears in *Beowulf*

---

[1] Conveniently reprinted in Klaeber's edition of *Beowulf*, pp. 290-292.
[2] *wettu irmingot (quad Hiltibrant)   obana ab heuane* ... – l. 30.
[3] *Welaga nu, waltant got (quad Hiltibrant),   wewurt skihit* ... – l.49.
[4] See, e.g., Elliott Van Kirk Dobbie, *The Anglo-Saxon Minor Poems*, pp.

itself as a digression,[5] and its principal characters are alluded to in *Widsith*.[6] This possibly early date and lack of Christian reference, however, do not justify the conclusion that the *Finnsburh* fragment is part of what must have been a 'pure' Germanic poem. It is quite possible that the two- or three-hundred line poem from which the fragment comes[7] contained some sort of Christian reference. One need only consider what conclusions would be drawn concerning the Christianity of *Beowulf* if only the Finn-episode from that poem were extant. There, in ninety-eight lines, the poet mentions the cremation of a number of slain warriors, but not a word about God or men's souls.

The same good fortune which has preserved the *Finnsburh* fragment has also saved from oblivion two fragments from an Old English poem about the well-known Germanic hero Walter of Aquitaine. Walter's Germanic pedigree is every bit as good as those of Finn and Hengest but, by chance, the two *Waldere* fragments, unlike *Finnsburh*, both contain apparently Christian references. In the first fragment, Hyldegyth urges Waldere to do valiant deeds while God protects him,[8] and the second fragment breaks off just as Waldere is about to tell Guthhere what it is that 'he who believes in the help of the Holy One' 'finds readily'.[9] Again, conclusions based upon a pair of fragments concerning the Christianity of the entire *Waldere* are dangerous. Here we have two probably Christian references in the space of sixty-three lines; in the *Waltharius*, which treats the same story in 1456 Latin hexameter lines, I have counted fifteen lines containing Christian material.[10] In other words, *Waldere* reveals its Christianity in one out of every thirty-two lines, *Waltharius* in one out

---

xviii-xix; C. L. Wrenn, *A Study of Old English Literature* (New York, 1967), pp. 89-90; Klaeber, *Beowulf*, p. 238.
[5] Ll. 1063-1159.
[6] Ll. 27 , 29.
[7] Dobbie, *Minor Poems*, p. xviii.
[8] *ðenden ðin god recce* – I, l. 23.
[9] *Se ðe him to ðam halgan   helpe gelifeð / to gode gioce,   he þær gearo findeð* ... – II, ll. 26-27.
[10] Ed. Karl Strecker (Berlin, 1947). The lines are 110, 225, 564-565, 570, 1161-1167, 1456.

of every ninety-seven lines. Based upon these statistics, then, the obvious conclusion is that *Waldere* must have been about three times as pious a poem as *Waltharius,* even though the latter is almost certainly written by a monk and is, according to its prologue, dedicated to a Bishop. One might further argue that the relative paucity of Christian references in *Waltharius* is a function of its having been written for entertainment,[11] while *Waldere* was probably written for some more pious purpose. On the other hand, one might refrain from idle speculation altogether.

Both *Widsith* and *Deor* treat the heroes and stories of Germanic legend and both are probably early compositions; indeed, parts of *Widsith* may be the earliest English verse extant. Yet both poems show traces of the influence of Christian tradition. In the list of tribes he claims to have visited, Widsith includes Israelites, Assyrians, Hebrews, Indians and Egyptians (82-83), and at the end of the poem he refers to prosperous lords as 'those whom God allows to rule the kingdom of men'.[12] Deor similarly observes that *witig dryhten* distributes weal and woe throughout this world (31-34). So far as I know, no one has argued that *Widsith* is a religious poem, and only one scholar has suggested that the attitude expressed by Deor is Boethian rather than simply stoical.[13] Nevertheless, it seems that neither poem is a 'pure' Germanic product.

Three of the so-called 'elegiac' poems in the *Exeter Book* contain no overt Christian references. These are *The Wife's Lament, Wulf and Eadwacer* and *The Ruin.* The first two named, together with *The Husband's Message,* are usually considered to be dramatic monologues in which the fictional speakers express states of intense emotion. Scholars have often suggested that the speakers of these three monologues are figures from heroic legend whom the original audiences would have been able to identify and place in the contexts of their proper stories.[14] If one ac-

11   *Ludendum magis est dominum quam sit rogitandum* ... – Prologue, l. 19.
12   *se þe him god syleð gumena rice / to gehealdenne* ... – ll. 133-134.
13   Murray Markland, "Boethius, Alfred, and *Deor*", *MP* LXVI (1968), 1-4.
14   See, e.g., Greenfield, *Critical History,* pp. 223-227; Wrenn, *Old English Literature,* pp. 83-85, 150-153.

cepts this hypothesis, he can make a case for *The Wife's Lament*
and *Wulf and Eadwacer* as examples of 'pure' Germanic poetry
from heroic tradition, and at the same time ignore various problems in the interpretation of the now lost stories behind them.
The fact is, however, that we do not know, and probably will
never know, what these stories were, or even if they ever existed.
Moreover, if these two poems do indeed represent fragments of
heroic legend, their lack of Christian reference may be entirely
fortuitous. *The Husband's Message,* which may likewise have
a lost heroic legend behind it, contains a reference to *alwaldend
god (32).* We simply do not know enough about the provenance
or intention of these poems, or of *The Ruin,* in which *wyrd*
rather than God appears as the dominant force in the world,
to decide with any confidence how Christian or pagan they
really are. The subject matter and sentiments of these three
poems seem entirely secular, so that they could conceivably be
remnants of pre-Christian tradition, but on the other hand hidden Christian implications cannot absolutely be ruled out. *The
Wife's Lament* has recently been interpreted as a call from the
Church to Christ,[15] and *The Ruin* as a description of Babylon.[16]
Doubtless a simple Christian solution to the knotty problems
presented by *Wulf and Eadwacer* may appear at any time now.

The longest and most complex Old English poem which treats
Germanic heroic subject matter is, of course, *Beowulf.* The
origins of Beowulf, Hrothgar, Hygelac, Finn, Sigemund, and the
other heroes whose names and deeds appear in the poem are
buried, some of them irredeemably, in the history, legend and
folklore of the Germanic past.[17] We cannot know what form

---

[15] M. J. Swanton, *"The Wife's Lament* and *The Husband's Message*; A
Reconsideration", *Anglia* LXXXII (1964), 269-290. W. F. Bolton, *"The
Wife's Lament* and *The Husband's Message*: A Reconsideration Revisited",
Archiv CCV (1969), 337-351.
[16] Hugh T. Keenan, *"The Ruin* as Babylon", *Tennessee Studies in Litera-
ture* XI (1966), 109-117.
[17] For full discussions of the various historical and fabulous elements in
Beowulf see the introduction of Klaeber's edition of the poem, and R. W.
Chambers, *Beowulf: An Introduction to the Study of the Poem with a Dis-
cussion of the Stories of Offa and Finn,* 3rd ed. (Cambridge, Eng., 1959).
A noteworthy recent attempt to unravel the Germanic pre-history of the

or forms the oral poetic antecedents of *Beowulf* took,[18] but few scholars question the basic assumption that the poem which we have today has its roots in Germanic heroic tradition.[19] Moreover, it should be tolerably clear from the preceding chapters that heroic ideals, embodied in the concepts which I have described, pervade the poem. [The conduct of Beowulf, Wiglaf, Hrothgar, and the other heroes of whom the poet speaks adheres strictly to a code based upon loyalty, vengeance and treasure, while the punishment for violating this code is exile. I hope I need not labor the point. At the same time, however, *Beowulf* appears to be a Christian poem insofar as its poet is certainly a Christian of some sort and his poem is liberally salted with Christian sentiments and allusions.] The problem with which we must deal here is that of determining as precisely as possible in what way and to what degree *Beowulf* is a Christian poem.

The Christianity of *Beowulf* continues to be the subject of apparently endless debate. As it is usually formulated, the main point of contention is whether *Beowulf* is an 'essentially Christian' or 'essentially pagan' poem. As I pointed out earlier, however, we are not at all concerned in this study with 'paganism' in the strict sense of the term. The concepts which I have described embody essentially secular moral values and have nothing apparent to do with Germanic religion. They are 'pre-Christian', 'Germanic', and 'heroic', but not 'pagan' or 'heathen'. Nevertheless, we are centrally concerned here with Christianity in Old English poetry and should, therefore, review the various scholarly opinions about the Christianity in *Beowulf*.

The predominant early view of the poem saw it as an essentially pagan poem, drawn from pre-Christian materials which

---

poem is G. V. Smithers, *The Making of Beowulf*.

[18]   Francis P. Magoun, Jr., has attempted to revive the theory that the poem consists of several originally independent songs stitched together to form one long poem. "*Beowulf A*: A Folk-Variant", *Arv* XIV (1958), 95-101. "*Beowulf B*: A Folk-Poem on Beowulf's Death", *Early English and Norse Studies Presented to Hugh Smith* ..., ed. Arthur Brown and Peter Foote (London, 1963), 127-140.

[19]   An exception is Dorothy Whitelock, *Audience*, pp. 3-4, who cautiously suggests that perhaps "there never was a heathen poem on *Beowulf*".

once existed without Christian sentiments and allusions. The Christian elements are of the most elementary nature and are mere 'coloring' added by a pious interpolator. This interpolation theory was forcefully formulated by F. A. Blackburn in 1897,[20] and by Hector Munro Chadwick in 1912.[21] Chadwick observes that the Christian references are so elementary that 'a pious Jew' could have supplied them, and suggests that Christian poems of the kind attributed to Caedmon could be the source of the poem's Christianity. Chadwick believed that the poem had been transmitted orally, however, and differs from Blackburn in suggesting that the interpolating must have been the work of poets or minstrels rather than scribes. As recently as 1967, Charles Moorman has renewed the argument for "The Essential Paganism of Beowulf," [22] relegating the Christian elements to the periphery of the poem and emphasizing the pagan spirit and view of life which pervades it.

In 1911 and 1912, Frederich Klaeber published an exhaustive study of the Christian elements in Beowulf,[23] on the basis of which he arrived at conclusions almost diametrically opposed to those of Blackburn and Chadwick. Summarizing his views in the introduction to his 1922 edition of the poem, he acknowledges that it "abounds . . . in supernatural elements of pre-Christian associations", but asserts that nevertheless "the general impression" is decidedly Christian. The "general tone" and "ethical viewpoint" are "predominantly Christian" and "the main story has been thoroughly imbued with the spirit of Christianity". Klaeber further suggests, very cautiously, that "we might even feel inclined to recognize features of the Christian Savior" in Beowulf. The theory that the Christian elements are the work of an interpolator is, of course, rejected.[24] R. W. Chambers,

---

[20] "The Christian Coloring in Beowulf", PMLA XII (1897), 205-225. Reprinted in Nicholson, pp. 1-21.
[21] The Heroic Age, pp. 47-56.
[22] MLQ, XXVIII (1967), 3-18. Moorman does not revive the interpolation theory, however.
[23] "Die Christlichen Elemente im 'Beowulf' ", Anglia XXXV (1911), 111-136, 249-270, 453-482; XXXVI (1912), 169-199.
[24] Klaeber, Beowulf, pp. xlviii-li.

in the year before Klaeber's edition appeared, came to similar conclusions, rejecting the interpolation theory and finding the poet a "devout, but not theologically-minded" Christian, who knows his characters are pagans but lets them speak as if they were Christians.[25]

Virtually all subsequent scholars accepted Klaeber's view that *Beowulf* is an essentially Christian poem. The degree to which they think the poem is Christian, however, varies considerably. W. W. Lawrence, for example, describes the Christian passages as "an integral part of the epic"[26] and finds the Christian attitude toward life pervasive there,[27] but at the same time reasserts the older view of the quality of the poem's Christianity:

The religion of the characters seems imposed upon them rather than natural to them. The poorest and weakest parts of the poem are to be found among the definitely Christian passages. The only thing that is naive about the poem is its theology. Here is untried material and a childlike attitude toward a new faith. Tradition had not yet taught the poet how to treat it with technical assurance. But, though ever present, the Christianity is all on the surface. The real vitality of the epic lies in its paganism.[28]

Marie Padgett Hamilton, on the other hand, argues that the poet's view of the past and his interpretation of the events and agents of his story are conditioned by Christian doctrines of Providence and grace found in patristic writers like Gregory, Jerome and Augustine.[29] Dorothy Whitelock has likewise attributed a rather sophisticated knowledge of Christian doctrine to the poet and to his audience.[30]

Unquestionably the most influential attempt to sort out and reconcile Christian and pagan elements in *Beowulf* is that of J. R. R. Tolkien in his famous lecture of 1936.[31] Tolkien describes the *Beowulf-poet* as a Christian possessing "an instinctive

---

[25] Chambers, *Beowulf: An Introduction*, pp. 121-128.
[26] *Beowulf and Epic Tradition* (Cambridge, Mass., 1928), p. 258.
[27] Lawrence, pp. 283-284.
[28] Lawrence, p. 9.
[29] "The Religious Principle in *Beowulf*", *PMLA* LXI (1946), 309-331. Reprinted in *Nicholson*, pp. 105-135.
[30] *Audience*, pp. 3-8.
[31] "*Beowulf*: The Monsters and the Critics", *Nicholson*, pp. 51-103.

historical sense"[32] who writes of a past which was "heathen, noble and hopeless".[33] The theme of *Beowulf* is the temporal tragedy of death and of the transitory nature of all earthly things. The poet has inherited his theme from the heathen past, but he can place it in a Christian perspective. ⌐*Beowulf* represents a fusion of pagan belief in monsters as the powers of darkness, evil and chaos, and Christianity, in which the foes of mankind in this world are also the enemies of God. Thus, the troll, Grendel, has become a member of the race of Cain, and Hrothgar "a Christian English conception of the noble chief before Christianity".⌐[34] In an appendix to his original lecture, Tolkien draws further distinctions between the Christian poet, the "wise and noble monotheist" Hrothgar,[35] and Beowulf, who believes in his own might and the power of a pagan *wyrd*.

Tolkien's arguments, that in *Beowulf* the Christian poet recreated a noble but pagan past and that he succeeded in fusing Christian and pagan views of life, have proved extremely persuasive. Many subsequent studies of *Beowulf* have attempted to elaborate upon or refine Tolkien's basic thesis. Peter F. Fisher, for example, argues that the unity of the poem "is to be found in the theme of redemption and judgment treated in a way which skillfully blends the Germanic hero with the Christian saint".[36] Arthur G. Brodeur similarly finds that "in the poem as in its hero, old and new, pagan and Christian, combine in a heroic synthesis . . .".[37] Brodeur, however, takes issue with Tolkien's identification of the monsters in *Beowulf* with the foes of the Norse gods, and rejects his distinction between the religion of Hrothgar and that of Beowulf. The poet represents both characters "as speaking and acting as his hearers would expect good and noble men to do",[38] even though he knows they are pagans.

---

[32]   Tolkien, "Monsters", p. 54.
[33]   Tolkien, "Monsters", p. 71.
[34]   Tolkien, "Monsters", p. 79.
[35]   Tolkien, "Monsters", p. 97.
[36]   "The Trials of the Epic Hero in *Beowulf*", *PMLA* LXXIII (1958), 171-183; 171.
[37]   *The Art of Beowulf*, p. 184.
[38]   *Art*, p. 206.

In order to make his originally pagan materials acceptable to a
Christian audience, the poet presents the Danes and Geats "as
Abraham and his descendants were presented in the Old Testament".[39] More recently, Charles Donahue and Larry D.
Benson
have attempted to explain the Christian poet's apparent admiration and sympathy for his pagan characters, the former by suggesting the influence of Irish Christian traditions,[40] and the latter
by introducing evidence that Anglo-Saxon Christians experienced
genuine sympathy for their heathen brethren on the Continent
because they had not had the opportunity to know the true God,
but might nevertheless be virtuous men.[41]

Klaeber explicitly rejects the view that *Beowulf* might be a
Christian allegory in which the hero could be identified as
Christ,[42] but his observation that the hero might be modelled
upon the Christian Savior apparently has furnished the initial
impetus toward a number of studies of the poem in the light of
Christian allegory, symbolism and typology. D. W. Robertson
identifies Grendel's pond and its environs as the evil garden of
Scriptures, and Grendel as "the type of the militant heretic or
worldly man" against whom Beowulf, the type of Christ, fights.[43]
Allen Cabaniss finds a parallel between Beowulf's descent into
Grendel's pond and Christ's harrowing of hell, and concludes
that the entire episode is "at the least a reflection of the liturgy
of baptism; at the most an allegory of it".[44] M. B. McNamee
argues that all three major episodes in the poem "tell the story
of salvation in allegorical terms" with Beowulf, again, as Christ-
the-Savior.[45] Margaret Goldsmith discovers a rather different

[39] *Art*, p. 219.
[40] "*Beowulf* and Christian Tradition: A Reconsideration from a Celtic
Stance", *Traditio* XXI (1965), 55-116.
[41] "The Pagan Coloring of *Beowulf*", *Old English Poetry: Fifteen Essays*,
ed. Robert P. Creed (Providence, R. I., 1967), pp. 193-213.
[42] *Beowulf*, pp. cxx-cxxi.
[43] "The Doctrine of Charity in Mediaeval Literary Gardens: A Topical
Approach Through Symbolism and Allegory", *Speculum* XXVII (1951),
24-49. Reprinted in *Nicholson*, pp. 165-188; p. 184.
[44] "*Beowulf* and the Liturgy", *JEGP* LIV (1955), 195-201. Reprinted in
Nicholson, pp. 223-232; p. 230.
[45] "*Beowulf* – An Allegory of Salvation?" *JEGP* LXI (1960), 190-207.
Reprinted in *Nicholson*, pp. 331-352; p. 347.

Christian message in *Beowulf*. In her "typological" interpretation, Beowulf is noble but imperfect; he is "found wanting by the Christian poet" who portrays him as "unregenerate man at his noblest and most magnanimous".[46]

Certainly the most effective method of determining the validity of the various allegorical and typological interpretations of *Beowulf* would be to examine them in detail, one at a time. This approach, however, would entail an excessive amount of space, so a few general observations must suffice here. Adrien Bonjour has wisely observed that allegorical interpretations of Beowulf depend heavily upon "the demon of analogy".[47] The critic begins with a simple, unarguable point of similarity – for example, that Beowulf, like Christ, is the savior of his people. Upon this single point he then erects a rather complex critical edifice composed of much less obvious points of similarity. In this process he emphasizes, and often distorts, all of the details favorable to the primary analogy, while ignoring any details which detract from or contradict the argument. If, however, an allegorical reading of any work of literature is to be at all convincing, the analogy must hold true consistently and continuously for the entire work, and in allegorical readings of *Beowulf* the various analogies do not hold up under close scrutiny. It is much easier to impose an allegorical interpretation upon a literary work than it is to verify that that interpretation was intended by the poet to inhere in the work itself. We have no evidence that the *Beowulf*-poet intended that his poem be read as allegory, Christian, pagan or otherwise.

John Halverson, in a witty and perceptive attack upon the current tendency of some scholars to read Christian meanings into *Beowulf*, remarks that "an allegory must have some coherence if it is to work".[48] Typology, on the other hand, does not

---

[46] "The Choice in *Beowulf*", *Neophil.* XLVIII (1964), 60-72; 63. In this article Goldsmith replies to objections raised against her two previous articles, "The Christian Theme of *Beowulf*", *MAE* XXIX (1960), 81-101, and "The Christian Perspective in *Beowulf*", *Brodeur Studies*, pp. 71-90. See also Goldsmith's *The Mode of Meaning of 'Beowulf'* (London, 1970).

[47] "Beowulf et le Démon de l'Analogie", *Twelve Beowulf Papers* (Neuchâtel et Geneve, 1962), pp. 173-189.

[48] "*Beowulf* and the Pitfalls of Piety", *University of Toronto Quarterly* XXXV (1966), 260-278; 264.

require extended similarities, but rather it depends upon single points of analogy. Thus Beowulf diving into Grendel's pond becomes for the moment the type of Christ in the act of harrowing hell. But, as Halverson observes, there is no reason why one cannot find precisely the same symbolism in the descent of Beowulf's Old Norse counterpart, Grettir-the-Strong, into the haunted mere in *Grettissaga*.[49] Isolated bits of supposed Christian symbolism in a literary work do not convincingly support coherent readings of the work as a whole, especially when the various symbols may depend upon fortuitous similarities not intended or recognized by the author himself. The critic must prove that the author is using typology and intends his audience to recognize his Christian symbolism if his critical argument is to be credible. In *Beowulf* criticism, the pursuit of Christian symbolism has proved to be a rather subjective critical method; scholars employ the same basic methods upon the same materials and emerge with readings diametrically opposed to one another. Beowulf turns out to be a type of Christ in one reading, and a sinner guilty of pride and avarice in another. We cannot believe both readings, and there is no particular reason why we should believe either one, or a third, or a fourth.

If we reject for lack of concrete evidence the argument that *Beowulf* is a Christian allegory of some sort, we are left with the problem of evaluating the importance of the overt Christian references and sentiments in the poem. In 1951, J. R. Hulbert briefly suggested that Chadwick's estimate of the Christianity of the poem might be more accurate than that of Klaeber.[50] A year later T. M. Gang began a debate concerning the credibility of Tolkien's arguments for the unity of *Beowulf*.[51] Adrien Bonjour defended Tolkien's symbolic approach,[52] but in 1955 J. C. Van Meurs published another attack upon Tolkien's findings, this time focusing upon the supposed connection between Norse mythology and scriptural tradition.[53] Of particular rele-

---

[49] Halverson, 264-265.
[50] "The Genesis of *Beowulf*: A Caveat", *PMLA* LXVI (1951), 1168-1176.
[51] "Approaches to *Beowulf*".
[52] "Monsters Crouching and Critics Rampant".
[53] "*Beowulf* and Literary Criticism".

vance here is Van Meurs' judicious observation that "the thorough
fusion of Christian and pagan elements in the poem is one of the
few established facts of criticism; yet it is by no means clear
how that fusion came about and what exactly its nature is".[54]
Bonjour again came eloquently to the defense of Tolkien's
approach to the poem, but did not consider specifically the
questions raised about the nature of the fusion of Christian and
pagan elements.[55]

In two recent articles William Whallon has attempted, I think
with a good deal of success, to assess the quality of the "fusion"
of elements in *Beowulf*. In the first,[56] he argues that "the epic
knows little of Christianity besides two stories from the first nine
chapters of Genesis",[57] the story of the Creation and the story of
Cain. Whallon finds no reason to assume that the poet was
writing allegory or that he had the sort of temporal perspective
to differentiate a pagan past and a Christian present. The poet
would have no great difficulty in reinterpreting traditional Germanic materials in the light of his rather elementary Christianity;
the account of Creation could have effected a displacement of
native sky-gods by the Christian Creator, while the story of Cain
could have accounted for the existence of evil and a Christian
conception of an originally Germanic hell. In the second
article,[58] Whallon demonstrates that the apparently Christian
vocabulary of *Beowulf* comes, for the most part, from traditional
Germanic poetic language. Words and phrases for God and the
devil probably had originally pagan associations: "For the words
fæder, alwalda and *meotod* are as biblical as *pater, omnipotens*
and *fatum* are in the *Aeneid,* and Beowulf is to this extent neither
Christian nor unChristian but pre-Christian".[59] One need not
assume that the words for God and His enemies were understood
by the audience of *Beowulf* in an exclusively pagan sense, but it

[54]   Van Meurs, 121.
[55]   "*Beowulf* and the Snares of Literary Criticism", *Etudes Anglaises* X
(1957), 30-36.
[56]   "The Christianity of *Beowulf*", *MP* LX (1962), 81-94.
[57]   "Christianity", 81.
[58]   "The Idea of God in *Beowulf*", *PMLA* LXXX (1965), 19-23.
[59]   "Idea of God", 20.

is quite clear that they do not by themselves indicate an essentially Christian background for the poem.

One can scarcely doubt that the poet who composed the poem we know as *Beowulf* was a Christian. One cannot determine, however, how much Christian doctrine and story he knew. The evidence of the text suggests that Chadwick was probably correct in his conclusion that the stage in the development of Christianity which we find in *Beowulf* is elementary and superficial. Whatever the actual degree of religious sophistication which the poet attained in his life, the degree of sophistication in his poem seems slight. I must agree with Kenneth Sisam that "in this work the poet was not much concerned with Christianity and paganism".[60] *Beowulf* appears to be a Christianized heroic poem, in which the Christianity is pervasive but superficial, and in the remainder of this chapter I intend to suggest how it was Christianized, and to examine the quality and function of its Christian elements.

Robert D. Stevick has offered a very plausible theory to explain how an originally pre-Christian heroic poem about Beowulf might have acquired its Christianity.[61] In essence, Stevick's theory is this: *Beowulf* existed for some time as an oral poem before it was copied down. In this pretextual stage, the poem was subject to extensive modification and alteration, and after the conversion of England to Roman Christianity it could have absorbed its Christian elements in the course of being sung by one or more converted oral singers. "... Christian elements in Beowulf derive first and significantly from the normal mutations and accretions in explanation, characterization and reflective commentary in oral literature of a cultural tradition whose religion had changed more radically than its narrative materials and poetic techniques".[62] Oral poets Christianized the Germanic heroic poem by adding material to suit themselves and their audiences as they composed the poem in recitation. In the light

[60] *The Structure of Beowulf* (Oxford, 1965), p. 78.
[61] "Christian Elements and the Genesis of *Beowulf*", *MP* LXI (1963), 79-89.
[62] Stevick, 88.

of oral-formulaic theory, the possibility of interpolation proposed by scholars like Blackburn and Chadwick takes on a new relevance. The spectre of a 'monkish scribe' tampering with a pre-Christian text, altering a word here and a line there in order to make the heathen king of the Danes sound like a Christian Sunday-School teacher, may be exorcised. Whatever praise or blame is due can be properly placed upon the poet whose version of the originally oral poem was finally copied down as *Beowulf*.

I do not mean to suggest, however, that the Christian elements have entered the text of *Beowulf* in merely random fashion. Quite the contrary, the poet (or poets) has inserted Christian comments and pious exclamations into his poem because he considers them necessary and appropriate. For example, several scholars have suggested that the poet makes his characters speak like Christians in order to make them as attractive as possible to a Christian audience.[63] Thus, when Beowulf and Hrothgar speak of God as the decider of battle, their pious comments are not fortuitous but functional; they serve to characterize the speakers. There is, however, some element of chance involved here; the poet may refrain from pious comment in a context where we might conceivably expect it, and we may attribute the omission to the poet's preoccupation with other matters, to negligence, or simply to chance. As Stevick has noted, the poet seems to have added references to God's influence upon the outcome of Beowulf's fight with Grendel's mother when he first narrates the episode (1518-1569), and when Beowulf recounts the battle to Hrothgar (1655-1666), but not when Beowulf tells the same story to Hygelac (2135-2141); there is no apparent reason for the omission.[64] We must assume that when a Christian element appears in the poem there is a reason for its appearance and that, since the poem is intended for oral presentation, that reason should be readily intelligible in the immediate context.[65]

---

[63]   See, e.g., Brodeur, *Art*, pp. 182-219; Sisam, *Structure*, pp. 77-78.
[64]   Stevick, 81-84.
[65]   On this point see Michael D. Cherniss, "*Beowulf*: Oral Presentation and the Criterion of Immediate Rhetorical Effect", *Genre* III (1970), 214-228.

On the simplest level, we find what might be called pious exclamations, uttered by the poet and his characters alike, in direct response to particular situations in the story. The major portion of these commonplace exclamations centers around the idea of God as the giver of worldly prosperity, success in battle, and good fortune in general. Almost everyone in the poem thanks God for something or asks Him for something. To mention but a few instances, Beowulf observes that *witig God, halig Dryhten* will decide the battle with Grendel as He thinks fitting (685-687), he attributes protection and aid in the fight with Grendel's mother to *ylda Waldend* (1655-1664), and he gives thanks to *Frean, Wuldurcyninge, ecum Dryhtne* for the treasures he wins from the dragon (2794-2798). Hrothgar attributes Beowulf's arrival to the favor of *halig God* (381-384), offers thanks to the *Alwealdan* for Beowulf's victory over Grendel (928-929), and again offers thanks to *Gode, mihtigan Drihtne,* for Beowulf's resolution to fight Grendel's mother (1397-1398). The Geats collectively thank *Gode* for their easy voyage to Denmark (227-228), and for Beowulf's safe return from the depth's of Grendel's pond (1626-1628). The Danish shore-guard wishes the Geats the favor of *Fæder alwalda* (316-318), Wealtheow thanks *Gode* for Beowulf's presence in Denmark (625-628), and Hygelac thanks *Gode* that Beowulf has returned safely home (1997-1998). A second major idea, that good men go to heaven after death while evil ones go to hell, controls all but a handful of the rest of the pious exclamations in the poem. I refrain from adducing examples in the interests of space.

One cannot doubt that, if the poet is a Christian, the God to whom he and his characters allude is the Christian God. When the characters offer thanks, they offer it to a single deity; when the poet in his own voice attributes the outcome of a battle to a supernatural power, he attributes it to a single deity; and when the poet tells his audience that his characters offer thanks, it is again to a single deity. In short, the poet makes no distinction whatever between his God and the God of his characters. Nevertheless, none of these pious exclamations seem very profoundly theological or devout, or indeed particularly Christian, any more than the remark of a contemporary that he 'hopes to God' he can find a parking space downtown or 'thanks God' for having found one. The Christian piety of these exclamations is all on the surface; it is not necessarily insincere, but it is merely formal. The poet speaks this way because he is a believer in the Christian God, and his characters speak the same way because they too, as virtuous and noble man, must appear to be believers. Every good man recognizes that God controls our fortunes in this world and knows that the good are rewarded and the evil punished in the next world.

A slightly different kind of commonplace statement, the maxim, is closely related to the pious exclamation in function and frequency. The *Beowulf*-poet appears rather fond of applying to the events of his story generalized statements of social, moral and religious truths much like those collected in the *Exeter Book* and the Cotton Manuscript of the Anglo-Saxon *Chronicle*. The maxims in *Beowulf* are at times essentially Christian, occasionally slightly pagan, but most often simply secular and heroic in sentiment. They are fairly evenly distributed between the poet and his characters. The nature of any given maxim seems to be determined primarily by the particular situation with which the poet is dealing. Thus, in the course of describing the rise to power of Scyld and his heir, Beowulf, the poet observes *lofdædum sceal / in mægþa gehwære man gepeon* (24-25), an appropriate heroic maxim. Later, he remarks that God gave Beowulf victory over Grendel, which leads him to make the Christian observation that *Soð is gecyþed, / þæt mihtig God manna cynnes / weold wideferhð* (700-702). Beowulf comforts Hrothgar's grief at the death of Æshere with the comment that *Selre bið æghwæm, / þæt he his freond wrece,   þonne he fela murne* (1384-1385), a rather un-Christian sentiment, even though Hrothgar thanks God for the young warrior's words (1397-1398). It seems reasonable to suggest that in many, if not most, situations which call forth statements of general truth, a secular truth will do as well as a religious one; the choice is apparently determined by whichever maxim seems appropriate to the poet at the time. It is perhaps the poet's fondness for general truths rather than his Christian piety which motivates the occasional moralizing in *Beowulf*.

No appraisal of the quality of the Christianity in *Beowulf* can depend upon conclusions drawn from the quantity of pious exclamations and maxims in the poem. Though these are abundant, their nature is elementary and superficial. They center around a relatively small number of simple ideas about the power of God and the promise of a future life after death, none of which are exclusively Christian. Further, none of these brief comments and allusions contain overt references to scriptural stories, to Christ, or to Christian dogma. *Beowulf* contains, however, several longer passages which many scholars hold to be more explicitly Christian in content, and which have suggested to them a more profound kind of Christianity in the poem. We must now examine these passages with an eye toward the depth and complexity of their Christian sentiments and toward their functions within their respective contexts. If, as I have suggested, they are additions to the originally heroic material of the poem, the reasons for their inclusion should be tolerably clear.

The first of these longer, more provocative, passages is the poet's description of a song about the Creation sung by a *scop* in Heorot before Grendel begins his nightly raids (90-98). Songs about the creation of the world need not, of course, be Christian; Klaeber points out that a court minstrel in the *Aeneid* (i, 742ff.) sings one, and we have remnants of Germanic creation-songs in *Voluspa* and Snorri's prose *Edda*. Nevertheless we should, I think, give our Christian poet the benefit of any doubt and assume that he has in mind here a Christian Genesis-lay. Certainly, the description of *se Ælmihtiga* creating the earth, the sun and moon for the benefit of its inhabitants, and finally life itself sounds like the story of Genesis. The poet may very well have in mind a poem like the Caedmonian *Genesis;* Chadwick suggested that two or three Caedmonian poems could have provided all of the Christianity in *Beowulf*,[66] and more recently Whitelock has argued that the audience of Beowulf was accus-

---

[66] *The Heroic Age*, p. 49.

tomed to hearing Christian poetry.[67]

The poet introduces the Creation-song as an example of the *dream . . . hludne in healle* (88-89) to which Grendel reacts so violently. Hall joys are of course a familiar heroic motif, intimately related to the ideal of the *comitatus*, and it is at least possible that, insofar as all songs are joys of the hall, the poet makes little distinction between Christian stories and stories from heroic tradition. This would not be surprising if he were accustomed to hearing both kinds of stories in a similar setting – whether it be the great hall of a lord or the refectory of a monastery – and considered them equally entertaining and appropriate. We cannot know whether *se þe cuþe / frumsceaft fira   feorran reccan* (90-91) is the same *scop* who later sings of Sigemund and of Finn, though Hrothgar seems to have only one *scop,* but certainly we never again hear of anyone singing a Christian song in Heorot.

Grendel's reaction to this joyous song helps to define him as an evil creature. Clearly, his hatred of the Danes' happiness in the hall reveals him as an outsider, making the opposition between him and his enemies explicit. One can carry the argument a bit farther and assume that Grendel's anger is directed specifically against the Christian content of the Creation-song, an assumption supported somewhat by the description of his descent from Cain in the succeeding lines. His motive for attacking Heorot, then, would appear to be his hatred of pious songs and this, in turn, would explain the poet's purpose in introducing the creation-song in this context. On the other hand, it is not clear whether it is the *scop's* Christian subject matter or simply the joy associated with songs in general which enrages Grendel. The decision rests largely upon one's conception of the poet's attitude toward Christian and heroic songs, and we have no evidence upon which to base a valid judgment. Grendel may be angry about the particular song, or he may be angry about songs in general.

The first of the two passages referring to Cain places Grendel directly in the race of the first murderer in the Old Testament (104-114). The passage functions primarily to identify and

[67]   *Audience,* pp. 8-12.

define Grendel at the point at which he becomes an actor in the narrative. The poet's impulse to define Grendel's character by his lineage seems identical with the genealogical impulse I have described in Chapter Four. It accounts for the poet's placing of Hrothgar in the Scylding line, for Hrothgar's associating Beowulf with his father Ecgtheow, for the various allusions to Hygelac's relatives, and for the introduction of Wiglaf's father, Weohstan. Just as noble ancestry suggests the inherent worth and virtue of a hero, so evil ancestry suggests an evil offspring; Grendel's relationship to the *untydras* (111) descended from Cain places him firmly in an evil line.

Miss Hamilton has cogently and judiciously discussed the theological background whereby monsters came to be associated with Cain, the *gigantes* of Genesis, and the inhabitants of Augustine's Earthly City in general, further suggesting that the poet only figuratively associated Grendel with this evil race.[68] There is, however, no indication that the poet knows this body of doctrine at first-hand. Whallon observes that "the Christian idea of the enemy of mankind affected the nature attributed in *Beowulf* to the ogres that preceded him, but the poet had no greater theological erudition than was necessary for appropriating the language used by a missionary in teaching the story of Cain".[69] The poet needs to know only that Grendel's ancestor, Cain, killed his kinsman, a crime thoroughly reprehensible to the Germanic code of conduct, and that from Cain descended a race of God-hating monsters whom God punished for their crimes. Whether he thinks of this punishment as the Flood, or damnation, or both, is not clear in this context.

Another factor which may or may not have influenced this first Cain passage is that, with the introduction of the song of Creation, the poet has worked himself into an immediate difficulty. He states unequivocally that God created *cynna gehwilcum   þara ðe cwice hwyrfaþ* (98), and then introduces a thoroughly malign creature, whose existence he may have felt impelled to account for. The story of Cain as he presents it here

[68] Hamilton, pp. 113-124.
[69] Whallon, "Christianity", 91.

gets him out of his difficulty by accounting for the existence of monsters like Grendel at the same time that he identifies him.

The second Cain-passage, like the first, functions to introduce a new actor, Grendel's mother, into the narrative (1260-1269). The nature of oral poetry explains the repetition of previously given information; the poet cannot rely upon his audience to remember Grendel's lineage. In this second passage the poet again mentions Cain's slaying of his kinsman, his subsequent exile, and his evil progeny, among whom he quite literally (*þanon* – 1265) numbers Grendel and, by implication, his mother. The references to Grendel as a 'hellish fiend', 'God's enemy', a 'heathen soul', and the companion of 'devils' probably depend upon his evil lineage and character rather than any explicitly theological concept of evil. This would help to explain why the dragon later in the poem does not receive similar epithets. While the poet conceives of Grendel as a troll, a human-like biped of the same race as *eotenas, ylfe, orcneas,* and *gigantas,* the dragon, in spite of his human motivations and reactions,[70] remains physically a member of the animal kingdom. Thus Grendel can receive a lineage and a kind of genealogy which is originally human while the dragon has no lineage at all, he simply appears and settles on the hoard (2270-2277). Grendel, as a member of the race of Cain, is *Godes andsaca* (1682), but the dragon, a dangerous animal, is only *se ðeodsceaða* (2278). This essential difference between Grendel and the dragon suggests that the Cain material in *Beowulf* has less importance as a theological explanation of evil than it does as a device for defining the characters of Grendel and his mother.

Possibly related to the Cain-passages is the description of the hilt of the sword with which Beowulf slays Grendel's mother (1677-1698). Blackburn thought that this passage originally referred to the Northern myth of the war between the gods and the giants,[71] but again I give the Christian poet the benefit of the doubt, and assume that he means to describe the flood in Genesis. The allusion to the Flood relates the sword explicitly to Grendel

---

[70]   See Chapter Four.
[71]   Blackburn, pp. 14-15.

and his race of *gigantas*, and suggests that the poet is still thinking of the Scriptural lineage of his trolls. Problems arise, however, if we seek consistency here. Since the race of giants died
in the Flood (1689-1690), we must, as Miss Hamilton suggests,[72] take Grendel's lineage figuratively. Again, if like all
wondrous creations of the past the sword is the 'old work of
giants' (1679),[73] why did its creator portray the beginning of the
strife which destroyed his race on it, and how did he manage it?
Did he simply carve the beginning of the enmity of God and the
giants before he was slain? Perhaps the poet did not remember
the story of the Flood and its interpretation very clearly. We
should probably not seek theological or mythological consistency
here. The emphasis in this passage falls primarily upon the
wonderful splendor and strangeness of the exotically carved
sword and, somewhat less certainly, upon its relationship to the
monsters who formerly owned it.

The Christian passage which causes scholars the most trouble
and raises the greatest difficulty for interpretation of the poem
as a whole is the so-called "Christian Excursus" (175-188). Here
the poet states quite clearly that the Danes are pagans who in
their search for a solution to the problem of Grendel's raids pray
to idols and do not know God. This passage seems radically at
variance with the apparently Christian tone of Hrothgar's
speeches, and with the poet's estimate of him as a perfect king.[74]
The poet's words indicate that this idol-worship is no temporary
apostasy from Christianity:

> Swylce wæs þeaw hira,
> hæþenra hyht; helle gemundon
> in modsefan, Metod hie ne cuþon,
> dæda Demend, ne wiston hie Drihten God,
> ne hie huru heofena Helm herian ne cuþon,
> wuldres Waldend. (178–183)

Tolkien's suggestion that only a part of the Danish people are
meant here seems unlikely.[75] Wealtheow and the shoreguard utter

---

[72] Hamilton, pp. 116, 120-124.
[73] Compare *Beowulf*, ll. 2616, 2717, 2774, 2979; *Wanderer*, l. 87; *Ruin*, l. 2.
[74] See e.g., ll. 1885-1886 (*þæt wæs an cyning / æghwæs orleahtre*).
[75] Tolkien, "Monsters", p. 101.

pious phrases like Hrothgar himself and, as Brodeur suggests, Hrothgar appears to be included in this description of Danish heathenism.[76] Blackburn rejected the entire passage as an interpolation,[77] while Tolkien[78] and Whitelock[79] find lines 181-188 suspect. The interpolation theory is attractive since without the Christian Excursus one would be free to take the other Christian material in *Beowulf* as a rather typical kind of medieval anachronism. The poet would seem no more confused about the religion of his characters than the composers of *Waltharius* or the *Nibelungenlied*.

Brodeur has argued that the poet is well aware of the Danes' paganism, and that he conceives of Grendel as a punishment sent by God for that paganism.[80] His conclusions concerning the Excursus are rather persuasive and are worth considering at some length:

In my opinion that passage is wholly genuine, and most deliberate. I believe the poet wished to put on record, once for all, the fact that Hrothgar and his Danes were pagans, and were punished for their idolatry; this was an almost necessary concession to his place and age. Even so, he could not permit himself to pronounce this judgment without reminding his hearers plainly that the paganism of this good king and his people was their misfortune, not their fault He could hardly have avoided the admission of Danish heathenism, since his audience surely knew that both Danes and Geats were heathen. The chief personages of his story were Danes and Geats; Beowulf must illustrate the heroic ideal, and Hrothgar must be shown as a great and good king. Therefore, he wisely admitted, early in the poem, the paganism of the Danes, explained it as their unfortunate heritage, and made the most of the tragic irony of the situation. Thereafter he was free to let them speak in those terms of gratitude and reverence for God which, by the standards of his own time and country, good men use. As Chambers has pointed out, the poet's avoidance of more strictly doctrinal terms, of reference to Christ or the saints, is to be explained on the ground that he knew the Danes and Geats *were* pagans.[81]

[76]   Brodeur, *Art*, pp. 197-198.
[77]   Blackburn, pp. 15-16.
[78]   Tolkien, "Monsters", pp. 101-103.
[79]   Whitelock, *Audience*, p. 78.
[80]   Brodeur, *Art*, pp. 204-205.
[81]   Brodeur, *Art*, p. 207.

Certainly, if one accepts the Christian Excursus as genuine, he must admit that the poet is aware that his characters are pagan. The argument that Grendel's visits are the punishment for that paganism, however, is open to serious doubts. If one takes the Creation song to be essentially Christian, then it seems more likely that Grendel, God's enemy, attacks because the Danes are Christian; to accept Brodeur's argument, one must assume the Creation song is a pagan one. Again, if as the poet says the Danes don't know the true God, Grendel's raids would seem, at least to an audience not well-versed in theological doctrine, a rather unjust punishment. If God is punishing the Danes, why should he suddenly relent and permit Beowulf to save them? Why, if the poet wishes to put on record the paganism of the Danes, does he wait until after he has suggested that they listen to what seems to be a Christian song in the hall? Why are the Geats never specifically identified as heathen like the Danes? Such questions could be resolved by a theological gloss on the poem, but one might doubt that a poet composing for oral performance would expect his auditors to be able to supply a running gloss as he recites his poem. Brodeur's explanation of the presence of the Excursus does not eliminate the inconsistency in the poet's treatment of his characters. Rather it makes the inconsistency appear to be a more serious aesthetic fault by suggesting that the poet is highly conscious of the paganism of his characters and in spite of this conciousness portrays them as Christians. It would seem wiser, perhaps, to acknowledge that such inconsistencies are very common in oral poetry,[82] and to minimize the importance of this particular inconsistency by

---

[82] As C. M. Bowra has observed, "The conditions of oral performance may mean that sooner or later a poet contradicts himself or muddles something in his narrative. There are few heroic poems in which some contradiction cannot be found. The poet so concentrates on his immediate task that he may not remember all that has gone before or forsee all that will come later. The chances are that any such slip will be of little importance, since, if the poet does not notice it, it is not likely that his audience will notice it either. But when his poem is written down and subjected to the sharp eyes of critical scholars, what was originally a trivial slip may be regarded as a grave error.... We must remember that most heroic poems are composed for one performance only and that the audience has no written text before

attempting to account for its presence not with reference to the poem as a whole, but with reference to its immediate context.

The Excursus is preceded by the introduction of Grendel and a general description of the demoralizing effect of his raids upon the Danes (115-146). The attacks continue for twelve years, and the wisest of the Danes are unable to make peace with or otherwise control Grendel (154-169). Aside from the devouring of Danish retainers, the most devastating effect of Grendel's ravages is the fact that the Danes are unable to inhabit the great hall after dark, which suggests the practical dissolution of the *comitatus* structure upon which heroic society is founded (138-146). Having noted the Danes' inability to prevent Grendel's raids, the poet goes on to describe them at council, where they seek a solution to their problem (170-174). Since the poet at this point in the narrative apparently thinks of his characters as pagans, he depicts them resorting, as pagans do when they need help, to idol-worship (175-178).[83] If he conceived of his characters as being to any degree Christian, he could easily have shown them praying to a Christian God, in which case the subsequent departure of Beowulf would appear to be God's answer to their prayers, and the inconsistency would not exist.

Idol-worship seems appropriate to a description of the Danes' search for a way out of their plight; it emphasizes their desperation and the futility of their efforts. The poet knows that pagan rites do not work very well, and he remarks upon their pagan character; they are the practice of those who don't know the true God (178-183). He does not say specifically that the Danes' paganism has caused their plight; he merely implies that their misdirected offerings will do them no good in their misery.

---

it . . . . The poet is therefore not much concerned to make everything consistent . . . ." *Heroic Poetry* (London, 1964), pp. 299-300. Beowulf's supposed 'inglorious youth' (2183-2188) is a typical example of this phenomenon.
[83] Sisam, *Structure*, p. 74, and Whitelock, *Audience*, pp. 78-79, suggest that the poet may have felt idol-worship to be a present danger to Christianity in the England of his time. This would account for the poet's recognition and condemnation of this particular practice, while he ignores the paganism of the more exotic practice of cremation with one's treasures, which had become an obsolete custom much earlier.

Indeed, he seems to be trying to alleviate the problem of having pagan heroes by attributing their paganism to 'custom' and ignorance. His observation about the Danes' paganism leads him directly into one of his frequent moral maxims, this one upon the relative merits of true and false belief – those who go to hell suffer woe, while those who go to heaven are happy (183-188). This maxim has no very direct bearing on the Danes' attempt to find a solution to their problem; it sounds like a sort of aside in which the poet is reacting to his own statement about pagans who don't know God. He is getting a bit off the track of his story, and he returns to it by picking up where he left off – he reiterates the difficulty the Danes experience in dealing with Grendel (189-193).

The poet's description of the dire circumstances of the Danes has prompted him to remark upon the dangers of pagan worship in much the same way that he remarks frequently upon the conduct of good retainers and good kings, and to make a statement about what he considers true religion. Once he has stated his beliefs, he quickly picks up the thread of his story. He never returns to the subject of the Danes' paganism because it is not really an important factor in the story. It would appear that the fact that his characters are pagans occurred to him and, having stated the fact, he felt obliged to excoriate them for such beliefs, after which he ignores these beliefs altogether. When describing Beowulf's departure for Denmark (193ff.), he does not attribute the imminent salvation of the Danes to God's grace, nor does he suggest that God has relented in His punishment of these pagans. By the time Hrothgar attributes Beowulf's arrival to God's favor (381-384), the audience might well have forgotten all about the idols. Certainly the sentiment expressed in the Excursus is Christian, and certainly it contradicts our impression of Hrothgar and his people, but it would probably be a mistake to attach much importance to it for the poem as a whole. It is, after all, as much an assertion of the poet's Christianity as of the Danes' paganism.

Critics often read Hrothgar's 'sermon' (1698-1784) as a Christian homily on the sins of pride and avarice. Brodeur, for example, consistently refers to Hrothgar's warning against *superbia,* attributes the poet's views on the subject, either directly or indirectly, to Augustine and Gregory, and finds in the 'sermon' the king's admission that he himself had been guilty of the sin of pride in building Heorot.[84] Margaret Goldsmith follows Brodeur's view of the 'sermon', but goes far beyond Brodeur in making the passage control her reading of *Beowulf* as a poem about pride and covetousness. As she would have it, ". . . Hrothgar, whose spiritual sloth had let envy and murder into Heorot, had seen his error, and so could beg Beowulf to guard himself against pride and covetousness, when the testing time should come.[85] Such readings of the passage, however, are by no means universally accepted. Halverson argues that "the point of Hrothgar's 'sermon' is practical and political; it is religious only to the extent that he attributes wealth and power to the favor of God, and even that is not an exclusively Christian notion".[86] Sisam notes of all Hrothgar's speeches: ". . . they put forward no characteristically Christian doctrine. Most intelligent men would agree that overweening is a vice, especially in the crude forms that Hrothgar thinks of – miserliness, rapacity and the wanton killing of companions (1709ff.). Reversals of fortune (1769ff.) are a commonplace subject of reflection and story among pagans. So are the shortness and uncertainty of human life (1753ff.) . . .".[87]

Hrothgar's speech is occasioned by the receipt of the wonderful swordhilt of which I have already spoken (1677-1698). Possibly the poet intends his audience to think that Hrothgar's words depend upon his Christian interpretation of the stories of Cain and Noah, but it seems more likely and more simple that, if he intends any connection at all, it is between the defeat of Grendel and his mother, and the hilt of a sword from their lair. Relics of battle usually remind one of the battles themselves; that is their purpose. Thinking of the defeated monsters, Hroth-

[84]   Brodeur, *Art*, pp. 208-215.
[85]   Goldsmith, "Perspective", p. 83.
[86]   Halverson, 263.
[87]   Sisam, *Structure*, pp. 78-79.

gar predictably begins by praising the might and wisdom (*mægen mid modes snyttrum* – 1706) of Beowulf, whose glory (*blæd* – 1703) is now assured. Such a hero, he observes, will become a great asset to his people (1707-1709). Hrothgar is thinking of Beowulf now as a prospective lord of the Geats, and he introduces Heremod as an example of a bad lord for instructional purposes.

A comparison between the Heremod passage in Hrothgar's speech (1709-1722) and the earlier Heremod passage (901-915) reveals the essential purpose of this later reference. In the earlier passage, Hrotgar's *scop* glorifies Beowulf's victory over Grendel by contrasting his service to the Danes with Heremod's failure to benefit them. Heremod was capable of performing valorous deeds, but he came to a miserable end and was a 'great sorrow' to his people. The Danes expected him to become a worthy lord, and therefore a *bote* for their *bealwa* (909), but he belied their expectations. No specific reason for Heremod's failure appears in this first passage, nor does the *scop* level any specific charge against him; the emphasis falls almost entirely upon the fact of his failure to benefit the Scyldings. The juxtaposition of statements at the end of the passage makes the point of contrast clear; Beowulf is 'a friend to all mankind' while 'evil took possession of' Heremod (913-915). Heremod failed to serve the Scyldings when they needed him, while Beowulf saved them from impending disaster.

In the Heremod passage of Hrothgar's 'sermon', the emphasis is slightly different. This later passage repeats some of the information given earlier – that Heremod failed to benefit his people and came to a bad end – but additional details alter the essential point of his story. Here Hrothgar offers Heremod explicitly as an example of a bad lord; he failed to give rings to the Danes according to their glory (*æfter dome* – 1720), and he slew his own retainers. While the function of the earlier passage was to glorify Beowulf's service to the Danes by contrasting that service with Heremod's failure to serve them, here the function is to glorify Beowulf's potential worth as a Germanic lord by contrasting him with a bad lord who violated the heroic code of loyalty and generosity. The earlier passage revealed no didactic intention, but here there is a warning implicit in the story of Heremod, a warning which Hrothgar will apply directly to Beowulf.

Heremod's story leads Hrothgar to offer a generalized description of the way in which a wise and powerful lord may degenerate, becoming a bane to his followers (1724-1757). God gives such lords great prosperity, and in their happiness they neglect to think of the future. Pride (*oferhygda dæl* – 1740) grows and the soul's guardian (*sawele hyrde* – 1742), conscience or perhaps reason, sleeps. Soon a metaphorical slayer (*bona* – 1743), an evil spirit, shoots 'arrows' which inflame the breast with strange desires. Then he grows greedy and fails to rule in proper heroic fashion. Finally he dies and a better ruler, one who gives treasure freely, succeeds him. All this may sound vaguely theological, but the morality being expressed remains essentially heroic and Germanic. The description of the *bona* and his arrows may derive from Christian homiletic descriptions of the devil, but as Halverson observes, it is being used in a secular context.[88] The 'pride' here is not theological *superbia* but temporal overweening, and the future with which a Germanic lord should concern himself may just as easily be his glory after death – which Heremod has sacrificed and the new lord who gives treasure freely will gain – as some sort of Christian afterlife among the angels.

Hrothgar next applies the lesson of his little discourse to Beowulf (1758-1768). He advises Beowulf to choose *ece rædas* (1760) by avoiding the *oferhyda* to which Heremod and his kind have fallen victim. *Ece rædas* might imply the eternal rewards of heaven, but the phrase may mean no more than 'advice which is always good' for a secular ruler. Hrothgar points out that misfortune, especially death, may strike at any time, and here again the implications may be entirely secular; if one dies ignominiously, he will be so remembered. Hrothgar offers himself as an example, not of the sin of *superbia*, nor of the secular pride

88   Halverson, 263.

of bad lords, but of the vicissitudes of fortune. His account of his recent difficulties may be no more than an extension of his general remarks on misfortune, or he may be suggesting indirectly that his future glory would have been severely injured had he died while Grendel still terrorized his people. He does not seem to be suggesting that he was responsible for Grendel's attacks. He simply thanks God in his usual manner for his present good fortune.

Hrothgar's 'sermon', then, need not be about theological pride and covetousness, even though pride and covetousness appear there as secular, heroic vices. Hrothgar concerns himself with the duties and proper conduct of Germanic lords, and with the glory which they may lose if they fail to fulfill the ideals upon which that glory is founded. The speech is not a Christian homily, even though it may contain echoes of the poet's Christian background. Significantly, at the end of the poem Beowulf dies confident that he has followed Hrothgar's advice: he has protected his people from their enemies (2732-2736), has not slain his kinsmen (2739-2743), and has, he believes, won treasure for his followers to enjoy after his death (2794-2798). The description of his funeral confirms the fact that he has won in his lifetime glory which will live after him (3155-3182). Hrothgar's 'sermon' is important, perhaps central, to the poem, not because it reveals a Christian view of life, but because it give expression to secular ideals which control the conduct of Germanic heroes.

The narrator and all of the important heroes who appear in *Beowulf* speak as if they are at least superficially Christian. Within the confines of the text itself, however, the Christianity appears rather elementary in quality; scriptural references are limited to perhaps two stories from Genesis, while references to theology or dogma are virtually impossible to identify with an appreciable degree of confidence. Germanic heroic ideals of conduct control the action of the poem; Christian piety is incidental to it. Without the various pious comments and Christian allusions in the poem, *Beowulf* would remain our finest Germanic heroic poem, far more highly developed in its artistry than the heroic

poems of the *Edda,* but scarcely more Christian. Without the
Christian Excursus, *Beowulf* would appear to be a nominally
Christian but essentially secular heroic poem like *Waltharius* or
the *Nibelungenlied.* As it stands, however, the poem is neither
entirely pagan nor essentially Christian. It is a hybrid, a
Germanic heroic poem composed by a Christian poet for a
Christian audience, and the contradictions which arise from the
process of hybridization will probably never be succesfully
resolved to the satisfaction of all.

Beowulf, like the Latin *Waltharius,* must, I think, be described
as a Christianized heroic poem. Its Christianity appears, to be
sure, pervasive, but nevertheless it remains 'coloring' in an otherwise secular poem. For this reason it would seem unwise to
overemphasize the importance of any or all of the Christian
elements in *Beowulf,* just as it would seem unwise to overemphasize the few traces of Germanic paganism there. I repeat,
Germanic heroic concepts provide the very fabric of the poem;
it is essentially secular, Germanic and heroic, not primarily either
Christian or pagan. It could quite conceivably be the product of
an illiterate *scop* who learned both heroic legend and Christian
religion by word of mouth. Indeed, he might have learned whatever he knew of Christian story and sentiment from the homilies
of preachers and from the sort of Old English poems which we
associate with the name Cædmon. We may now turn our attention
to that larger group of Old English poems which deals with
Christian subject matter.

VII

GENESIS B

No one has ever seriously challenged the critical view that the majority of Old English narrative poems dealing with Christian stories and themes contains pre-Christian, Germanic elements. That much is apparent from the most casual reading of Old English poetry. The Germanic heroic elements in *Genesis B*, the first of the Christian poems which we shall consider here, have been noticed by many scholars, most of whom have restricted their observations to brief remarks upon the fact that Satan is presented as the disloyal retainer of a God who appears Himself to be a Germanic lord. Having paid their respects to the Germanic ancestors of the poem, however, scholars have been quick to focus their attention upon the Christian antecedents, literary and theological, of *Genesis B*. The pre-Christian concepts which we have been discussing have received cursory treatment, and the extent to which they influence the Anglo-Saxon poet's manner of telling his story has been largely ignored.[1]

The poet who originally conceived *Genesis B* took his story from Judaeo-Christian tradition. The plot and characters of the story, as it unfolds itself in *Genesis B,* come from scriptures, from apocryphal documents and, possibly, from exegetical commentaries upon Genesis and from Eastern sources. The cosmology of the poem is likewise Christian, although the three realms of heaven, earth and hell are paralleled in the pagan cosmos of Northern mythology as it survives in the two Icelandic eddas.

[1] A notable exception is J. M. Evans, *"Genesis B* and Its Background", *RES*, n.s., XIV (1963), 1-16, 113-123, to which we will have occasion to refer in the course of this chapter.

These Christian elements are self-evident and require only passing notice here, but less evident is the dominance of pre-Christian heroic concepts in the poem. The ideals and attitudes by which the conduct of the characters is judged, and which, therefore, establish the moral climate of the poem, are virtually identical with those which govern the conduct of the heroes of Germanic legend. In spite of several clearly heroic passages, the primacy of these ideals is often obscured by an apparently Christian vocabulary and by the smoothness with which the Christian story and the heroic concepts are joined. The violent conflict inherent in the story, the hierarchic world in which it is set, and the absence of complex theology make it possible for the Germanic poet to tell this Christian story using techniques originally developed for pagan heroic verse. Yet the poet, whatever the sophistication of his Christianity, could not, and indeed did not try to, avoid presenting and evaluating his characters and their acts according to the concepts which we find embedded in Germanic tradition for "his first concern seems to have been to write a poem which would be acceptable to an audience familiar with secular Germanic literature".[2]

The profusion of heroic elements in *Genesis B* may, at least partially, be accounted for by its somewhat peculiar provenance. The poem which we know as *Genesis B*, or the *Later Genesis*, consists of six-hundred and sixteen lines (235-851) which have been interpolated into the long Genesis-paraphrase, *Genesis A*, in the *Junius Manuscript*.[3] *Genesis A* is a 'Cædmonian' poem which was probably composed around the year 700,[4] but the interpolated poem is of considerably later date. According to B. J. Timmer, the most recent editor of *Genesis B*, "The evidence of phonology and vocabulary shows that the L[ater] G[enesis] was translated from the Old Saxon about the time of King Alfred, or shortly afterwards"[5] — that is, about the year

---

[2]   Evans, 123.
[3]   Ed., George Philip Krapp (New York, 1931). All citations from *Genesis B* are from this edition, pp. 9-28.
[4]   Krapp, *The Junius Manuscript*, pp. xxvi-xxvii.
[5]   *The Later Genesis*, ed. B. J. Timmer (Oxford, 1948), p. 43.

900. The immediate source of *Genesis B* is an Old Saxon poem of which three fragments, one corresponding to lines 790 to 816 of the Old English poem and two for which there are no known Old English counterparts, exist today.

In the seventh century, English missionaries travelled to the Continent in order to convert the Germanic tribes to Christianity. By the eighth century, the English influence in Germany was extensive, and English culture had spread widely through the Germanic peoples. Timmer takes the traditional point of view and conjectures that Saxon scholarship, aided greatly by the similarity of the Old Saxon and Old English languages, grew, and in the second quarter of the ninth century the Old Saxon poems *Heliand* and *Genesis,* modelled upon Old English religious poetry like *Genesis A,* were composed. Also during the ninth century, many Saxon monks journeyed to England, bringing with them manuscripts among which was doubtless one containing the Old-Saxon *Genesis.* Thus, it was in England that *Genesis B* was translated from Old Saxon to Old English.[6] Thus, although the date of composition of *Genesis B* is comparatively late, the persistence and prominence of heroic elements in the poem may be attributed to its being a translation of a poem written in a Germanic country more recently converted to Christianity than England, and itself modeled upon English poems roughly contemporary with *Beowulf.*

Very nearly a century of scholarship has failed to discover a single, unquestionable source for *Genesis B* and its Old Saxon counterpart, and only the *Vulgate* is almost unanimously accepted as a partial source. Because the story of the Fall in the poem differs in several important details from the scriptural account, scholars have searched assiduously for parallel details in the Christian documents of the period, with only limited success. The two most recent scholars to deal with the problem of sources, J. M. Evans and Rosemary Woolf, come to quite different conclusions, the former concluding that the poet used 'literary' sources like the poems by Avitus and Dracontius on

---

[6] For a more detailed discussion of the origins of *Genesis B* see Timmer's edition, pp. 43-45.

the Fall,[7] the latter favoring the theological tradition of apocryphal and exegetical documents.[8] In the absence of any unanimity or certainty concerning either partial of complete sources, Timmer's conclusions remain the most readily acceptable: the poet may have worked with some apocryphal document which has been lost, but "So long as the document which presumably is the source of the *Genesis* does not turn up, we may ascribe the poetical elaborations and the emotional and dramatic details to the originality of the poet. This would naturally hold both for the [Old Saxon] *Genesis* and for L[ater] G[enesis] . . .".[9]

If the composer of the Old Saxon *Genesis* had no single source from which he took his story whole, and we have no evidence that he had such a source, then we are free to attribute not only "the poetical elaborations and the emotional and dramatic details" but also the overall structure of the poem to his originality. For example, we may assume that, since the *Vulgate* Genesis does not describe Satan's Fall, the poet is himself responsible for the inclusion of this description (no matter what his source for it) in the place in which it appears in *Genesis B*. We may further assume that in placing this description within the story of the Fall of Man the poet had some structural purpose in mind, and we may speculate upon what that purpose might be. Such speculation, however, must begin with the assumption that *Genesis B* has structural unity, while the evidence which we have concerning the original form of the Old Saxon *Genesis* seems to contradict this assumption. The Old Saxon fragment which corresponds to lines 791 through 817 of *Genesis B* is one of four Old Saxon poetic fragments written in six blank spaces in a manuscript discovered in 1894 in the Vatican Library. There can be no doubt that the passage in *Genesis B* is a translation of its Old Saxon counterpart.[10] One of the Old Saxon fragments is from the *Heliand,* while the other

[7]   Evans, 1-16.
[8]   Rosemary Woolf, "The Fall of Man in *Genesis B* and the *Mystère d'Adam*", Brodeur Studies, pp. 187-199.
[9]   Timmer, edition, pp. 47-48.
[10]   See Timmer, edition, pp. 48-50.

three, if as is customary they are assumed to be from the same poem, suggest that there existed an Old Saxon Genesis-poem as long as, or longer than, the Old English *Genesis A,* and that the Old Saxon equivalent of *Genesis B* was but a small portion of that poem.

Scholars assume that the three fragments which Behaghel calls "Der Sündenfall" (1-26), "Kain" (27-150) and "Der Untergang von Sodom" (151-337),[11] are taken from a single long poem but, as will become apparent in the course of our discussion of *Genesis B,* there is a thematic and structural unity within the six-hundred and sixteen lines of that poem which seems to deny the assumption that it, at least, is only a fragment of a much longer translation. This paradox might be explained in several ways. The Old Saxon fragments which do not correspond to *Genesis B* might be from another poem (or other poems) than the fragment which does correspond to the Old English. The presence of the fragment from the *Heliand* proves that the copyist had more than one poem before him. The remaining three fragments are, however, all based upon Genesis, and it is perhaps extravagant to hypothesize two or three Old Saxon Genesis-poems. If the three fragments are all from a single poem, this would not preclude the possibility that the translator-poet's intended scope was narrower than that of his Old Saxon source. He may have rearranged portions of the Old Saxon *Genesis* to make a new, unified structure and, as Timmer has suggested,[12] he may have added material of his own. The fragment which corresponds to *Genesis B* is too short to be of help in proving or refuting these speculations. Tentatively, then, one is free to conclude that *Genesis B* is complete, or almost complete, in its present form, and that the originality and contribution of the translator to the original version cannot be determined.

The primary unity of *Genesis B* is that of the plot itself. The story of the Fall of the Angels, and the subsequent Fall of Man, from a state of grace, is treated as a single, unified plot in *Genesis B,* just as it is in *Paradise Lost.* The addition of the story

[11] *Heliand und Genesis,* ed. Otto Behaghel (Halle, 1903), p. 204.
[12] Timmer, edition, pp. 59-60.

of the Fall of the Angels to the story of the Fall of Man which appears in Genesis makes the scriptural story more intelligible and, from a Christian point of view, more reasonable to an audience. The story of Satan's Fall provides theological background and, consequently, comprehensible motivation, for the events in the Genesis story. With the motives of God for creating Man, and of Satan for tempting him, the history of Man's life in, and expulsion from, Paradise forms a more or less self-contained and self-explanatory whole. This unity of plot is reinforced by the poet's use of heroic concepts to give the story its thematic structure. The theme of the poem is loyalty, and recurring motifs which center about the heroic attitude toward loyalty and the related attitudes toward vengeance, treasure and exile serve to link the episodes in the poem securely to one another. Just as in Germanic heroic poetry, the concept of loyalty, of the duty of a retainer to serve his lord, is at the core of the ethical system by which the behavior of the characters in this Christian story is judged. God and His angels, Satan and his devils, and God and Adam are all related as Germanic lords and their retainers. Like Satan, Adam and Eve fail in their duty to their lord, and the poet is careful to differentiate Man's Fall through duplicity from Satan's Fall through pride. Essential differences in attitude between Satan and his followers on the one hand, and Adam and Eve on the other, are contrasted throughout the poem. A detailed examination of *Genesis B* should help us determine how completely heroic concepts supply the ethical foundation for the poet's treatment of his plot material, and to what extent they control his shaping of that material.

In its present condition, *Genesis B* begins with the last words of a speech by God to Adam and Eve in which He warns them against eating the forbidden fruit (235-236). God says that, so long as Adam and Eve obey His injunction, *Ne wyrð . . . wilna gæd* (236). God's promise echoes that of Hrothgar to Beowulf on the evening of his fight with Grendel – *Ne bið þe wilna gad* (660) – and the similarity of the two promises suggests that like Hrothgar's speech, God's speech is essentially that of a Germanic lord promising rewards for loyal service. This suggestion gains

additional support from the succeeding lines (237-245) in which
we learn that, like Beowulf,[13] Adam and Eve hold their land
through the generosity of their *stiðferhð cyning* (241). The poet
emphasizes the relationship between the loyal obedience of Adam
and Eve to their lord, God, and their resultant prosperity:

>   Stod his handgeweorc
> somod on sande,   nyston sorga wiht
> to begrornianne,   butan heo godes willan
> lengest læsten.   Heo wæron leof gode
> ðenden heo his halige word   healdan woldon. (241–245)

Like all good Germanic retainers, Adam and Eve will remain
leof to their lord and prosperous so long as they *læsten* Him
properly.

The poet next describes the creation and fall of the angels
(246ff). Since angels were created before Man, this description
is out of chronological order and it seems likely that it parallels
a missing passage prior to line 235 in which the creation of
Adam and Eve had been described. This description of the
angels' failure to obey God, when seen in the light of God's
instructions to Adam and Eve, serves to emphasize the importance of those instructions, and to illuminate the parallel between
the situations of the angels and Man before their respective falls.
God created the angels as His personal *comitatus,* and trusted
them to carry out His wishes:

> Hæfde se alwalda   engelcynna
> þurh handmægen,   halig drihten,
> tene getrimede,   þæm he getruwode wel
> þæt hie his giongorscipe   fyligan wolden,
> wyrcean his willan ....   (246–250)

Satan is the foremost retainer in this angelic *comitatus,* holding
a position analogous to that of Beowulf in Hygelac's court. He
is a mighty, courageous warrior (*swa swiðne geworhtne,* / *swa
mihtigne on his modgeþohte* – 252-253), who 'rules so much' that
he is second in power to God alone (253-254). All of a retainer's
possessions come from his lord, and Satan's are no exception; his

---

[13] *Beowulf*, 2190-2199.

very form (*wæstm*) *him com from weroda drihtne* (255). Like any worthy retainer, Satan is expected to win glory for his lord, thereby repaying the favors which he has received:

> Lof sceolde he drihtnes wyrcean,
> dyran sceolde he his dreamas on heofonum,   and sceolde
>   his drihtne þancian
> þæs leanes þe he him on þam leohte gescerede –
>   þonne læte he his hine lange wealdan.
>
>   (256–258)

When Satan begins to 'raise strife' with God, the emphasis is upon his failure to serve properly, and we are told that this failure is the result of 'pride' (*ofermod*):

> Deore wæs he drihtne urum;   ne mihte him bedyrned
>   weorðan
> þæt his engyl ongan   ofermod wesan,
> ahof hine wið his hearran,   sohte hetespræce,
> gylpword ongean,   nolde gode þeowian. . . . (261–264)

Ofermod (262, 272) in *Genesis B* is synonymous with *oferhygd* (328); *oferhygd*, as we have observed in the context of Hrothgar's sermon to Beowulf (*Beowulf*, 1740), manifests itself in violations of the heroic code of conduct.[14] From a purely heroic point of view, Satan's conduct is morally reprehensible, for he is a 'dear' retainer who boasts that he will abandon his lord, build his own hall (*getimbro* – 276), and serve no longer.

In his first speech (278-291), Satan declares that he needs no lord, and is powerful enough to rule a *comitatus* of his own; a dangerous attitude, in an heroic world where, as we see in the opening lines of *Beowulf*, rulers who live within reach of more powerful lords are usually forced to become tributaries to them. Ironically, Satan boasts of the loyalty of the followers who will support him in his undertaking:

> Bigstandað me strange geneatas,   þa ne willað me
>   æt þam striðe geswican,
> hæleþas heardmode. Hie habbað me to hearran gecorene,

---

[14] Rosemary Woolf, in "The Devil in Old-English Poetry", 6-8, observes that the use of the lord-retainer relationship in *Genesis B* solves for the poet the problem of presenting pride as evil to an Anglo-Saxon audience. Pride becomes, in the context of this poem, the violation of the social hierarchy.

rofe rincas;   mid swilcum mæg man ræd geþencean,
fon mid swilcum folcgesteallan.   Frynd synd hie mine
georne,
holde on hyra hygesceaftum.   (284–288)

Satan, a secondary heroic lord (in the same way that Beowulf
is lord of his small troop of Geats in Denmark), expects loyalty
from his retainers at the same time that he is plotting disloyalty
to his own lord. An audience accustomed to hearing Germanic
heroic poetry would immediately recognize the hypocrisy
reflected by this paradoxical demand. Further, such an audience
would be aware that a band of retainers who had broken faith
with one lord should scarcely be cause for the boasting of their
new lord. While it is acceptable for retainers to 'choose' a new
lord if their old one has died, they are bound to serve the old
lord so long as he lives and dispenses favors to them. No respectable lord would, like Satan, accept into his service retainers whom
he knew to have been disloyal to their former lord.

When God learns of the crime which Satan and his followers
are plotting against Him, He reacts precisely as we would expect
a Germanic lord to react. He becomes angry (*gebolgen* – 299),
and takes vengeance upon the rebels – *sceolde he þa dæd
ongyldan* (295). The poet comments that warriors who raise
strife against their lords are always properly punished:

Swa deð monna gehwilc
þe wið his waldend   winnan ongynneð
mid mane wið þone mæran drihten.   (297–299)

This bit of gnomic wisdom applies equally to the situations of
the angels and of Man in the poem, and would be equally
appropriate in a purely secular heroic context. The poet wisely
refrains from describing the strife between God and His angels
in detail, while making it quite clear that the loss of their lord's
favor results in the angels' exile from Heaven – *hyldo hæfde his
ferlorene, / ... Forþon he sceolde grund gesecean...*' (301–
302). The angels' attempt to dishonor their lord, their failure
to win a victory over Him, and their exile are set in a causal
relationship by the poet:

Forþon heo his dæd and word
noldon weorðian,   forþon he heo on wyrse leoht
under eorðan neoðan,   ællmihtig god,
sette sigelease   on þa sweartan helle.   (309–312).

The opposition which the poet sets up between heaven and hell is the same as the opposition which we find in secular heroic poetry between the hall and the lands of exile. In heaven, the loyal angels continue to live happily under their lord (320–321), while the disloyal angels dwell in hell, a physically unpleasant place, dark (*leohtes leas* – 333) and dangerous (*fyres fær micel* – 334). Significantly, the only punishment which the rebel angels suffer is that worst of all possible fates for a Germanic warrior, physical exile. The poet, it is true, tells us that the rebel angels were transformed into 'devils' (308-309), but he does not elaborate upon the nature of this transformation. Nowhere does he develop any concept of spiritual damnation, beyond the obvious spiritual implications of heroic exile.

Greenfield describes Satan in defeat as "the undaunted Germanic warrior, not the lamenting exile of *Christ and Satan*",[15] but in fact Satan's great speech (338-441) reveals both of these aspects of his character. The earlier part of this speech, which he speaks 'in sorrow' (347) from an 'overflowing heart' (353-354), is very clearly the lament of an exile. He begins with the typical exile's lament over the place in which he finds himself, and his sense of loss is intensified by his memories of his former situation in the service of his lord:

Is þæs ænga styde   ungelic swiðe
þam oðrum ham   þe we ær cuðon,
hean on heofonrice . . . .   (356–358).

He refuses to admit his own guilt, and accuses God of wronging him (360), but of course the audience would immediately recognize the justice of the punishment of disloyalty by exile. His sense of personal dishonor is reflected in his lament for his lost position, his *stronglican stol* (366), and in his resentment of the

15   Greenfield, *Critical History*, p. 151.

'joy' (*wynne* 367) of his successor, Adam. His description of himself, *rices leas* (372), bound in the *laðran landscipe* (376) of hell, exactly coincides with the ordinary exile's lament over his poverty, his physical surroundings, and his personal hardships. Just as an ordinary exile is outside of Man's law, in that he lives isolated from human society, so Satan declares himself and his followers outside of God's laws (390-393) and, since there is no chance of regaining God's favor (402-403), his mind turns to thoughts of avenging his lost honor.

When he begins to think of vengeance, Satan ceases to regard himself as an exile and reassumes the role in which he met his downfall, that of an heroic lord. He cannot take vengeance on God directly (393-394), but by causing Adam to be disloyal he can at once dishonor God (by depriving Him of his new race of retainers) and Adam (by causing him to violate the heroic code of conduct). God will be deprived of followers, Adam and his race will lose the favors by which he is more honored than Satan, and Satan will gain honor by increasing the numbers of his *giongrum* (407). Satan again ignores the fact that followers who come to him in disgrace will bring him little honor. With the words, *Onginnað nu ymb þa fyrde þencean!* (408), Satan begins to exhort his retainers to do 'battle' for his glory. In his role as lord of a *comitatus,* he reminds his retainers of their duty to repay with loyal service the treasures which he has given them:

> Gif ic ænegum þægne   þeodenmadmas
> geara forgeafe,   þenden we on þan godan rice
> gesælige sæton   and hæfdon ure setla geweald,
> þonne he me na on leofran tid   leanum ne meahte
> mine gife gyldan,   gif his gien wolde
> minra þegna hwylc   geþafa wurðan ....   (409–414).

Again we have irony in Satan's appealing to his retainers' gratitude for his generosity after he has failed to show similar gratitude to his own lord, and after their devotion to him has already cost them their places in heaven. He tells his followers that Adam and Eve now possess the 'wealth', and therefore the honor, which was once their own:

> ... þær geworht stondað
> Adam and Eue   on eorðrice
> mid welan bewunden,   and we synd aworpene hider
> on þas deopan dalo.   Nu hie drihtne synt
> wurðran micle,   and moton him þone welan agan
> þe we on heofonrice   habban sceoldon,
> rice mid rihte . . . .   (418–424)

If Adam and Eve should fail to serve God loyally, they will
lose their 'wealth' – *siððan bið him se wela onwended* (431) –
and Satan will, he thinks, be able to 'rest easily' in his fetters
gif him þæt rice losað (434). To whatever thane can bring about
Man's fall, Satan promises the highest honor which a lord can
bestow upon a retainer, a seat next to himself:

> Se þe þaet gelæsteð,   him bið lean gearo
> æfter to aldre,   þæs we her inne magon
> on þyssum fyre forð   fremena gewinnan.
> Sittan læte ic hine wið me sylfne,   swa hwa
>   swa þæt secgan cymeð
> on þas hatan helle . . . .   (435–439)

The second-highest seat in *þas hatan helle* is, of course, an honor
of questionable magnitude. Satan inverts the values of the heroic
hierarchy by speaking of a seat next to the lord of hell as if it
were equivalent in honor to a seat next to the Lord of heaven.

At this point in the narrative the relationship of Man to the
fallen angels should be quite clear. Adam is now in a position
parallel to that of Satan before his fall; he is heir to the wealth
and honor which belonged to Satan when he was God's foremost
retainer. Satan, however, would like Adam to be his heir in
misery as well, and wishes Mankind to serve the fallen angels.
The poet has very carefully set forth the circumstances of Satan's
fall. Because of *ofermod* he not only failed to serve his lord
properly, but indeed he attempted to supplant Him. He was cast
by force into exile in hell, where he is afterwards actively hostile
to God. He will not admit his guilt, and he desires only revenge.
The poet expects his audience to remember these circumstances
and, in fact, frequently recalls them during the ensuing account
of the Fall of Man. Adam, too, will prove disloyal to his lord's
commands, but his crime will, as we shall see, be somewhat less

reprehensible from a heroic, though not a theological, point-of-view.

After a gap in the manuscript (two pages are missing), the poet describes the preparations and journey to Eden of the subordinate devil who will tempt Adam and Eve. The tempter is in effect undertaking the task of avenging his lord, and so he is presented as a warrior arming himself for battle. The 'helmet of invisibility' (*hæleðhelm* – 444) which is part of his *frætwum* introduces a note of the supernatural which recalls the heroic mythology of the North.[16] When the tempter arrives in Eden, we are introduced to the trees of life and death, the latter of which has sent generations of scholars searching for non-scriptural precedents.[17] Whatever the poet's source for the dark and gloomy tree of death, it is clear that he has chosen to depict the two trees in such a way that Man's alternatives would be readily understood by his audience. On these two trees, he says, the children of men must choose *godes and yfeles . . . / welan and wawan* (465-466). The tree of life is equated with 'good' and 'wealth', which in heroic poetry are virtually identical, while the tree of death is equated with 'evil' and 'woe'. The tree of life offers Man all that a Germanic warrior could desire; a healthy, joyous life with his lord's favor in this world as well as the next (467-476). The tree of death offers a life of 'sweat' and 'sorrow' (482), the loss through old age of those things which Germanic heroes hold dear, 'deeds of valor, joys and lordship' (*ellendæda / dreamas and drihtscipes* – 484-485), and, after death, perpetual service in 'the darkest of lands' (487). Certainly the most pagan auditor would immediately recognize which tree is the more desirable.

The tempter, in his first attempt to convince Adam to eat the fruit, appeals primarily to Adam's sense of loyalty to his lord. He claims to be God's personal messenger (497-499), and says that God has 'commanded' (*het* – 500) that Adam eat. He reminds Adam of his duty as God's follower, while praising his steadfast loyalty:

[16] See Timmer, edition, note to l. 444 (p. 106).
[17] See e.g., Evans, 10.

                              Nu þu willan hæfst,
hyldo geworhte   heofoncyninges,
to þance geþenod   þinum hearran,
hæfst þe wið drihten dyrne geworhtne.   Ic
     gehyrde hine þine dæd and word
lofian on his leohte   and ymb þin lif sprecan. (504–508)

As the devil would have it, Adam will eat the fruit because
he is loyal to his lord. God's original command that he not eat
is uppermost in Adam's mind (523-529), and he fully intends to
carry out God's wishes:

                    Ic wat hwæt he me self bebead,
     nergend user,   þa ic hine nehst geseah;
     he het me his word weorðian   and wel healdan,
     læstan his lare.   (535–538)

Adam's obvious devotion to duty in this first speech stands in
direct contrast to the lack of devotion revealed by Satan in his
first speech (278-291). Satan made a rash decision, but Adam
is cautious, and so he questions the authenticity of 'god's messenger', who has shown him no 'token' *(tacen* – 540) of his trust-
worthiness. Adam acknowledges the debt which he owes his lord
for the 'gift' of his being – *þe me mid his earmum worhte* (544) –
unlike Satan, who never acknowledged that God created him, too,
mid his handum (251). Finally, Adam recognizes the flaw in his
tempter's argument, for he knows that, *He mæg me of his hean
rice / geofian mid goda gehwilcum,   þeah he his gingran ne
sende* (545-546).

   The tempter next turns his attention to Eve and, significantly,
he begins his temptation of her with the statement that God will
be angry wih Adam and Eve for Adam's failure to obey His
command (551ff). He places the burden of amending this failure
squarely upon Eve (557ff), and repeats his argument about
Man's duty to his lord:

                         Span þu hine georne
     þæt he þine lare læste   þy læs gyt lað gode,
        incrum waldende,   weorðan þyrfen.   (575–577)

While the temptation of Adam was founded upon a direct lie,
the temptation of Eve is founded partially upon the truth of her

duty to Adam. Miss Woolf has argued that the tempter's suggestion that Eve 'guide' (*gestyran* – 568) Adam is an appeal to her vanity and an attempt to make her violate her place in the hierarchy of Creation. She cites doctrinal precedents for the inferiority of women, but she is forced to admit that in *Genesis B* this doctrinal point is by and large neglected.[18] One cannot argue with Miss Woolf's theology, but theology plays a minimal part in this poem, and in heroic terms Eve's duty, like that of any queen in Germanic heroic poetry, is to serve and advise her husband and to protect him, if possible, from the dangers which might beset him as the result of a wrong decision. No one, after all, criticizes Wealtheow for urging Hrothgar to give generous gifts to his visitors at Heorot (*Beowulf*, 1169ff).

Eve is so conscious of her duty to Adam that she fails to recognize the questionable nature of the 'command' which he has refused to obey. If there is a flaw in the tempter's argument, it consists in his words to her that he will hide Adam's supposed error from God (578-580). An omniscient God can of course never be deceived, but this seems a rather subtle theological point in this context, and one which the audience, as well as Eve, might easily miss. Eve is more susceptible to error than Adam – *hæfde hire wacran hige / metod gemearcod* (590-591). After she has eaten the fruit, the poet expresses his incredulity over the course of events. His words raise serious doubts in our minds about his theological competence, and thereby lend support to our view of the poem as an essentially Germanic heroic work:

> þæt is micel wundor
> þæt hit ece god   æfre wolde
> þeoden þolian,   þæt wurde þegn swa monig
> forlædd be þam lygenum   þe for þam larum com.
> (595–598)

Whatever the poet's doctrinal deficiencies, this passage does emphasize the essential difference between Man's fall and Satan's fall. That Satan could be disloyal to his lord because of pride, and consequently be driven from his lord's favor, is under-

---

[18] Woolf, "The Fall of Man ...", pp. 194-196.

standable, but that Eve, and later Adam, could be tricked into disobedience and yet have to suffer the consequences of their acts is 'a wonder' to the poet. The false vision which Eve has after she has eaten helps the tempter to convince her of the truth of his words, and so she is deceived into tempting Adam. The poet introduces the second temptation of Adam by recapitulating the theme of loyalty as it applies to Man's relationship with God. At the same time he continues to extenuate Eve's crime by means of references to her having been deceived (*forlæd mid ligenum* – 630), because of her weaker mind (*wifes wac geþoht* – 649) into believing in the tempters' loyalty (*his holdne hyge*–654). The poet does not attempt to excuse the crime completely, nor does he minimize its consequences, but he certainly transfers much of the guilt from Eve (and later, Adam) to the tempter. Eve's attempt to convince her lord (*hearran* – 654, *frea* – 655), Adam, to eat is not made with evil intent on her part, for she believes that she is helping him and that the tempter has spoken the truth. She wants Adam to please the 'messenger' because she thinks he can 'intercede' for them with God (665) and, indeed, she thinks that because she has eaten the fruit she can see heaven (666ff). The heaven which she sees looks like a Germanic *comitatus* – the lord is *welan bewunden* (668), his followers *wereda wynsumast* (671) – but this is the consistent idea of heaven throughout the poem and thus cannot be considered deceptive on that account. After her speech, the poet again contrasts her motives with those of the tempter (694–714). The tempter knows that he has been disloyal and that he has broken God's commands with *ligenwordum* (699) in order to *forlæranne* (703) God's loyal followers, but Eve has acted with a 'loyal mind' and has erred through ignorance:

> Heo dyde hit þeah þurh holdne hyge,   nyste þæt
>   þær hearma swa fela,
> fyrenearfeða,   fylgean sceolde
> monna cynne,   þæs heo on mod genam
> þæt heo þæs laðan bodan   larum hyrde,
> ac wende þæt heo hyldo   heofoncyninges
> worhte mid þam wordum   þe heo þam were swelce
> tacen oðiewde   and treowe gehet ....   (708–714)

As soon as Adam has eaten the fruit, the tempter rejoices in his triumph and, in the course of his speech he restates the major heroic themes of the poem. He begins by boasting that he has served his lord (Satan) well and thus earned his 'favor' (726-728). Adam and Eve will lose God's favor and the joys of heaven – ... *monig forleton / on heofonrice heahgetimbro, / godlice geardas* (738-740). Man's loss of Paradise parallels the angels' loss of heaven, and the tempter recalls without remorse the disloyalty and subsequent exile of his comrades (740-750). Satan can be happy, for 'both things are now accomplished' (751); Man has lost heaven and will join Satan's retinue, and God has been dishonored (750-755). He claims that all has been avenged – ... *ealle synt uncre hearmas gewrecene / laðes þaet wit lange poledon* (759-760) – and resolves to return in triumph to his lord (760-762). The victory is an empty one, however, for the victor must return to hell where nothing has really changed. The poet underscores the irony here by observing that Satan, the victim of God's vengeance, still 'lies in chains' (764-765).

When Adam and Eve realize that they have been deceived, they repent immediately having broken faith with their lord (765ff), a reaction for which there is no scriptural precedent. They fall to prayer and, unlike Satan, who showed no contrition, they ask God to punish them (776-783). Adam regrets ever having seen Eve because she has led him astray, and she is equally sorry for her part in the crime (816-826). The punishment which Adam expects is conceived of entirely in terms of physical suffering, and calls to mind the sufferings of the exiled warrior; he and Eve will endure hunger and thirst, the cold of the Winter and the heat of the Summer (805-815). While Satan desired revenge, Adam wishes only to atone for his crime, and he volunteers to undertake a life of exile in the form of a sea-journey because no service can compensate him for the loss of his lord:

> Gif ic waldendes willan cuðe,
> hwæt ic his to hearmsceare habban sceolde,
> ne gesawe þu no sniomor, þeah me on sæ wadan
> hete heofones god heonone nu þa,
> on flod faran, nære he firnum þæs deop,

merestream þæs micel,   þæt his o min mod
                         getweode,
ac ic to þam grunde genge,   gif ic godes meahte
willan gewyrcean.   Nis me on worulde niod
æniges þegnscipes,   nu ic mines þeodnes hafa
hyldo forworhte,   þæt ic hie habban ne mæg.
                         (828–837)

Finally, Adam and Eve pray that God will show them how to live (841-851), throwing themselves upon God's mercy, unlike Satan who grew even more hostile to Him. *Genesis B* ends at this point, and thus it lacks the account of Man's expulsion from Paradise, which would parallel the account of Satan's punishment and logically complete the poem (as it does in *Paradise Lost*). The poet has, by drawing attention to the differences between the Fall of the angels and the Fall of Man, prepared the way for an account of Man's less severe punishment, but we can only speculate as to whether he really made any such point about the expulsion from Paradise. Perhaps there was a concluding passage, and the scribe who copied the text of *Genesis B* into *Genesis A* chose, with unfortunately poor judgment, to use the account of the expulsion which he had in the older poem (*Genesis A,* 852-964).

There can, I think, be little doubt that *Genesis B,* in the incomplete form in which we have it, has a unity which is not accidental, but rather is revealed not only in its plot but also in its thematic structure. By contrasting the actions and attitudes of Satan and his followers on the one hand, and Adam and Eve on the other, the poet is able to tell a story in which the heroes, Adam and Eve, violate the heroic code of conduct and yet remain both intelligible and acceptable to a secular audience. Satan and Adam are both retainers of the same essentially Germanic lord, and both violate the code of conduct dictated by the heroic concept of loyalty, but there is an essential difference between the disloyalty of Satan and the disloyalty of Man. Satan rebels through pride, he receives the customary punishment for disloyalty, exile, and he is never contrite nor honest about his guilt. Adam (and Eve) is tricked into being disloyal, repents immediately, and nobly awaits his punishment. As Greenfield

observes, the points at which the story in *Genesis B* differs from
the scriptural account of the fall of Man seem "to lead to the
conclusion that the Old Saxon poet endeavored to depict the
Fall not to show man's moral disobedience but to stress the
deception of innocence by malevolence and fraud, to remind us
of the forces of destruction that lurk behind human choices of
action, however good our motivations." [19] That is to say, the
poem is not about religious doctrine but about life in the secular
world.

The absence of strict Christian orthodoxy in the poet's
portrayal of the story of the Fall of Man is directly related to the
heroic tradition in which he is working. The moral and ethical
climate of *Genesis B* is controlled completely by the heroic
concepts which we have been examining and principally by the
concept of loyalty. In the heroic world, loyalty to one's lord is
the primary virtue, and disloyalty the worst vice. A poet wishing
to tell the story of the Fall would have no difficulty portraying
Satan as a disloyal retainer, but portraying Adam and Eve in like
manner would create a problem because they must, for the sake
of the secular audience, be presented as being disloyal but not
totally reprehensible. As Evans says, the poet of *Genesis B*
circumvents this problem: "At every stage of the story the Saxon
poet has gone out of his way to present Adam and Eve in the
most favorable possible light." [20] The crime of Adam and Eve is,
in heroic terms, still a crime, but their pure motives make their
conduct understandable and acceptable to a secular Germanic
audience. It is not moral depravity, but rather their zeal to be
loyal to their lord which ultimately causes them to be disloyal.
Though they are theologically culpable, they remain, from an
heroic point of view, respectable human beings.

Genesis B is unusual among Old English poems in that its
composer has used irony rather frequently, and in his use of
irony, the poet again reveals his absolute reliance upon the
validity of heroic concepts. In the instances where irony is used
to obtain a poetic effect, it is never used to make an adverse

[19]   Greenfield, *Critical History*, p. 153.
[20]   Evans, 113.

comment upon heroic ideals. Quite the contrary, the effect obtained by dramatic irony in the poem depends upon the audience's acceptance of these ideals. Generally speaking, the poet achieves irony in *Genesis B* by making his characters give voice to heroic ideals at the same time that they are violating them. Thus Satan appeals to the loyalty of his retainers (284ff), and claims service for his gifts to them (409ff), in spite of the fact that he has shown neither loyalty nor gratitude toward his own lord. The tempter's words to Eve are ironic in a slightly different way because they reveal only a part of the truth:

> ... wæs seo hwil þæs lang
> þæt ic geornlice   gode þegnode
> þurh holdne hyge,   herran minum,
> drihtne selfum ....   (584–587)

Like his evil lord, the tempter claims to be the hero which he once was but is no longer. The way in which the poet uses irony helps to reveal the nature of evil in his poem. Evil consists in the divergence from heroic ideals of conduct, and when a character consciously and maliciously gives voice to these ideals while violating them himself, he is thoroughly reprehensible.

Genesis B, then, is essentially a heroic poem, based upon the concepts which govern the behavior of the heroes of secular Germanic verse. The poet has managed to compose a Christian poem in which secular, heroic ideals maintain positive value, are never questioned, and do not conflict radically with the Christian story. Indeed, the heroic concepts of loyalty, vengeance, treasure and exile give the story moral significance for the Germanic audience. Nowhere in Old English Christian verse do Christian and pre-Christian, heroic elements reside so harmoniously together; for this reason *Genesis B* is probably the finest fusion of Christian and Germanic tradition which we have in Old English.

VIII

ANDREAS

The pre-Christian concepts with which we are concerned in this study appear in *Andreas,* but they are not nearly so essential to the moral climate and overall design of that poem as they are to *Genesis B. Andreas* is more thoroughly informed by the spirit of Christianity and, in consequence, owes considerably less of its effectiveness to the spirit of the Germanic heroic world. Whereas moral judgments in *Genesis B* are based primarily upon heroic concepts of conduct, such judgments in *Andreas* are based upon essentially non-heroic Christian concepts; judgments based upon heroic concepts seem largely incidental to the view of the world which controls *Andreas.* Heroic concepts in *Andreas* appear along side of, but not necessarily in harmony with, doctrines and sentiments very different from those which are central to *Genesis B,* so that the overall impression given by *Andreas* is that of a Christian poem containing remnants of an earlier, pre-Christian tradition of thought and expression.

Andreas is one of that group of Old English Christian poems which scholars traditionally associate with the so-called 'Cynewulfian school' of verse. On the evidence of language, style and meter, however, Krapp concludes that *Andreas* is not by Cynewulf himself.[1] Claes Schaar, the most recent scholar to evaluate the Cynewulf canon on stylistic grounds, also finds numerous stylistic differences between *Andreas* and the signed poems of Cynewulf, and so rejects *Andreas* from the canon.[2] If

[1] *Andreas and the Fates of the Apostles*, ed. George Philip Krapp (Boston, 1906), p. li.
[2] Claes Schaar, *Critical Studies in the Cynewulf Group* (Lund, 1949), pp.

the poet must therefore remain anonymous, then the date of composition of the poem is likewise almost impossible to determine with much confidence; Kenneth R. Brooks, the most recent editor of *Andreas,* cautiously offers on linguistic evidence a mid-ninth century date, but the evidence appears less than conclusive.[3]

The traditional scholarly association of *Andreas* with the poems of Cynewulf suggests, however, that we might expect the Christianity of that poem to be of a more sophisticated variety than that of the presumably earlier 'Caedmonian' poems with which *Genesis B* is associated. In other words, if, as I shall attempt to demonstrate, *Andreas* is less 'heroic' and more 'Christian' than *Genesis B,* this distinction is not necessarily inconsistent with the traditional (and highly speculative) chronology of Old English verse. Even though *Andreas* was probably composed before *Genesis B,* the less rigorous brand of Christianity in the latter poem can be attributed to its having been modeled upon the poems of an earlier era in Old English Christian verse.

While no immediate source exists for *Andreas,* there is general agreement among scholars that the poem is based upon a lost Latin translation of the Greek *Acts of Andrew and Matthew in the City of the Man-Eaters.*[4] The Greek story differs from the Old English poem in a few details, but the two plots are almost identical, and some of the speeches in the poem reproduce the substance of those in the Greek with almost perfect fidelity. The Greek story is definitely the source of a few extant fragments of a Latin version which, in turn, may have been the immediate source for *Andreas,* and for a later Old English prose legend of Saint Andrew.[5] Krapp comments upon the poet's use of his

---

34-41. See also S. K. Das, *Cynewulf and the Cynewulf Canon* (Calcutta, 1942), pp. 228ff.

[3] *Andreas and the Fates of the Apostles* (Oxford, 1961), pp. xviii-xxii, xxxi-xxxix.

[4] Translated into English in *The Ante-Nicene Fathers,* ed. Alexander Roberts and James Donaldson (Buffalo, 1886), Vol. VIII, pp. 517-535.

[5] The Old English prose legend is reprinted in James W. Bright, *An Anglo-Saxon Reader* (New York, 1917), pp. 113-128. Brooks reprints the most important Latin fragment, pp. 177-178.

sources that, "The framework of the story of both poems [*i.e.,* *Andreas* and *Elene*] was given in their sources . . . . There is not a single incident in the action of *Andreas* which was not suggested by its source."[6]

Despite the apparent fidelity with which the *Andreas*-poet follows the events, and even some of the speeches, of his source, his poem contains an abundance of Germanic heroic elements. The frequency with which one is confronted with heroic elements reminiscent of *Beowulf,* together with various similarities of action and phraseology, has led several scholars to speculate that the poet used *Beowulf* as a model for *Andreas.* This view, taken by Krapp[7] and Klaeber[8] among others, has been challenged by Leonard J. Peters, who points out that incidents and details common to the two poems can be found in the Greek version of the story, while verbal similarities between them can be the result of both poets' drawing upon a common Old English poetic vocabulary.[9] The oral-formulaic theory would seem to support Peters' argument by accounting for the persistence of heroic phrases, motifs and concepts in Old English Christian poems. Brooks, after reviewing the question, takes a middle-ground, concluding that it would be unwise to absolutely deny the possibility that *Beowulf* influenced *Andreas,* even though that influence cannot finally be proved.[10] Rosemary Woolf apparently rejects Peters' arguments altogether, and argues that the *Andreas*-poet flaunts his borrowings from *Beowulf:* "Lines or even pairs of lines are repeated for the sake of the allusion rather than for their propriety in the new context. It is clearly part of the author's technique to recall *Beowulf* in the same way it was Milton's to recall the *Aeneid* by his Latinisms and echoes of it in *Paradise*

---

[6]   Krapp, *Andreas,* p. li. Krapp also discusses in detail the source of *Andreas* in relationship to other versions of the story, pp. xxi-xxix. See also Brooks, pp. xv-xviii.

[7]   Krapp, *Andreas,* pp. lv ff.

[8]   Klaeber, *Beowulf,* p. cxi.

[9]   "The Relationship of the Old English *Andreas* to *Beowulf*", *PMLA* LXVI (1951), 844-863.

[10]   Brooks, pp. xxii-xxvi.

Lost." [11] She finds that the heroic elements in *Andreas* are largely inappropriate to the story, clumsily introduced, and in general an ill-advised attempt to recall the heroic quality of *Beowulf*.

Contrary to Miss Woolf, I would argue that the *Andreas*-poet introduces heroic elements into his poem not because he wishes to remind his audience of *Beowulf,* but because he finds them natural and useful in telling his story. After all, we do not know that *Beowulf* was held in the same high reverence by the audience of *Andreas* that the *Aeneid* was by audience for whom Milton intended *Paradise Lost.* Further, if as seems likely either *Beowulf* or *Andreas* or both were intended primarily for oral presentation, it would be rather extravagant of the *Andreas*-poet to expect his audience to recognize brief allusions to and quotations from the older poem. If the poet's use of heroic elements often appears mechanical or incongruous, it is because he is unable to adopt his Germanic poetic heritage to the demands of his Christian subject matter. I shall attempt to demonstrate precisely how the poet uses (or misuses) his heroic material in the following pages, and the Greek version of the story will, because of its closeness to *Andreas,* prove useful for my purposes. Where one finds evidence of the presence of heroic concepts and motifs in the poem, the Greek version can sometimes reveal what the poet's purpose is in introducing these elements into his narrative. It is not in the events that make up the plot of *Andreas* that one finds heroic concepts in evidence, but rather in the poet's expression and explanation of these events for his Anglo-Saxon audience. The Greek version, because it is itself remote from Germanic tradition, can upon occasion help us to evaluate the Germanic content of the poem.

The opening lines of *Andreas* in some measure epitomize the way in which the poet employs heroic concepts in his poem. These lines, often compared to the opening lines of *Beowulf,* are typical of the beginning of an Old English heroic poem:

> Hwæt! We gefrunan　　on fyrndagum
> twelfe under tunglum　　tireadige hæleð,

[11] "Saints' Lives", *Continuations and Beginnings: Studies in Old English Literature,* ed. Eric Gerald Stanley (London, 1966), p. 51.

þeodnes þegnas.　　No hira þrym alæg
camprædenne　　þonne cumbol hneotan,
syððăn hie gedældon,　　swa him dryhten sylf,
heofona heahcyning,　　hlyt getæhte.
　　þæt wæron mære　　men ofer eorðan,
frome folctogan　　ond fyrdhwate,
rofe rincas,　　þonne rond ond hand
on herefelda　　helm ealgodon,
on meotudwange.　　　　　　　　(1–11)[12]

The poet is speaking of the twelve apostles, but one would never recognize them from this description. They appear here as members of a Germanic *comitatus,* and if we had no more of the poem than these eleven lines, we would be justified in assuming that, because they are clearly excellent warriors, they behave and are to be judged in accordance with the concepts of loyalty, vengeance, treasure and exile which govern pre-Christian heroic verse. Of course, this description is grossly inaccurate both in terms of Christian tradition and in the context of the poem which follows it. We may translate *þeodnes þegnas* (3) in such a way as to deprive the formula of its connotations of martial service, but what are we to do with 'war, where banners clash' (4), 'leaders bold and fierce in battle, brave warriors, when hand and shield protected the helmet on the battle-field' (8-10)? Nowhere in Christian tradition, so far as I know, are the apostles represented as literally participating in physical combat and, more important, the two apostles whom we meet in *Andreas* never do any fighting for their Lord or anyone else. Further, I must agree with Kenneth Sisam that the 'Christian Knight' concept derived from St. Paul is not implied here.[13] There is no indication that any such metaphor is being used, and it is unlikely that a poet would thrust such a metaphor without warning upon an audience accustomed to hearing poems about men who are, in a literal sense, warriors. I suggest that a reasonable explanation for the presence of this passage is that the poet considered the

---

[12]　The text cited is that of G. P. Krapp, ed. *The Vercelli Book* (New York, 1932), pp. 3-51.
[13]　Kenneth Sisam, "Cynewulf and his Poetry", *Studies in the History of Old English Literature* (Oxford, 1962), p. 16.

conventional heroic opening, with all of its essentially pre-Christian, martial connotations, the most effective one for his purposes, and used it accordingly. Once he has gained the attention of his audience, and thus obtained the desired effect, he is free to let the heroic aspects of his story drop and revert to them only when he has some reason to do so, and this is precisely what he does.

The poet is apparently unaware of, or else does not consider himself obligated to pursue, a consistently heroic point-of-view in telling his story, and the heavy emphasis upon Christian doctrine and sentiment in his source would make such an approach to his material impracticable. Indeed, the theme of the story, in both the Greek source and the Old English poem, is the temptation of Saint Andrew. Through the action and dialogue we see the saint as he grows from a slightly timorous disciple into a full-fledged worker of miracles in the name of Christ. A brief discussion at this point of the structure of *Andreas* should make clear this essentially Christian theme.

The narrative begins with a description of the sufferings of Matthew, who is a prisoner of, and prospective meal for, the Mermedonians (11-160). Matthew, because he has attained perfect Christian faith, and has placed himself entirely in God's hands, functions as a contrast to Andrew, who is subsequently introduced. God tells Andrew to go to Matthew's rescue, but Andrew seems reluctant to undertake the task and offers excuses (161-201). Andrew has logical reasons for doubting his own abilities, but his doubts reveal that his faith in God's help is less than it should be. God rebukes him, implicity in the Greek story and explicitly in the poem, for his lack of faith, and sends him off to Mermedonia (202-224). Andrew has failed his first test.

Andrew performs much better on his second test, which consists of making the proper responses to the questions of the sailor (Christ in disguise) from whom he seeks passage. This entire episode has a very formal tone – Andrew asks the proper questions and gives appropriate answers in a fitting manner. When requesting passage, he makes his finances clear, and offers

only a 'reward with God' (275). He politely refuses to be
deterred by the threat of imminent death (286-289), and when
the sailor points out that travel is difficult without money and
that Andrew and his followers will go hungry (307-314), practical arguments similar to those which Andrew himself offered
earlier to God, Andrew rebukes the sailor for his proud words
and admonishes him to be more humble (317-339). Andrew, by
refusing to be deterred from his journey, has passed this test and
is taken on board.

On the journey, Christ examines the various aspects of
Andrew's Christianity. His prayers of thanksgiving for his
passage (355-358) and for his food (386-390), reveal his humility
and his gratitude for the gifts sent to him by God. He shows
proper concern for his followers in their distress on the rough
seas (391-394) and, after they have refused to abandon him,
at the instigation of the divine sailor, he encourages them. His
speech to his followers is properly religious in its emphasis, and
reveals his ability to lead men (429-460). Andrew suffers a slight
setback in his testing, however, when he asks how the sailor is
able to sail swiftly and smoothly over the turbulent seas (471-
509). The sailor replies that the sea is following the will of God
by not oppressing His disciples (526-531). This seems to be a
mild rebuke to Andrew, who should have known that God is
protecting and aiding him.

Next, the sailor begins asking Andrew questions about Christ
and His miracles (555-627). After answering two questions,
Andrew asks why the sailor is asking questions to which he
obviously knows the answers (629-631), and is told that it is for
the pure joy of hearing about Christ (634-642). Since the sailor
is Himself Christ, and since no one else is listening (the followers
are asleep), this answer seems evasive. The corresponding passage
in the Greek story makes the point of this questioning more
explicit. Andrew asks, 'O man, who hast the spirit of inquisitive-
ness, why dost thou put me to the test?' [14] Christ is giving Andrew
his final 'test' in Christian lore. Satisfied with the sailor's answer,

[14]   *The Ante-Nicene Fathers*, p. 519.

Andrew delivers a one-hundred-and-seventy-two-line discourse on Christ's miracles (644-816), after which he falls asleep, and awakens in Mermedonia. Andrew's homily is correspondingly long in the Greek source and is based upon the Gospel accounts of Christ's life and teaching. It serves the dual purpose of revealing Andrew's competence in teaching Christianity and of edifying the reader or auditor of the story. As we might expect, this homily in verse is almost entirely devoid of heroic elements. It should be clear that this first half of *Andreas* (and its source) is intended to depict the spiritual, intellectual testing of Andrew. Only after he has proved his understanding of the cerebral aspects of his religion, and shown the firmness of his faith, is Andrew ready to face the coming physical trials.

The second half of the story describes the physical anguish through which the saint must pass on his journey to beatitude, and the appearance of Christ to Andrew marks the transition to this second phase of Andrew's temptation (910ff). Andrew asks why he was not permitted to know that Christ was on the ship with him (920-924), and is told by Christ that the reason was that he had faltered in his faith (926-932), and that now Andrew has redeemed himself and knows the power of the Lord (932-935). Christ reveals Himself to Andrew only after He has tested and is sure of him. Christ goes on to warn Andrew of the suffering which he must endure, and exhorts him to remain steadfast (950ff). Andrew then enters the city, frees Matthew, and remains to await his physical trials.

Christ promises to aid and protect Andrew during his sufferings, and to save him from attempts to take his life (954-956). He helps him to free Matthew, and hides him during the Mermedonians' attempt to eat a child, but ultimately He must abandon him to his tormentors for a while (1208-1218). The Mermedonians torture Andrew for three days but, though severely injured, he maintains his faith in God. The poet does not dwell in detail upon the torments which Andrew suffers, but he makes it clear that they include physical abuse and mental anguish. Andrew prays frequently throughout his ordeal and keeps his faith even when visited by the Devil and his followers who, unable to slay him (1335-1336), scorn and mock him (1356-1358). On the third day, Andrew prays for his immortal soul, God encourages him, gives him a sign of His presence and, that night, He heals Andrew's wounds and sets him free.

His trials over, Andrew's victory begins. He has now completely proven himself to be a saint and is able to perform miracles, and so he begins by calling forth water from a pillar (1498ff). God, of course, makes the miracles performed by Andrew possible, but where before God had told Andrew exactly what he should do, now Andrew himself is in charge and God simply does whatever he asks. Andrew carries out his mission by converting the cannibals to Christianity, has the city redecorated in Christian decor and, after one false start, returns to Achaia. The episode in which God tells Andrew to postpone his departure from Mermedonia for seven days is perhaps intended to show that God's hand still guides Andrew in his holy works.

This synopsis of *Andreas* suggests that the essentially Christian theme of beatitude through suffering is inseparable from the events which comprise the story which the poet is telling. Moreover, it does not in summary sound like a story which is particularly suited to the inherited materials of a heroic poetic tradition. It contains no physical combat, no heroic feasting or giving of gifts, and no instances of vengeance. The titular hero is a pauper who willingly endures torture and insults and, when he is finally in a position to avenge himself, forgives his enemies. While not primarily a theological treatise, the poem does contain considerably more Christian lore and Christian doctrine than *Genesis B* which, unlike *Andreas* (1680-1686), does not even contain a reference to the triune God.

Moving from thematic structure to matters of character exposition, we discover that here, too, the emphasis is Christian rather than heroic. Take, for example, the portrayal of Matthew, the secondary hero of *Andreas*. We meet Matthew immediately after the heroic prologue (1-11), and are told that he is one of the *þeodnes þegnas* (3). The prologue has led us to expect that Matthew will be presented as a Germanic warrior, and we might further expect that, because of his present plight in an alien land, some aspect of the concept of exile will be used to express his misery. None of these expectations is realized, however, for Matthew turns out to be every inch a Christian. The closest we get to an heroic battle between Germanic warriors is the poet's description of the Mermedonians, the *deofles þegnas* (43), going to meet Matthew:

> Eodon him þa togenes,   garum gehyrsted,
> lungre under linde,   (nalas late wæron),
> eorre æscberend,   to þam orlege.   (45–47)

Of course, no fight ensues; they capture and bind Matthew without encountering any resistance (48–51). Matthew's loyalty to his Lord finds expression not in his doing physical battle for Him but rather in his continued faith in and praise for Him. Matthew's 'valor' (*elne* – 54) consists in his honoring God with praise from his prison. Superficially, such loyalty seems no different from that of the unfallen angels in *Genesis B,* but in that poem the centrality of the heroic concept forces us to think of the loyal followers of God as warriors, while in *Andreas* it is quite clear that the disciples' loyalty to God is not that heroic loyalty which is revealed in combat.

In recasting Matthew's prayer (59–87) in Old English verse, the poet follows the (ultimately) Greek source idea by idea, and does not develop those elements which might be expressed in terms of Germanic concepts. For example, the fact that Matthew is *eðelleasum* (74) might well suggest to the poet that he portray Matthew as an exile, but he does not do so. The prayer is neither an exile's lament nor an heroic affirmation of loyalty in the face of danger, but rather a weeping expression of complete submission to the Will of God. Matthew's loyalty manifests itself in suffering rather than action. His willingness to die for his Lord (70–75) conforms to heroic ideals, but his desire to endure the insults (*edwitspræce* – 81) of his enemies is wholly a Christian sentiment (76–81). Indeed, because this prayer is an affirmation of Matthew's suffering, if it were expressed in terms of the heroic concept of exile it would necessarily have to negate that concept in order to remain a Christian prayer at all. Exiles in heroic poetry never affirm the beneficial aspects of their condition.

In *Genesis B* morality is determined primarily by heroic concepts of good and evil conduct, but such is not the case in *Andreas*. In the heroic world the primary virtue is loyalty to one's lord in battle and, while in *Andreas* loyalty remains a virtue and disloyalty a vice, loyalty is no longer heroic loyalty but rather it is Christian faith. One achieves 'victory' not by defeating his lord's enemies in battle, but by maintaining his faith in God while suffering their tortures (113–117). The Mermedonians are evil not by any heroic criterion but because they don't believe in the mildness of God – *Rihtes ne gimdon, / meotudes mildse* (139-140) – and because they are unconcerned with salvation:

> Feorh ne bemurndan,
> grædige guðrincas, hu þæs gastes sið
> æfter swyltcwale geseted wurde. (154–156)

Fierce martial heroic loyalty, and the lasting glory on earth which such loyalty earns for a warrior, has given place in the scale of values to the gentler loyalty to God and His precepts, and the glory of eternal salvation. As we examine the instances in *Andreas* in which heroic concepts continue to function, we become increasingly aware that they are no longer central to the world which the poet is depicting.

The Christian God portrayed in *Andreas* reveals few of the heroic traits which he possesses in *Genesis B*. Nevertheless, the *Andreas*-poet's conception of heaven and of the devil are at times similar to that of the poet of *Genesis B*. The heaven which Andrew's followers see in their vision (857-891) is an ideal Germanic *comitatus* where angels dwell with God, *þegnas ymb þeoden* (872), honor Him with their praise, and live in 'joy' (*dream* – 874). The blessed souls are a *dugoð domgeorne* (878) who sing *soðfæstlic lof* of their *sigedryhtne* (877). There is 'glorious joy, glory of warriors, noble actions, and no strife' (*þær wæs wuldres wynn, wigendra þrym, / æðelic onginn, næs þær ænigum gewinn* (887-888). 'Exile' (*wræcsið* – 889) is the lot of those who become estranged from these 'joys' (*gefeana* – 890) and journey hence. The Greek version and the corresponding Latin fragment account for almost nothing in this description. Its heroic tenor, which is reminiscent of descriptions of the Danish and Geatish courts in *Beowulf,* is no doubt to be attributed to the difficulty the poet encounters when he attempts to express the inexpressible. Heaven is, after all, perfect beyond human conception and, while an ideal human society is not heaven, it is perhaps the closest equivalent to heaven which the poet can describe.

It is a good deal easier for an Anglo-Saxon poet to portray the devil since, as Miss Woolf has pointed out,[15] the presentation of the devil as a disloyal retainer neatly solves the problem of presenting pride as evil to an audience accustomed to hearing heroic poetry. Disloyalty, the violation of the hierarchy, is evil in both Christian and Germanic traditions: "... the heroic formulae, when applied to Christ and his apostles and saints, always remained separate from the fundamental conception, whereas, when applied to the devil, they became fused with the Christian idea and produced a deeper meaning."[16] Thus, Andrew chides the devil because he is an exile who must endure forever his 'hard existence' (*drohtaþ strengra* – 1385). The devil plans to win personal glory by defeating Andrew and forcing him to 'break his boast' (*gylp forbegan* – 1333). In this Christian context it is entirely fitting that the devil should give expression to the heroic concept of vengeance, and that he should be the only character to do so. He exhorts his followers, the Mermedonians, to avenge the injury which Andrew has caused them by freeing their prisoners:

> Nu ge magon eaðe   oncyðdæda
> wrecan on gewyrhtum.   Lætað wæpnes spor
> iren ecgheard,   ealdorgeard sceoran,
> fæges feorhhord.   Gað fromlice
> þæt ge wiðerfeohtend   wiges gehnægan.
> (1179–1183)

The poet reveals the country of Mermedonia to the audience from two points-of-view, both of which depend heavily upon

---

[15] Rosemary Woolf, "The Devil in Old English Poetry", 6-8.
[16] Woolf, "The Devil ...", 12.

heroic concepts. When viewed from the outside, as it is before Andrew arrives there, the forbidding qualities of Mermedonia and its inhabitants make it appear to be the traditional heroic land of exile. As an 'island' (*igland* – 15) or 'borderland' (*mearcland* – 19), it is conceived of as being remote from the homeland of the heroes of the poem and as being a dangerous place for all strangers (14ff). The principal danger comes, of course, from the Mermedonians themselves, who are akin to Grendel and to the wild beasts which traditionally oppress exiles. The fact that they 'long not for the joys of man' (*hie ne murndan æfter mandreame* – 37) reflects their estrangement from the normal social customs of Germanic tribes. Descriptions of them often reflect the poet's conception of them as a tribe of Germanic warriors:

>   Duguð samnade,
> hæðne hildfrecan, heapum þrungon,
> (guðsearo gullon, garas hrysedon),
> bolgenmode, under bordhreoðan. (125–128)

They are, however, *deofles þegnas* (43), a tribe hostile to all other human beings, into whose hands it is certain death to fall. The sea-journey by which Andrew must reach Mermedonia is traditionally associated with heroic exile, and his initial reluctance to embark on this journey reflects this heroic association. His objection that he has not sufficient time to reach the distant land (190-198) comes from the Greek source, but the poet has added Andrew's observation that he has no friends or acquaintances there (198-200). This remonstrance is not necessary to our knowledge of Andrew's situation, since only a few lines earlier (174-188) God has made quite clear the Mermedonian's hostility to foreigners. The poet seems to have added this detail to enforce the association in the minds of the audience of Andrew's task with heroic exile and to show that, initially, Andrew is somewhat hesitant at the prospect of undergoing the kinds of hardships traditionally associated with the life of the exile.

Once Andrew has arrived in Mermedonia and we are able to observe the Mermedonians at first hand, we discover that they constitute an heroic society which has been disordered by calamity and in which normal heroic pursuits have been suspended. The poet conceives of the Mermedonians as a Germanic *comitatus* and often applies heroic epithets to them, even when they behave least heroically:

> þrymman sceocan,
> modige maguþegnas,　　morðres on luste,
> woldon æninga,　　ellenrofe,
> on þam hysebeorðre　　heafolan gescenan,
> garum agetan.　　((1139–1143)

The warrior who offers his son to the hungry Mermedonian host rather than be eaten himself is nevertheless referred to in respectful terms as an *ealdgesiða* (1104), a wise man and a leader of the troops (1103-1106). The city itself is described in terms which suggest its magnificence (840-843). The famine which has plagued Mermedonia is the cause of the unheroic behavior of its inhabitants. Their hunger has caused them to abandon the normal pursuits of the *comitatus*:

> þeod wæs oflysted,
> metes modgeomre,　　næs him to maðme wynn,
> hyht to hordgestreonum.　　(1112–1114)

Treasure, and therefore heroic honor, has no attraction for a society which is dying of hunger. This same point is emphasized a bit later on:

> Hreopon friccan,
> mændon meteleaste,　　meðe stodon,
> hungre gehæfte.　　Hornsalu wunedon,
> weste winræced,　　welan ne benohton
> beornas to brucanne　　on þa bitran tid,
> gesæton searuþancle　　sundor to rune
> ermðu eahtigan.　　Næs him to eðle wynn.
> 　　　　(1156–1162)

As in *Beowulf* (129ff), the disruption of normal heroic pursuits and failure to partake of the joys of the hall is symptomatic of social disorder. We are led to assume that the reason for this disorder is that the Mermedonians have a bad lord; they are 'the devil's thanes' and are being punished by famine for their misguided service. After Andrew converts them, their city becomes once again a *goldburg* in which they partake of the hall-joys of men. Andrew is about to depart from the city:

> Sægde his fusne hige,
> þæt he þa goldburg ofgifan wolde,
> secga seledream ond sincgestreon,
> beorht beagselu, ond him brimþisan
> æt sæs faroðe secan wolde. (1654–1658)

The prosperity and social stability of the Mermedonians has returned with their new loyalty to a proper 'lord', in both the Christian and Germanic senses of the term.

It is not difficult to see why the poet has employed heroic concepts, nor why he has in essence given us two views of Mermedonia, in his presentation of that city and its inhabitants. The concept of exile helps him to suggest to his audience the hardships which Andrew and Matthew must endure in the service of their Lord. Thus Mermedonia, the place of their trials, becomes in some degree associated with the exile-land of Germanic heroic tradition. On the other hand, since the Mermedonians are to be converted and to become the allies of Andrew in the service of Christ, the poet must somehow temper the monstrosity of their heathen behavior. He does this by suggesting that they are essentially a worthy Germanic *comitatus* which, under evil leadership, must suffer severe hardships and disorder. Once they have pledged their loyalty to their rightful Lord, they can live as an heroic tribe should live.

Although in portraying Andrew the poet follows his source closely, there are nevertheless instances in which the hero of *Andreas* takes on some of the coloring of a Germanic warrior. The suggestion of the poem's opening lines that the apostles are warriors who do battle for God reappears occasionally with specific reference to Andrew, as, for example, when he is called *þegn þeodenhold* (384). As we have observed earlier, his initial reluctance to journey to Mermedonia reflects the Germanic warrior's distaste for an exile's journey. When God rebukes Andrew for his hesitation, He accuses him, in a passage not paralleled in the Greek version, of lack of faith:

> Ne meaht ðu þæs siðfætes   sæne weorðan,
> ne on gewitte to wac,   gif ðu wel þencest
> wið þinne waldend   wære gehealdan,
> treowe tacen.   (211–214)

These words would be equally appropriate as a rebuke to a timorous Christian and a faltering Germanic warrior, and God's description of Andrew's task makes him seem more the latter than the former:

> þu scealt þa fore geferan   ond þin feorh beran
> in gramra gripe,   ðær þe guðgewinn
> þurh hæðenra   hildewoman,
> beorna beaducræft,   geboden wyrðeð.
>
> (216–218)

In spite of his previous reluctance to go on his journey, Andrew is presented nevertheless as a resolute Germanic warrior as he leads his troop of *þegnas* (237) to the shore to seek passage to Mermedonia:

> þa wæs ærende   æðelum cempan
> aboden in burgum,   ne wæs him bleað hyge,
> ah he wæs anræd   ellenweorces,
> heard ond higerof,   nalas hildlata,
> gearo, guðe fram,   to godes campe.   (230–234)

The phrase 'God's battle' may or may not be intended to be taken figuratively in this context but, even if it is intended as a metaphor for the spiritual strife in which the saint is to participate, this does not alter the fact that the figurative 'battle' is equated with specifically Germanic heroic combat, and that the 'warrior' is conceived of in heroic terms and his conduct for the moment governed by heroic concepts. Without the underlying complex of heroic ideas about battle and warriors, the Christian idea of 'God's battle' or 'God's warrior' would be ineffective as a metaphor. Thus, in *Andreas* in particular, and in Old English Christian poetry in general, whenever we encounter a description of a saint as a Germanic warrior, the question of whether or not the poet means his description literally should not obscure the possibility that heroic concepts may underlie even a figurative description.

While Andrew at times appears to be a *þegn*, in the full heroic sense of the term, God, in His relationship with Andrew, scarcely ever appears to be a Germanic lord. When Christ appears to Andrew before the gates of Mermedonia, He exhorts him to do 'battle' (*guð* – 951, *heardum heoruswengum* – 952), and reminds him to be 'eager for glory' (*Wes a domes georn* – 959), just as a Germanic lord might exhort his retainer, but, when He goes on to offer His own suffering at the hands of His enemies as a model for Andrew to emulate in his coming 'battle', any expectation that Christ may turn out to be a Germanic lord is disappointed (950-976). It is quite impossible to conceive of a pre-Christian Germanic lord being willing to endure suffering himself or advising his retainer to endure such humiliation at the hands of his enemies. Further, the fact that Andrew follows Christ's instructions throughout his sojourn in Mermedonia indicates clearly that, whatever heroic elements have been employed in his portrayal, he is not conceived of as an ideal Germanic hero in any very consistent manner. He willingly endures severe physical torture and insults for three days, never thinks of worldly glory, and takes no vengeance upon his enemies when he finally has opportunity to do so.

The most striking instances of the use of heroic concepts in *Andreas* occur in isolation, answering to the immediate needs of the poet, and the most striking of these is the passage in which Andrew's followers refuse to desert him (396-414). The sailor suggests that, since the followers are terrified of the storm at sea, they be set ashore to await the return of their leader. Their reply is immediate and unambiguous:

> Hwider hweorfað we   hlafordlease,
> geomormode,   gode orfeorme,
> synnum wunde,   gif we swicað þe?
> We bioð laðe   on landa gehwam,
> folcum fracoðe,   þonne fira bearn,
> ellenrofe,   æht besittaþ,
> hwylc hira selost   symle gelæste
> hlaforde æt hilde,   þonne hand ond rond
> on beaduwange   billum forgrunden
> æt niðplegan   nearu þrowedon.   (405–414)

Like any worthy troop of Germanic warriors, Andrew's thanes

will not violate the heroic code of loyalty by deserting their lord in the face of danger. If their loyalty should falter, they would become 'lordless' and, scorned in every land where warriors remain loyal in battle to their lords, they would become homeless exiles.

In the Greek story the followers likewise refuse to abandon Andrew, but they give no specific reason for their refusal, saying only, 'If we go away from thee, may we become strangers to the good things which the Lord hath provided for us.' [17] The ideal of heroic loyalty in battle, and the related concept of heroic exile, seems incongruous here since Andrew's followers are not really warriors and since Andrew himself does not really do any fighting in Mermedonia. Furthermore, in spite of this avowal of steadfast loyalty, Andrew's followers do not in the poem accompany him into the city, and he accomplishes his task, as we might expect of a saint, without human assistance. We must conclude that the poet has made use of heroic concepts in this instance to emphasize the devotion, suggested in his source, of Andrew's followers to their leader. Having accomplished his immediate purpose, he need not and does not concern himself with this relationship at any later point in his narrative. Since the poet is not attempting to portray a consistently loyal heroic *comitatus*, once Andrew enters the city his followers can disappear from the narrative and never be mentioned again.

Another, somewhat less obvious, aspect of the concept of exile appears in the course of the poet's description of Andrew's first night in prison. As soon as Andrew has been locked up for the night, the poet gives us an eleven-line description of the bitterly cold winter weather outside (1255-1265), a description which is not suggested in the various prose versions of the story. As we have seen earlier, winter weather is one of the most common hardships which the exile in heroic poetry must endure, and its sudden appearance here, at the beginning of Andrew's period of suffering, together with the fact that it is never mentioned again, suggests that this description is intended to emphasize the severity

---

[17]   *The Ante-Nicene Fathers*, p. 518.

of the hardships which Andrew (himself in some respects an exile) must endure. The poet has selected one of the components of the exile theme which is appropriate to a description of his hero's physical condition. He goes on, however, to describe Andrew's state-of-mind:

> Bliðheort wunode
> eorl unforcuð,   elnes gemyndig,
> þrist ond þrohtheard   in þreanedum
> wintercealdan niht.   (1262–1265)

While the exile of heroic tradition laments the cold as one of his afflictions, the Christian saint remains *bliðheort*, and praises his God in prayer (1265-1269). We cannot conclude from this passage that the poet is conscious of denying the validity of the heroic concept of exile, but in effect that is precisely what he is doing. In heroic tradition exile is the condition most to be feared and lamented, for it is the worst fate which can befall a warrior. By representing his hero as being happy in spite of his suffering at least one of the hardships of the exile state, the poet in this instance weakens the force of the heroic concept as a means of expressing human misfortune. In the light of the previously discussed passage in which Andrew's followers refuse to become exiles by abandoning him, it seems highly unlikely that the poet consciously intended to attack the validity of the heroic concept of exile; comparison of the two passages underscores the inconsistent nature of his use of heroic concepts in this poem.

If we examine the instances in which treasure appears or is mentioned in *Andreas,* we discover that it does not always play the role assigned to it in the heroic system of values. The first instance occurs when Andrew seeks passage to Mermedonia (270ff). He asks the sailor to convey him and his followers over the sea, even though he has 'few rings, treasure-honor' to give, and he offers a 'reward with God' if the sailor will be generous to him (270-276). Although the words Andrew uses are, in heroic poetry, associated with the concept of treasure as we have outlined it earlier, his speech as a whole sounds, in the poem as in the Greek version, like an attempt to defer not the heroic exchange of gifts but the payment of a fee for a service. In the pre-Christian

world of heroic poetry, where heroes are never poor and trade is
unknown, payment for a service with money or treasure of any
kind would be impossible. The ensuing dialogue between Andrew
and the sailor helps to confirm our impression that the heroic
concept of treasure has given place to more modern notions of
exchange. The sailor asks for *gafulrædenne, sceattas gescrifene*
once more (290-298), and Andrew again enumerates the kinds of
wealth which he does not possess:

> Næbbe ic fæted gold   ne feohgestreon,
> welan ne wiste   ne wira gespann,
> landes ne locenra beaga,   þæt ic þe mæge lust ahwettan,
> willan in worulde,   swa ðu worde beswist.   (301–304)

The sailor observes that travel *maðmum bedæled* (309) is very
difficult because one cannot buy food or drink (*hlafes wiste
ne hlutterne / drync* – 312-313) along the way (305-314). Clearly,
we are not in an heroic world where strangers are either given
hospitality as friends or driven off as enemies, but rather in a
world where one may buy his sustenance from disinterested sellers.
Andrew rebukes the sailor for his proud words; one who has
welan ond wiste   ond woruldspede (318) given him by God
should, as Christ taught, be kind to everyone, and especially to
the impoverished *þegnas* (323) of Christ (315-342). The words
of Christ which Andrew cites sound very like the promises which
Germanic lords make of rewards for loyal service:

> Ne ðurfan ge on þa fore   frætwe lædan,
> gold ne seolfor.   Ic eow goda gehwæs
> on eowerne agenne dom   est ahwette.   (337–339)

The context of this exchange between Andrew and the sailor,
however, forces a non-heroic interpretation of *goda* and *eowerne
agenne dom* in this passage. Throughout this dialogue we are
dealing not with treasure in its heroic function as a material symbol of honor, but with treasure as money.

A few lines later we encounter another reference to treasure,
but in this second instance it is much more difficult to draw conclusions as to the precise nature of the 'treasure' being described.

Andrew and his companions set out to sea, and the poet describes
their ship:

Æfre ic ne hyrde

þon cymlicor   ceol gehladenne

heahgestreonum.   Hæleð in sæton,

þeodnas þrymfulle,   þegnas wlitige.   (360–363)

If we take this passage literally, we cannot but wonder where
Andrew and his companions, who have had to beg passage, got
this sudden wealth. The poet, it would seem, has added this detail
because, in Germanic heroic tradition, heroes necessarily possess
treasure. The *heahgestreon* reflects the great worth of the men in
the ship, and the poet is again relying upon a heroic concept for
his immediate purposes. Just as the treasures on Beowulf's ship
when he journeys to (213-214) and from (1896-1899) Denmark
indicate the quality of the Geat and his thanes, so the 'ship laden
with high-treasures' indicates the quality of the Christian troop in
Andreas. On the other hand, however, the juxtaposition of the
two sentences quoted above may mean that the poet intends the
word *heahgestreonum* figuratively, as a metaphor for the *þeodnas*
and *þegnas* themselves. If this is the case, then we can no longer
consider the passage to be a contradiction of the earlier emphasis
upon Andrew's poverty, but nevertheless the heroic concept of
treasure may still be implicit in the metaphor. 'Treasure', even in
its metaphorical context, must mean more than just 'money',
especially since we have already heard Andrew discourse upon
the relative merits of worldly wealth and heavenly rewards (270-
276, 315-342). To equate a saint and his companions with money
or its equivalent would be to demean them, while to equate them
with the kind of treasure which represents heroic honor and
worthiness would be, if not wholly consistent with Christian values, at least a more fitting comparison.

After the travelers are well under way, Andrew expresses his
admiration for the skill of the sailor, and asks for his friendship,
but he phrases his request in a rather peculiar way:

Ic wille þe,

eorl unforcuð,   anre nu gena

bene biddan,   þeah ic þe beaga lyt,

> sincweorðunga,   syllan mihte,
> fætedsinces.   Wolde ic freondscipe,
> þeoden þrymfæst,   þinne, gif ic mehte,
> begitan godne.   (474–480)

The sailor knows Andrew is poor, and has given him passage, he says, because he is Christ's disciple (343-348). Thus Andrew's emphasis here upon his poverty does not seem to be an expression of the embarrassment of a poor man asking a favor of a rich one. Andrew's words imply his preoccupation with the heroic custom of gift–giving as an expression of mutual loyalty, and so they invite comparison with the passage in *Beowulf* (2144ff) in which Beowulf and Hygelac exchange gifts. Andrew is in fact apologizing for his inability to offer gifts which would bring as much honor to the sailor as the sailor's gift of friendship would bring to Andrew.

Andrew goes on to offer, in place of the treasure which the sailor would traditionally receive, *haligne hyht   on heofonþrymme* (481). Possibly, the poet is attempting here to supplant the heroic concept of worldly glory with the Christian notion of eternal reward in heaven for one's noble deeds and generosity, but when we consider the capricious way in which he uses heroic concepts to serve his immediate poetic needs, such a deliberate and conscious juxtaposition of the two traditions seems very doubtful. In this connection we may recall that he uses the heroic concept of treasure in its traditional form in his portrayal of the plight of the Mermedonians. Before their conversion, because famine has disordered their society, they 'receive no joy from treasure' (1113), and 'do not enjoy wealth' (1159), but after they convert to Christianity and order is reestablished, they have 'treasure, bright ring-giving' (1656-1657). Andrew, it is true, wishes to leave this scene of heroic prosperity (1654-1658), but the poet gives us no indication that either Andrew or God Himself disapproves of it. If the poet consciously desired to negate the heroic concept of treasure, he would surely not have had God tell Andrew to remain seven more days in the *salu sinchroden* (1673), nor would he have made the Mermedonians seem the good Christians which they are at the end of the poem.

From the foregoing discussion we may conclude that, at times, Germanic heroic concepts appear in *Andreas*, and that they appear with many, if not all, of the implications which they have in the most typically heroic Old English poetry which we have. These concepts do not form a consistent ideological background for the narrative, however. Sometimes the poet ignores them altogether, while at other times he contradicts them, so that it becomes impossible for us to tell whether he believes in their validity, is indifferent to them, or consciously disbelieves them. It does seem evident that the poet is not conscious of employing two traditions, the Christian and the Germanic, in telling his story. Whenever it serves his purpose, he mixes Christian and Germanic concepts and sentiments without the least indication that he is aware of incongruity or inconsistency. The essential difference, then, for our purposes, between *Genesis B* and *Andreas* is that in the former heroic concepts underlie the moral system which governs the world of the poem, and thus control its meaning, while in the latter heroic concepts are largely incidental to the morality and meaning of the poem. We may in all fairness say that *Genesis B* is a heroic poem based upon a Christian story, while *Andreas* is an essentially Christian poem in which heroic concepts and motifs play a secondary role.

IX

JULIANA AND *THE SEAFARER*

As we have seen, heroic concepts play a definite role in *Andreas,* but the status of these concepts in the world which the poet has portrayed is equivocal. One cannot be certain from one passage to the next whether the heroic values embodied in the concepts of loyalty, vengeance, treasure and exile are still operative and acceptable to the poet and his audience. When we turn to *Juliana* and *The Seafarer,* however, we find ourselves on more solid ground. Heroic concepts, to be sure, appear in these poems, but the role which they play is a basically negative one. The poets use these concepts in such a way that they become the secular concepts and inadequate values against which the Christian concepts and values work. In these two poems we may observe Christian values displacing the pre-Christian values in ways which lead us to believe that the poets are conscious of the conflicts of ideology between the two traditions, and that they desire to show in a consistent manner that Christian doctrine must take precedence over Germanic heroic custom. Thus, the Christianity of *Juliana* and *The Seafarer* is more thorough and more consistently presented than that of any of the poems which we have examined previously.

Juliana has been preserved in the *Exeter Book,* and is one of the four poems with the runic signature of the poet Cynewulf (675-731).[1] Charles W. Kennedy considers *Juliana* an early work of Cynewulf because, "The style is that of a writer who has not yet mastered narrative verse."[2] Rosemary Woolf, the most recent

---

[1] Line references are to the edition of G. P. Krapp and E. V. K. Dobbie, *The Exeter Book* (New York, 1936), pp. 113-133.

[2] Charles W. Kennedy, *The Poems of Cynewulf* (New York, 1910), p. 21.

editor of the poem, thinks it Cynewulf's last work because, "The general effect of the poem ... is that of uninspired competence rather than that of the technical hesitancy of a poet working towards his maturity",[3] and points out that it could have been written at any time from the very late eighth century to about 900.[4] Actually, there is no reason why Cynewulf could not have produced a mediocre work during the years of his best writing, particularly since much of the praise or blame for the quality of *Juliana* may be attributed to the Latin source which Cynewulf follows quite closely. Thus, the best we can do insofar as a date is concerned is to place *Juliana* within the lifetime of Cynewulf, which most scholars date about the first half of the ninth century.[5] As we have noted in the preceding chapter, Brooks dates *Andreas* around the middle of the ninth century, and so we may consider *Juliana* to have been written a bit earlier than *Andreas*, so long as we remember that we have no concrete evidence upon which to establish the relative chronology of these poems.

The generally accepted source for *Juliana* is the Latin life of St. Juliana published as "Acta auctore anonymo ex xi veteribus MSS" in the Bollandist *Acta Sanctorum* under the date February 16.[6] Krapp concludes his discussion of the source of *Juliana* by stating that, "In the absence of any closer Latin version, the text of the *Acta Sanctorum* may be accepted, for all practical purposes, as Cynewulf's original."[7] That the Bollandist text is the probable source of *Juliana* is substantiated both by the close correspondence of incident between the two stories, and by frequent verbal parallels and echoes of the Latin text in the Old English.[8] Cynewulf follows the *Acta* closely for his story, but he

[3]   Rosemary Woolf, ed., *Juliana* (London, 1955), p. 7.
[4]   Woolf, *Juliana*, pp. 5-7.
[5]   Albert S. Cook, ed., *The Christ of Cynewulf* (Boston, 1900), p. lxx, gives the approximate dates 750-825. Kenneth Sisam, "Cynewulf and His Poetry", pp. 1-7, places him in the ninth century. See also Woolf, *Juliana*, pp. 5-7; Brooks, *Andreas*, p. xxii.
[6]   Reprinted in *The Juliana of Cynewulf*, ed. William Strunk (Boston, 1904), pp. 33-49.
[7]   Krapp and Dobbie, *The Exeter Book*, p. xxxvii.
[8]   Among those I have noted are:

omits various details and expands his source in a few places. Strunk has noted that Cynewulf eliminated certain unattractive characteristics such as deceitfulness, vindictiveness, cruelty and coarseness of speech from the picture of Juliana drawn in the *Acta*.[9] Strunk fails to note, however, that the Latin version, judging by its language and presentation, was probably written for schoolboys, who would naturally be less sensitive to these incongruities than Cynewulf, who was no doubt writing for an adult audience. While Cynewulf's alterations of plot and character portrayal have little relevance here, occasionally his use of heroic concepts and motifs may be verified by noting that they are neither contained in, nor suggested by, his Latin source.

The opening lines of *Juliana* are superficially similar to the heroic opening of *Andreas,* but if one examines these lines at all closely he discovers that the heroic implications of the opening of *Andreas* are in effect negated here. The first three lines follow the familiar pattern of the first lines of *Andreas* and *Beowulf,* and thus would probably have aroused in the Anglo-Saxon audience the momentary expectation that they were about to hear a heroic poem extolling the martial deeds of a Germanic warrior:

> Hwæt! We ðæt hyrdon   hæleð eahtian,
> deman dædhwate,   þætte in dagum gelamp
> Maximianes,   se geond middangeard .... (1–3)

The elements in these lines are all conventional: the initial *Hwæt,* designed to attract the listener's attention; the 'we heard' formula which, together with the reference to the past (*in dagum*), estab-

---

Juliana line		*Acta* paragraph	
95	*minra eagna leoht*	2.	*lux oculorum meum*
244	*engles hiw*	6.	*in figura angeli*
312	*mid minum broþrum*	7.	*cum fratribus meis*
418	*unclæne gæst*	10.	*immunde spiritus*
491	*butan godes tacne*	11.	*non habentes signaculum Christi*
595	*ongon his hrægl teran*	18.	*scidit vestimenta suo*
610–	*þæt hyre endestæf*	/ 18.	*eo quod appropinquasset*
611	*of gewindagum weorþan sceolde*		*finis certaminis ejus*

[9] Strunk, pp. xxxiii ff.

lishes the tale as an old one; the vague reference to the hero's
sphere of activity; and the name of the hero. The expectation that
we are to hear a poem about the famous lord Maximian is stifled
when, in line four, we learn that Maximian was a 'cruel king'
(*arleas cyning*), and by line eight we know that he is no hero, but
rather a 'heathen prince' (*hæþen hildfruma* – 7) who persecutes
the righteous people (*ryhtfremmendra* – 8) who are Christian.
Cynewulf goes on to describe Maximian and his followers in
words which suggest that he thinks of this heathen as a powerful
Germanic lord who commands a band of warlike retainers:

> Wæs his rice brad,
> wid ond weorðlic   ofer werþeode,
> lytesna ofer ealne   yrmenne grund.
> Foron æfter burgum,   swa he biboden hæfde,
> þegnas þryðfulle.   Oft hi þræce rærdon....
>
> (8–12)

The 'strife' in which these thanes engage, however, consists in
'evil deeds' (*dædum gedwolene* – 13), the murder of God's faithful followers. Thus Cynewulf begins his narrative by speaking of
the martial exploits, the wealth and the power of an apparently
Germanic lord and his retainers, but at the same time he makes
them thoroughly evil, the villains of his story. He sets up the
principal opposition between heathen and Christian which will
control the action of his narrative, while suggesting through his
choice of words that the heathens are to be identified with the
lords and warriors of Germanic heroic poetic tradition. In this
context, victorious acts of war are evil and the defeated Christians, *godes cempan* (17), are obviously expected to arouse the
sympathy and approval of the audience. Unlike the *Andreas*-
poet, Cynewulf apparently does not think it necessary to disguise
Christian martyrs and teachers as Germanic warriors; quite the
contrary, he seems to have enough confidence in the Christianity
of his audience to make characters who would appear as heroes
in pre-Christian tradition the villains of his poem.

Cynewulf's use of the phrase *godes cempan* (17) in the introductory lines, and of *Cristes þegnas* later in *Juliana* (299-303),
again raises the question, discussed earlier in connection with

Andreas, of whether these and other formulas which have martial denotations in heroic poetry are intended in a strictly figurative sense in this particular poem. In *Andreas* one can almost never be certain that the poet is using martial imagery and language metaphorically when he describes his peaceful Christians as if they were Germanic warriors, and more often than not one suspects that he thinks quite literally of his Christians as warriors. In *Juliana*, however, one finds no confusion between the conduct of good Christians and the conduct of good Germanic warriors, so that, when one encounters martial imagery and language applied to Christians, he can be reasonably certain that it should not be taken literally. Christians are called *godes cempan*, but seldom is the warrior imagery elaborated in the same manner which arouses our suspicions in *Andreas*. One might argue that, since the only Christian of any importance in *Juliana* is the heroine herself, Cynewulf had no real opportunity to indulge in the kind of heroic description which the *Andreas*-poet lavishes upon his male heroes, but in fact there is enough martial imagery and language in the poem for us to decide with some confidence whether or not Cynewulf uses such images and words with any literal intent.

In the course of her interrogation of the devil whom she has captured, Juliana asks him for an account of his tactics as he goes about attempting to seduce God's servants into evil (345-350). His reply contains much sustained martial imagery which is not contained in the Latin source, which is clearly figurative, and which calls to mind the imagery of Ephesians 6, xii-xvii, and of medieval psychological allegories like Prudentius' *Psychomachia*. He begins by telling Juliana in a straightforward manner how he turns the faithful from the paths of salvation by introducing evil desires into their minds (362-381). His attack is not physical, but psychological:

> Ic him geswete   synna lustas,
> mæne modlufan,   þæt he minum hraþe,
> leahtrum gelenge,   larum hyreð.   (369–371)

Under his influence men turn from prayer and devotion to God to lives of vice. By having the devil begin his account with a literal description of the way in which he tempts the faithful, Cynewulf ensures that the warfare imagery which he is about to introduce will not be mistaken for a literal description of physical battle between the devil and the faithful Christian. Sometimes, says the devil, he encounters a 'warrior of God' (*metodes cempan* – 383) who is 'valorous' (*ellenrofne* – 382) and 'courageous' (*modigne* – 383), and will not 'bow from battle' (*bugan from beaduwe* – 385). Such a 'warrior' raises his 'shield' (*bord* – 385) against the devil's 'storm of arrows' (*flanþræce* – 384). The 'arrows' are clearly the evil thoughts to which the devil has already referred, and the 'shield', as Cynewulf carefully has him explain, is 'a holy shield, spiritual armor' (*haligne scyld, / gæstlic guðreaf* – 386-387). God's warrior 'fights' by standing firmly at prayer (388-389), thus forcing the devil to depart lamenting his failure to 'win the battle' (*guðe wiðgongan* – 393). The devil goes off to seek a 'worse warrior' to do battle with:

> ... ic geomor sceal
> secan oþerne   ellenleasran,
> under cumbolhagan,   cempan sænran,
> þe ic onbryrdan mæge   beorman mine,
> agælan æt guþe.   (393–397)

As he proceeds with his confession, the devil's imagery becomes a bit more elaborate, but Cynewulf sees to it that he prepares his audience so that they cannot misunderstand him. In describing his more successful attack upon the 'worse warrior', the devil employs the imagery of a siege, but before he does so, he tells Juliana that he begins this new campaign by scouting the 'defenses' within the enemy's mind:

> ... ic beo gearo sona,
> þæt ic ingehygd   eal geondwlite,
> hu gefæstnad sy   ferð innanweard,
> wiðsteall geworht.   (398–401)

This unambiguous statement makes the images of wall, gate, and tower which follow (401ff) intelligible; the description of the victim's mind as a walled town should not confuse the audience, since they have been told beforehand what the devil is talking about. He makes his metaphor even more explicit by identifying the *torr* (402) with the *breostsefan* (405) into which he sends the 'flight of arrows' (*eargfare* – 404) which are 'bitter thoughts' (*bitre geþoncas* – 405). Finally, lest anyone miss the point that the devil is speaking of warfare against the human soul rather than the body, he summarizes his goals for us:

```
                                     Ic þære sawle ma
     geornor gyme      ymb þæs gæstes forwyrd
     þonne þæs lichoman,    se þe on legre sceal
     weorðan in worulde    wyrme to hroþor,
     bifolen in foldan.                (413–417)
```

In the light of this long passage it is, I think, impossible to read the other martial images and words which Cynewulf uses as literal descriptions. The care which he takes to make his figurative language unambiguous further suggests that he does not wish his audience to confuse his Christian characters with the warriors of heroic poetic tradition, and that when we discover heroic concepts in *Juliana* we should examine their functions with some care.

Eleusius is, from a strictly heroic, Germanic point-of-view, an admirable man. Although his reputation as a warrior is scarcely mentioned, he nevertheless possesses the wealth and power befitting a lord in Germanic poetic tradition. Heroic connotations of lordship and treasure permeate the words with which he is introduced into the poem:

```
     Sum wæs æhtwelig      æþeles cynnes
     rice gerefa.     Rondburgum weold,
     eard weardade      oftast symle
     in þære ceastre      Commedia,
     heold hordgestreon.              (18–22)
```

Like all the lords of Germanic tradition, he is 'rich in possessions', 'of noble lineage', 'ruler of the shield-town', guardian of the *eard* in which he dwells, and the possessor of the treasure-hoard. He is, of course, famous, as would be any hero who had won honor commensurate with his great wealth – *hæfde ealdordom / micelne ond mærne* (25-26). Later in the poem we find passing references to his *domsetle* (162, 534), and his *duguð* (162). Into this first, heroic description of Eleusius, however, Cynewulf introduces one element which is not traditionally emphasized in the portrayal of the lords of heroic poetry; he is heathen:

> Oft he hæþengield
> ofer word godes, weoh gesohte
> neode geneahhe. (22–24)

By identifying Eleusius both as a heathen and as a worthy Germanic lord, Cynewulf has taken a position from which he can, in the process of discrediting false religion, also discredit heroic ideals as a part of the heathen view of the world, and that is precisely what he does. From the point at which Juliana enters the narrative (26ff), the opposition is established between Christianity and Christian ideals on the one hand, and paganism and heroic ideals on the other. Eleusius develops a desire for Juliana (*hine fyrwet bræc* – 27), but she loves Christ (26-31). She is not interested in Eleusius, in spite of his wealth:

> Hire wæs godes egsa
> mara in gemyndum þonne eall þæt maþþumgesteald
> þe in þæs æþelinges æhtum wunade.
> þa wæs se weliga þæra wifgifta,
> goldspedig guma, georn on mode,
> þæt him mon fromlicast fæmnan gegyrede,
> bryd to bolde. Heo þæs beornes lufan
> fæste wiðhogde, þeah þe feohgestreon
> under hordlocan hyrsta unrim
> æhte ofer eorþan. (35–44)

This passage, with its heavy emphasis upon Eleusius' 'treasure', constitutes a clear and specific rejection of the heroic concept of treasure. If treasure is the material manifestation of human worth, then Eleusius is certainly a worthy man and, consequently, a desirable husband. Juliana, however, is Christian to the core, and does not judge a hero by his wealth. She rejects Eleusius not specifically because he is wealthy, but rather because he is a pagan (44-57); but in doing so she places the criterion of true religion higher than that of heroic worth and honor on the scale of human valuation. Moreover, since treasure is the symbol of heroic loyalty, the reward of the worthy avenger and one of the good things of which the exile is deprived, by rejecting the concept of treasure Cynewulf's heroine implicitly rejects the other three major heroic concepts with which we have been dealing. By coupling the rejection of heathenism with the rejection of treasure, Cynewulf suggests that treasure is a heathen value which has no place in the life of a true Christian.

The relationship of Eleusius to Juliana's father, Affricanus, is that of a Germanic lord to his retainer. Cynewulf describes their first meeting as that of two 'warriors' taking peaceful counsel together:

> Reord up astag,
> siþþan hy togædre   garas hlændon,
> hildeþremman.   (62–64)

Just as in his first description of Eleusius as a Germanic lord, so here Cynewulf inserts a reminder that both the participants in this meeting are heathens (64-65). In his speech (66-77), which has no counterpart in the Latin source, Eleusius emphasizes the insult which he has received from Juliana. Like all Germanic heroes, he resents a personal insult every bit as much as he would a physical attack; an insult *fore þissum folce* (74) which goes unavenged means a loss of heroic honor. Eleusius takes Juliana's rejection of his suit as an insult in two respects; it is a personal 'insult' (*orwyrðu* – 69) to him because she doesn't care about his affection for her (68-71), and an 'insult' (*fraceðu* – 71) to his religion because she has advised him to convert to Christianity (71-77). Once again, Cynewulf has managed to associate the heroic value placed upon personal honor with the heathen religion of Eleusius.

Affricanus' reply to Eleusius (78-88) reflects the heroic loyalty which a worthy retainer is expected to show to his lord. Affricanus' lord has been offended, and it is Affricanus' duty as a loyal retainer to avenge that offense if he can. Heathen religion and heroic concept are again united as Affricanus swears in one breath to repay both the favor he has received from his god and the favor he has received from his lord:

Ic þæt geswerge   þurh soð godu,
swa ic are æt him   æfre finde,
oþþe, þeoden, æt þe   þine hyldu
winburgum in . . . .   (80–83)

The actual situation, of course, precludes Affricanus' going to battle in the service of his lord, but he does swear to render up the life of his lord's enemy, just as if she were a warrior herself. Considered in abstract terms, then, the situation presented in this scene is very similar to that in which Beowulf pledges his aid to Hrothgar after Grendel's mother has carried off Æschere (Beo., 1381ff.); the loyal retainer promises to repay the favors of his lord by avenging an affront which the lord has received. According to the heroic concepts of loyalty and vengeance, Affricanus is acting properly, but the fact that his cause, heathen religion, is evil negates the propriety of his conduct and in consequence, denies the universal validity of the concepts themselves.

Affricanus' words to his daughter (89-104) again reveal that he thinks like a Germanic warrior. He does not in this first speech to her rebuke her specifically for her religious views, but rather for her 'foolishness' (geaþe – 96) in refusing so worthy a husband as Eleusius. From Affricanus' point-of-view, Eleusius is an excellent catch:

Wiðsæcest þu to swiþe   sylfre rædes
þinum brydguman,   se is betra þonne þu,
æþelra for eorþan,   æhtspedigra
feohgestreona.   He is to freond god.   (99–102)

Affricanus' equation of 'better' with 'more noble' and 'wealthier in treasure' recalls the observation made by the Beowulf-poet that Hygelac retained more wealth than Beowulf because he was 'better' (2196-2199). Affricanus thinks according to heroic concepts which equate personal wealth with personal merit. His remark that Eleusius is also 'a good friend' perhaps suggest that Eleusius gives generously of his wealth to his loyal retainers. It is no wonder that Affricanus tells Juliana that she would be acting worthily (is þæs wyrþe – 103) by accepting his lord's suit. Juliana, however, is more enlightened than her father, and so she rejects his proposal that she marry a man who chooses to remain a pagan

(105-116). At the same time she again rejects the notion that Eleusius' treasure reflects his merit by implying that his wealth is of no importance to her:

> He þa brydlufan
> sceal to oþerre   æhtgestealdum
> idese secan;   nafað he ænige her.   (114–116)

Affricanus' threat that if she persists in her Christianity she will be killed fails to move her from her devotion to Christ (118-129); no torture, says she, will force her to alter her decision (130-139).

I have previously observed that by implying the concept of vengeance in the first exchange between Eleusius and Affricanus (58-88), Cynewulf has likewise implied a relationship between vengeance and paganism, and thus denied the validity of vengeance as an ideal of proper conduct. Other references to vengeance in the poem support the contention that Cynewulf desires to discredit this ideal, for only the villains ever seek vengeance. Thus, when he has Juliana in his power, Eleusius makes a vow (*beotwordum spræc* – 185) that, if she does not cease her blasphemy and accept his god, he will be forced to take vengeance upon her (184-208). 'Torture' (*witebrogan* – 196) will be her 'reward' (*lean* – 195) if she does not offer sacrifices to his god. He states quite clearly that he intends to 'avenge' the 'strife' which she has raised with his god:

> Læt þa sace restan,
> lað leodgewin.   Gif þu leng ofer þis
> þurh þin dolwillen   gedwolan fylgest,
> þonne ic nyde sceal   niþa gebæded
> on þære grimmestan   godscyld wrecan,
> torne teoncwide,   þe þu tælnissum
> wiþ þa selestan   sacan ongunne,
> ond þa mildestan   þara þe men witen,
> þe þes leodscype mid him   longe bieode.
>   (200–208)

Of course, the god whom Eleusius serves, and whom he is so zealous to avenge, is Satan, and so his loyalty to his 'lord', which by heroic standards is admirable, becomes in this context reprehensible.

Juliana, unlike her tormentors, never speaks of vengeance either for the torments which she herself has undergone or for the crimes which the devil tells her he has perpetrated against other human beings. In revealing no malice toward her oppressors, of course, she behaves as a Christian should. Unlike her counterpart in the Latin *Acta*, she even releases the devil after he has revealed his secrets to her (553ff). This devil shows his gratitude for her mercy by returning to demand that vengeance be taken upon her for her Christian faith (an insult to his lord, Satan), and for the personal humiliation which he has suffered:

> Gyldað nu mid gyrne,   þæt heo goda ussa
> meaht forhogde,   ond mec swiþast
> geminsade,   þæt ic to meldan wearð.
> Læteð hy laþra   leana hleotan
> þurh wæpnes spor,   wrecað ealdne nið,
> synne gesohte.   Ic þa sorge gemon,
> hu ic bendum fæst   bisga unrim
> on anre niht   earfeða dreag,
> yfel ormætu.   (619–627)

Juliana says nothing in reply, but her glance is enough to frighten her accuser into flight (627-634). The devil's cowardice effectively reduces the essentially heroic demand for vengeance to absurdity. He acts out of fear and hatred, not out of a heroic sense of honor, and he must rely upon misguided heathens to carry out his wishes. If such cowards are the proponents of vengeance, Cynewulf seems to imply, then vengeance cannot be a very worthy enterprise.

The concept of exile appears only once in *Juliana*, and at first glance it seems as if Cynewulf is employing this one heroic concept, in precisely the same way that it is employed in pre-Christian heroic tradition, to depict severe human suffering. After Juliana's death, in both the Latin source and the poem, Eleusius and his followers become frightened and flee Nicomedia on a ship in which they ultimately drown. Cynewulf enforces the traditional associations of exile inherent in descriptions of sea-journeys by adding formulas which emphasize the miseries which the voyagers endure. The 'band of warriors' (*secga hloþe* – 676) dies in 'severe misery' (*þurh þearlic þrea* – 678), in a storm *(þurh wæges wylm*

– 680), 'lowly with their lord, deprived of joy' (*heane mid hlaford, hroþra bidæled* – 681). One might argue that Cynewulf has here fallen back upon a heroic concept in order to emphasize the wretchedness of his villains, and that, even though he has at various points in the narrative cast doubts upon the other three major heroic concepts, he nevertheless retains this one. We must bear in mind, however, that this most terrible of all heroic fates befalls those characters who live according to heroic values. Cynewulf does not suggest that exile is a miserable fate for both Christians and pagans; he does suggest that, even by their own system of values, these heathen Germanic warriors end their lives in misery.

Cynewulf goes on to speak of the fate after death of the heathen host. It is not a happy one:

> Ne þorftan þa þegnas   in þam þystran ham,
> seo geneatscolu   in þam neolan scræfe,
> to þam frumgare   feohgestealda
> witedra wenan,   þæt hy in winsele
> ofer beorsetle   beagas þegon,
> æpplede gold.   (683–388)

In its emphasis upon wretched physical surroundings and deprivation of the joys of the hall this description of 'life' in hell sounds very like a description of exile. Further, we have learned earlier in the poem that Satan, the 'lord' whom heathens like Eleusius serve, is not a 'mild lord' (*frea milde* – 328) but a 'terrible' one (*egesful ealdor* – 329). Cynewulf seems to be saying here that heathen Germanic warriors not only do not go to the true heaven, but that they are disappointed in their expectation of what their false heaven, which is hell, will be like. Hell is not an ideal *comitatus*, but rather it is the equivalent of permanent heroic exile.

On the other hand, Cynewulf does not suggest that the true heaven to which Juliana goes is at all like the ideal *comitatus* which Germanic heroes expect, and in this he is unlike the poets of *Genesis B* and *Andreas*. Indeed, he wisely refrains from attempting to describe heaven at all, for *seo þrynis   þrymsittende / in annesse* (726-727) is scarcely describable in any words, and certainly not in terms of the formulas of Old English heroic tradition. Of Juliana's ultimate fate he says only that *hyre sawl wearð*

/ *alæded of lice*   *to þam langan gefean* (669-670). The implication of this final passage of the narrative (669-695)[10] is that the heathen die in misery but do not therefore attain the heaven which they desire, while the Christian heroine dies in similarly unpleasant circumstances and consequently does attain the heaven which she deserves. To die a heathen in heathen misery is unprofitable, while to die a Christian in Christian martyrdom is actually beneficial. Thus Cynewulf does in a way negate the heroic concept of exile by showing that the suffering which the exiled heathen endures is of no importance to his salvation, and does not end with his death, while the suffering which the Christian endures in this world helps to pave his way to heaven.

In *Juliana*, then, Cynewulf uses heroic Germanic concepts in a manner which differs from that used by the poets of *Genesis B* and *Andreas*. By making only his heathen villains speak and act in accordance with the concepts which underlie the heroic view of the world, and by making his Christian heroine reject these concepts in word and deed, he effectively equates the heroic view with paganism and thus rejects it. Unlike the composers of *Genesis B* and *Andreas*, he seems to be aware of the incompatibility of the Christian and heroic views of life, and conscious of the fact that the concepts of loyalty, treasure, vengeance and exile, as we find them in heroic poetry, are the integral, cohesive framework upon which the heroic view rests. By specifically identifying heroic ideals with paganism, Cynewulf leads one to suspect that he recognized that, at least in England, heroic poetic tradition precedes chronologically the Christian tradition as he knows it, and that Christianity and Christian ideals must displace heroic ideals in the hierarchy of absolute human values.

The only major heroic concept which Cynewulf treats at all ambiguously in *Juliana* is that of exile. But even if we consider Cynewulf's treatment of the concept of exile equivocal, we cannot place the same criticism upon the anonymous poet who composed *The Seafarer*, for in that poem exile plays a central role.

[10] The concluding lines of the poem (695-731) consist of Cynewulf's plea for the prayers of his audience and his runic signature.

Indeed, *The Seafarer*, like *The Wife's Lament*, is a monologue[11] about the exile's condition, spoken by one who claims to have experienced the hardships of exile at first hand. But where *The Wife's Lament* presents the traditional pre-Christian view of exile as the worst of human conditions, *The Seafarer* deviates sharply from the traditional view in that it presents exile as, ultimately, a benefical and desirable condition. Like *Juliana, The Seafarer* can be read, at least in part, as its poet's conscious rejection of the concepts which control pre-Christian heroic poetry.

So much has been written in recent years concerning the interpretation of *The Seafarer* that it would be both inordinately time-consuming and largely irrelevant to our purposes for us to concern ourselves with an extensive consideration of earlier criticism.[12] Greenfield has conveniently summarized the two basic critical views commonly taken of *The Seafarer* in his observation that, "Either we can take the proposed sea-journey [of the narrator] literally, seeing in it an ascetic resolution to forsake the things of this world for a *peregrinatio pro amore Dei*, or we can take it as an allegory of man's passage to the land from whence he was exiled in the Fall of Adam, the heavenly *patria*, his earlier voyaging being an allegory for his life on earth, as in the sea-voyage simile at the end of *Christ II*."[13] As we shall see, a careful examination of the poet's use of heroic concepts contributes rather heavily to the literal view, first proposed by Dorothy Whitelock,[14] of the narrator as a *peregrinus*, but any direct refutation of allegorical readings of the poem lies outside the scope of our immediate concern and will not be attempted.

Of the various critical comments upon the heroic elements in

---

[11]   But see J. C. Pope, "Dramatic Voices in *The Wanderer* and *The Seafarer*", in *Franciplegius*, pp. 164-193, for the view that there are two voices in the poem. Stanley B. Greenfield, "MIN, SYLF, and 'Dramatic Voices in *The Wanderer* and *The Seafarer*'", *JEGP* LXVIII (1969), 212-220, offers a convincing refutation of Pope's view.

[12]   For more extensive surveys of various interpretations of the poem see Greenfield, *Critical History*, pp. 219-221, and *The Seafarer*, ed. I. L. Gordon (London, 1960), pp. 1-12.

[13]   Greenfield, *Critical History*, pp. 220-221.

[14]   "The Interpretation of *The Seafarer*". See also Henry, *The Early English and Celtic Lyric*.

The Seafarer, the most provocative, and most nearly suggestive of the view which I shall develop here, is that of Mrs. Gordon in the introduction to her edition of the poem:

Both *The Wanderer* and *The Seafarer* are the work of poets to whom it is natural to use the terms of Germanic secular poetry to express their homiletic themes. The picture of the vanished life of the hall in *The Wanderer*, and the glories of the "golden age" of the past in *The Seafarer* 80–90, though clearly derived from the homiletic *ubi sunt* motif, are expressed in a form that would have a special significance to an audience familiar with Germanic heroic poetry. And the process was evidently a conscious one, since the same tendency to exploit the terms of heroic poetry, though for a different purpose, is seen in the way in which the poet of *The Seafarer* plays upon the double meaning of certain words.[15]

She goes on to cite Greenfield's comments [16] upon the poet's use of the words *dryhten* in lines 41-43, *dream, duguð,* and *blæd* in lines 64-88, and *lof* in lines 73 and 78 with both secular and Christian meanings, and concludes, "These double meanings were, of course, current in the language itself, but in understanding them thus the poet points the contrast between the heroic and the Christian ideal." [17]

The dating of *The Seafarer*, as Mrs. Gordon points out, "must to some extent depend on the interpretation we give to its subject matter",[18] and is extremely difficult to ascertain with any sort of confidence. Sisam's speculations concerning the compilation of the *Exeter Book* give Mrs. Gordon a basis for taking the approximate date 940 as a *terminus ad quem* for the composition of the poem. While she offers no *terminus a quo*, she seems to favor a late, rather than an early date, and points to the mid-ninth or early tenth century as the periods most favorable to the poem's composition. Since Cynewulf's death is thought to have occurred around the middle of the ninth century, *The Seafarer*, if Mrs.

---

[15] Gordon, *The Seafarer*, p. 26.
[16] Stanley B. Greenfield, "Attitudes and Values in *The Seafarer*", *SP* LI (1954), 18-20.
[17] Gordon, *The Seafarer*, p. 27.
[18] Gordon, *The Seafarer*, p. 29.

Gordon's speculations are correct, may be a somewhat later poem than *Juliana*.[19]

No one, I think, could seriously dispute the contention that the personal experience about which the Seafarer speaks is (at least on a literal level) exile, in the pre-Christian sense of the word. Indeed, he is quite explicit about the nature of his seafaring. He says that he will tell his audience of his wretched, lordless life on the sea:

> hu ic earmcearig   iscealdne sæ
> winter wunade   wræccan lastum,
> winemægum bidroren. . . .   (14–16)[20]

We have observed earlier that the sea in Germanic heroic poetry is preeminently a place of exile, and especially so when the seafarer is separated from his lord and his fellow warriors. Unlike the two brief journeys of Beowulf to and from Denmark (*Beo.*, 210-228, 1903-1919), the Seafarer's travels have been 'a time of misery' (*earfoðhwile* – 3). He has endured cold, hunger and, no doubt, physical danger when his ship *be clifum cnossað* (8-12). His statement that the cries of birds replaced the convivial sounds and pastimes of the hall reflects the solitude of exile:

>   Hwilum ylfete song
> dyde ic me to gomene,   ganetes hleoþor
> ond huilpan sweg   fore hleahtor wera
> mæw singende   fore medodrince.   (19–22)

His frequent remarks upon the contrast between the life of the seafarer and that of the *esteadig secg* (56) remind us of the poverty which is commonly the lot of the exile.

In spite of the severity of the suffering which the Seafarer has endured, and in spite of the introduction of the 'elegiac mood' in his monologue (80ff.), the poem is not an exile's lament in the same way that the speech of the 'last survivor' in *Beowulf* (2231ff.) is a lament. Two key elements common to the traditional heroic exile's lament are conspicuously absent; the Seafarer

[19] For a thorough discussion of the date and place of origin of the poem see Gordon, *The Seafarer*, pp. 27-32.
[20] Line references are to G. P. Krapp and E. V. K. Dobbie, eds., *The Exeter Book* (New York, 1936), pp. 143-147.

expresses neither nostalgic longing for the vanished joys of the past, nor desire to acquire a new lord. Indeed, this particular exile is 'lordless' only in the heroic sense of the term, for he has a 'Lord' in Heaven, the Christian God. Thus, as Greenfield has pointed out,[21] the play upon the word *dryhten*, meaning first a warrior's temporal lord (*his dryhten* – 41) and then God (*dryhten* – 43), suggests the poet's approach to the concept of exile in this poem. The poet's Christian values, expressed through the mouth of an exile, make his poem an affirmation of, rather than a lament for, the condition of exile. Christian doctrine, stressing renunciation of this world, makes exile, which in the heroic system of values is the worst of all possible fates, a desirable condition. In the process of affirming exile, the poet necessarily elevates Christian values above heroic values, the Christian *dryhten* above the temporal *dryhten*, and thus questions the ultimate validity of the complex of concepts which control Germanic heroic poetry. By examining *The Seafarer* in some detail, one can see how the poet manages this displacement of inherited Germanic values.

In the first twenty-six lines of *The Seafarer*, the speaker describes in a straightforward manner the condition of exile which he has experienced. The hardships which he describes are typical of those suffered by any exile in Germanic heroic poetry, and the language in which he describes these hardships is likewise common to the heroic theme of exile. The audience is given no reason to suspect that this poem will express anything but the traditional heroic concept of exile. Indeed, the phrases *bitre breostceare* (4), *ceare seofedun* (10), and *ic earmcearig* (14) suggest that, like all heroic exiles, the Seafarer deplored his hard fate. His use of the past tense in these opening lines suggests that his condition is no longer that of an exile, leading the audience to believe that perhaps he has found a new lord and a new *comitatus*. In this context, the contrast between his hardships on the sea and the life of 'the man whose lot is most happy on land' (12-17) seems to be drawn only for the sake of rhetorical emphasis. In reality, of course, this contrast between the prosperous Germanic warrior, living with his lord *on foldan* (13), and the exile, living *winemæ-*

gum bidroren (16) on the *iscealdne sæ* (14), will acquire deeper significance in the course of the poem. This contrast between *comitatus* life and exile gains additional emphasis from the speaker's subsequent statement of his isolation (19-22), which is expressed in terms of his deprivation of the hall-joys which all fortunate Germanic warriors enjoy – *gomene* (20), *hleahtor wera* (21), and *medodrince* (22). Likewise the final remark that 'no protecting-kinsman could console [his] wretched spirit' (25-26) seems here to mean simply that he had no lord, but it foreshadows the contrast which the Seafarer will draw between the power of temporal lords and the power of God.

At this point in his monologue, the Seafarer alters his emphasis slightly and offers what would be, for an audience expecting an exposition of the heroic concept of exile, a paradoxical, enigmatic statement (27-38). As a brief summary of his previous remarks, he begins by reiterating the notion that the hardships of exile are so severe that the prosperous, happy warrior cannot even conceive of them (27-33). However, having emphasized once more this contrast between prosperity and exile, he goes on (33-38) to say that *Forþon*, for this very reason (*i.e.*, that such misery as the exile endures is unknown on land), he desires to return to a life of exile and 'seek far hence a foreign land' (37-38). This statement, in a strictly heroic context, seems to make no sense. It would doubtless astonish a pre-Christian audience, and would probably perplex an audience which, even if it were entirely Christian, had been led to expect a poem about heroic exile. The Seafarer welcomes exile precisely because it is the worst of fates in a heroic world, but he is not yet ready to explain why he has made this choice.

Instead, the Seafarer now makes a series of general statements in the third person about both the difficulty and the desirability of the exile's journey (39-57). In this section of the poem he further eleborates upon the contrast between the succesful Germanic warrior and the unfortunate exile. He begins by saying that no man, no matter how secure his position within the *comitatus*, can contemplate a sea-journey without feeling anxiety about his fate (39-43). The poet implies by this observation that the ideal life from a heroic point of view – *a modwlonc mon* (39), who is *in geoguþe* . . . *hwæt* (40), *in his dædum* . . . *deor* (41) and who has a *gifena* . . . *god* (40), *a dryhten* . . .*hold* (41) – is inadequate because ultimately the most devoted of temporal lords (*dryhten* – 41) cannot protect any warrior from the Lord (*drythen* – 43). For this reason, a voluntary exile thinks only of *yða gewealc* (46), of the time when he is completely in the hands of the Lord, and ignores the rewards of loyal service to a temporal lord (*hearpan hyge, hringþege, wife wyn* – 44-45). Likewise, the pleasures of nature are of no account to him. The beauty of the spring land-scape and the song of the cuckoo, *sumeres weard* (54) only re-mind him (*gemoniað* – 50; *monað* – 53) of his exile's journey, and they cannot compensate him for the hardships which he must endure (48-55). Finally, he again remarks upon the ignorance of prosperous men concerning the rigors of the exile's life (55-57). Thus, the Seafarer has moved from the bare statement that he welcomes exile (33-38), to the intimation that this preference is the result of his consciousness of the inadequacy of the benefits of secular heroic life and heroic values (39-57). He has hinted that, if the positive values of Germanic heroic tradition are un-satisfactory, then the negative values embodied in the concept of exile may indeed be more beneficial. It remains for him to show precisely why this inversion of heroic values is desirable.

Up to this point in the poem, we have been given only veiled intimations as to why the Seafarer prefers the deprivation of exile to heroic prosperity. Now, however, he moves back to the first person to make an unambiguous statement of his personal beliefs (58-71). This statement will lead us into a specifically Christian explanation of the anti-heroic view of exile which he has been expounding. His mind, he says, projects itself out of his body, passes far out over the sea, the *hwæles eþel* (60), a place of very real danger to the voyager, and then returns to 'incite' (*hweteð* – 63) him to travel (58-64). He goes on to tell us that this is not an irrational longing for the dangers of the unknown:

> Forþon me hatran sind
> dryhtnes dreamas   þonne þis deade lif,
> læne on londe.   (64–66)

While earlier in the poem he had merely contrasted exile with life on land, now he refers specifically to 'God's joys' as distinct from the traditional joys of men within the *comitatus*. Thus exile, the condition in which the warrior lacks the joys of men, is offered quite clearly as the condition in which he can gain the joys of God, joys which he suggests are not transitory (*læne*) like earthly joys.

The Seafarer then remarks that he does not believe that 'earthly wealth stands eternally' (*eorðwelan   ece stondað* – 67) for the man who lives 'this dead life' because the threat of death always hangs over him (66-71). This initial remark upon wealth leads him into a series of reflections upon earthly heroic glory. Earthly wealth and the heroic ideal of glory are intimately associated in the Seafarer's mind, just as they are in the mind of the *Beowulf*-poet. The statement that such wealth is not a warrior's eternal possession, which to a modern reader sounds rather obvious in its implications, would probably seem somewhat ambiguous to an audience familiar with the idea of wealth which one finds in Old English heroic poetry. Such an audience might well wonder whether the Seafarer simply means that, at a warrior's death, his possessions pass on to his heirs, or that the heroic ideal of *dom* with which, at least in heroic poetry, wealth is associated, is itself somehow invalid. The succeeding lines are therefore necessary to develop and clarify the meaning of the Seafarer's original statement.

The Seafarer once again shifts to the third person in order to make a series of general observations intended to cast doubt upon, and ultimately negate, certain values inherent in the heroic view of life (72-102). He says that the praise (*lof* – 73) of the living is the 'best fame after death' (*lastworda betst* – 73), just as in *Beowulf* the hero says:

> Ure æghwylc sceal   ende gebidan
> worolde lifes;   wyrce se þe mote
> domes ær deaþe;   þæt bið drihtguman
> unlifgendum   æfter selest.   (1386–1389)

But while in *Beowulf* such lasting glory is won by bold deeds against mortal enemies, in the Christian world of *The Seafarer* it

is won by *deorum dædum   deofle togeanes* (76), and this more
worthy warfare results in glory which lives eternally not only
among men, but among the angels as well (77-80). 'Praise' in this
context becomes more than one of the joys of men, for it is 'joy
amidst the troops' (*dream mid dugeþum* – 80) in heaven. The
Seafarer supplants the heroic goal of achieving glory (*dom*)
through praise (*lof*) on earth alone by offering the additional
possibility that one particular kind of 'warfare' not considered in
the heroic scheme of values can result in even greater glory, that
glory which is conferred by the praise of angels in heaven.

The Seafarer goes on to suggest reasons why the glory of heaven
available to Christians is superior to, and more durable than the
heroic *dom* sought by Germanic warriors (80-96). The great glory
which the heroes of the past won *þonne hi mæst mid him
mærþa gefremedon / ond on dryhtlicestum   dome lifdon* (84-
85) has not saved them from death. Lesser men (*wacran* – 87)
have inherited the world, and its 'nobleness grows old and withers,
just as does every man throughout the world' (89-90). If the
quality of earthly glory has degenerated with time, and if all of
the warriors who possess such glory must ultimately die, as the
Seafarer says they must (91-96), then the implications are clear:
earthly heroic glory neither hinders the coming of death nor significantly benefits a warrior after he is gone. The heroic maxim,
lof se gewyrceð, / hafað under heofonum   heahfæstne dom
(Widsith, 142-143), is most valid if the *lof* is earned through
Christian deeds, but the *dom* won thereby is far more lasting than
the songs of the *scop*. The Seafarer does not categorically deny
the validity of the heroic ideal of *lof* and *dom*, but rather he
reveals its inadequacy within the larger context of his Christian
view of this world and the next.

Six lines follow which Mrs. Gordon calls "probably the most
disputed passage of the poem".[22] It appears in the manuscript as
follows:

<pre>
    þeah þe græf wille   golde stregan
    broþor his geborenum,   byrgan be deadum,
    maþmum mislicum   þæt hine mid wille,
</pre>

[22] Gordon, *The Seafarer*, p. 45n.

> ne mæg þære sawle   þe biþ synna ful
> gold to geoce   for godes egsan
> þonne he hit ær hydeð   þenden he her
>   leofað.   (97–102)

Mrs. Gordon, following Sisam, amends *wille* (99) to *nille*, but the passage makes perfectly good sense as it stands if we bear in mind that 'treasure' (*gold* – 97, 101, *maþmum* – 99) in the heroic world represents a warrior's glory and worth, and that such treasure may properly be interred with its possessor. In the light of our knowledge of the heroic concept of treasure, we find that this passage simply reiterates the Seafarer's previous comments upon the transitory nature of earthly heroic glory. The honor and glory which a warrior has won in his lifetime, and which, from a heroic point-of-view, 'will go with him' (that is, 'remains his possession in death'), cannot save his soul from God's Judgment. This is but another way of saying that worldly, heroic glory should not be the ultimate goal for which men strive. The heroic value of *dom* embodied in the concept of treasure must give place to the Christian value placed upon eternal salvation.

The poem ends with the Seafarer's exhortation to his audience to fear God's wrath and to live Christian lives (103-124). A man, he says, should recognize that his hope for eternal glory lies with God, and should strive to reach his heavenly home:

> Uton we hycgan   hwær we ham agen,
> ond þonne geþencan   hu we þider cumen,
> ond we þonne eac tilien,   þæt we to moten
> in þa ecan   eadignesse,
> þær is lif gelong   in lufan dryhtnes,
> hyht in heofonum.   (117–122)

A man's first concern should be for his immortal soul and this, finally, is the reason why exile is a desirable condition for a Christian. His final 'home' is not among the members of a *comitatus*, but in heaven. The values and code of conduct reflected in heroic concepts are inadequate for salvation and, indeed, may lead him away from a Christian life. The goal of the Germanic hero is glory in this world; he obtains this glory by living in the *comitatus* and by acting in accordance with heroic concepts. The exile by definition is deprived of the pleasures and the glory of heroic life, but this very deprivation is, from a Christian point-of-view, beneficial for the salvation of his soul. The man who willingly renounces his heroic preoccupation with the glory of this world at the same time prepares himself for eternal glory in the next world.

The poet of *The Seafarer* thus affirms Christian values by inverting and displacing the heroic values inherent in pre-Christian heroic poetic tradition. In Germanic heroic poetry, treasure is desirable because it represents the ultimate worth and honor of the warrior who possesses it, while exile is to be avoided because it means the deprivation of everything worth having. In *The Seafarer*, however, treasure represents the vanities and false values of this world and so should be shunned, while exile (at least, if it is voluntary) means the renunciation of earthly vanities and the embracing of the eternal values of Christianity. By confronting heroic concepts with Christian concepts, the poet has displaced the heroic view of life, and replaced it with the Christian view, in an absolute hierarchy of ultimate validity and worth. He has used heroic concepts in full consciousness of their implications for a Christian world, and used them to make a Christian statement about the relative importance of this world and the next. His intention, insofar as heroic concepts are concerned, is the same as that of Cynewulf in *Juliana*, but his method is a bit more subtle. Cynewulf discredits heroic concepts by attributing them to heathens, who are *prima facie* villains in his story; the *Seafarer*-poet discredits heroic concepts by showing that the benefits gained by living according to Christian concepts are vastly more desirable than those of the *comitatus*.

X

CHRIST II AND *GUTHLAC A*

In the preceding chapter we discussed two poems, *Juliana* and *The Seafarer*, in which the poets set up contrasts between two clearly opposed sets of values, the secular values of Germania and the spiritual values of Christianity. In this chapter, we shall examine two poems, *Christ II* and *Guthlac A*, in which the poets seem to have moved beyond the point at which they find it necessary and desirable to directly confront the Germanic, heroic view of the world with the Christian view. Christian values, presented in a specifically Christian frame of reference, have in these poems absorbed heroic concepts and motifs to such an extent that it becomes increasingly difficult to identify passages which clearly express heroic concepts. When heroic elements appear, they have either been adapted to the expression of Christian ideas and sentiments or else they have simply lost their original heroic implications altogether. Much of the vocabulary which, in the poems discussed previously, had essentially heroic denotations and connotations, in these poems seems to have lost its original meaning and, under the influence of Christian Latin literary tradition, taken on new, slightly different, meaning.

One cannot pinpoint a moment in the development of Old English Christian verse at which the heroic view of the world ceases to be treated by poets as a coherent, cohesive matrix of ideas either necessary or useful in the building of a poetic argument. Literature and literary traditions do not develop according to a neat, orderly, linear progression in time. Consequently, such a moment must remain purely hypothetical, a figment, albeit a useful figment, of the literary historian's imagination. One cannot say precisely when Old English poetry ceases to be either essentially Germanic and heroic in character or at least frequently dependent upon heroic concepts and ideals and, under the steadily increasing influence of Christian tradition becomes instead essentially Christian poetry containing only vestiges of heroic tradition. One can, however, demonstrate that in particular poems the Christian view of life has become so thoroughly familiar to poet and audience alike that the poet no longer finds it necessary to present his ideals of order, harmony and virtue exclusively in terms of an ideal Germanic *comitatus*, or to treat heroic concepts and motifs as aspects of a consistent scheme of values.

In *Christ II* and *Guthlac A,* heroic concepts and motifs in general seem to function figuratively, as metaphors. By this I mean that the heroic concepts which I have discussed and the motifs associated with them may be used by the poets in such a way that they represent Christian concepts with which they are clearly not identical. This metaphorical function of heroic concepts differs essentially from the basic functions of these same concepts in the poems we have examined thus far. In *Genesis B*, the poet seems to conceive of the structure of the universe literally as being that of a Germanic *comitatus*. He makes no distinction between the physical world and the spiritual; God is a Germanic lord who rules the heavenly *comitatus*, Adam is His retainer and Satan is an exiled warrior. In *Juliana* and *The Seafarer*, the poets make a distinction between the physical, temporal world of this earth with its secular values, and the spiritual, eternal world of God. They reject the heroic, mundane world in favor of the spiritual, Christian world; God's joys are placed above the joys of the *comitatus* on an absolute scale of values. Nevertheless, the ideals of the heroic world, based upon Germanic concepts of loyalty, vengeance, treasure and exile, remain intact; they are simply subordinated to a Christian set of ideals.

In poems like *Christ II* and *Guthlac A,* where the basic frame of reference is entirely Christian, heroic concepts or aspects of these concepts may function as metaphors for spiritual or psychological conditions, and it is generally clear that the poet does not wish that his heroic, secular terminology be taken literally. The poet may, for example, describe the relationship between God and His followers in terms of the loyalty between a Germanic lord and his retainers. Nevertheless, he will at the same time attempt to make clear that he is describing a spiritual phenomenon rather than a literal situation. The popular metaphor of the saint as Christian warrior appears frequently in these poems, and when a poet describes a saint as a warrior, the highly conventional, traditional diction and vocabulary of Old English poetry will transform the saint into a particularly Germanic kind of warrior. The description, however, will usually include details like 'spiritual armor' and 'arrows of sin' which prevent the audience from assuming that the saintly warrior participates in physical warfare against a physical enemy. Whether Germanic or Semitic, he is a warrior only in a figurative sense. We have already observed an isolated instance of this technique in Cynewulf's treatment of the confession of the devil in *Juliana*.

If, in any given poem, the predominant function of the ideological material of Germanic heroic tradition is figurative, and if that material is completely subordinated to the Christian story and Christian attitudes and values, then it is reasonable and accurate to say that the Christian literary tradition has absorbed the Germanic. Christian ideals will pervade and dominate the poem so that the poet may, if he so desires, employ heroic concepts to express spiritual ideas in intelligible terms without fear that his audience will misinterpret his intention. Further, the poet will not treat heroic concepts or aspects of those concepts as integral parts of a consistent, organic way of viewing the world. Consequently, because one aspect of a concept need not imply the entire concept or any other concept (as it would in poetry dependent upon heroic ideals), the poet need not concern himself with the problem of heroic ideals conflicting with Christian ideals. Heroic ideals in such poems will appear in emasculated form by virtue of their having been detached from their ideological matrix. The poet may take whatever details he considers useful for the spiritual-physical metaphor he wishes to construct, and omit whatever details he considers inappropriate or superfluous. Thus, he may depict God as a Germanic lord insofar as He exhibits devotion to his followers, without implying the concomitant heroic motif of giving rings from a treasure-hoard. In *Christ II* and *Guthlac A*, one finds passages in which basically heroic concepts are suggested but not very fully developed, and this phenomenon is especially apparent where elaboration would impair the main point of similarity in the poet's metaphor.

Christ II is one of the four signed poems of Cynewulf and therefore was probably written in the first half of the ninth century.[1] It is concerned with the ascension of Christ and is based principally upon the ascension sermon of Pope Gregory the Great.[2] Albert S. Cook, in his edition of *Christ*, cites as a possible secondary source an ascension hymn ascribed to Bede which exhibits some similarities in concept and phrasing to Cynewulf's poem.[3] Thus, in its sources, its subject matter and its ideological assumptions, the poem is thoroughly Christian. Nevertheless, one finds heroic locutions frequently in *Christ II*; words, phrases and even entire passages suggest at first glance that we have a sub-stratum of heroic concepts operative throughout. A closer reading of the poem, however, doet not support the conclusion that Cynewulf thinks of his Christian universe as corresponding precisely in structure to a secular world built upon heroic ideals, nor does it seem that he desires that his audience think of the spiritual world as an intangible replica of the physical world of heroic poetry. Phrases and descriptions which suggest that the Christian, spiritual world conforms to heroic, secular ideals of moral perfection are not intended to be taken literally, but figuratively, as metaphorical approximations of supernatural phenomena.

Three passages, based directly upon Gregory's sermon (*Hom. in Evang.*, 29:10), which contain no suggestion of heroic concepts and owe nothing to Germanic tradition, but which are clearly intended metaphorically, should indicate how thoroughly accustomed Cynewulf is to conceiving of and describing spiritual phenomena by analogy. First, he follows Gregory in taking the bird in

---

[1]   See Chapter IX, n. 5. Cook, *The Christ of Cynewulf*, pp. lxviii-lxx, thinks it the latest of the signed poems; Woolf, *Juliana*, p. 7, places *Juliana* later.

[2]   *Patrologiæ Latinæ*, LXXVI, 1218-1219.

[3]   *The Christ of Cynewulf*, pp. 116-118.

Job 28 : 7 – *Semitam ignoravit avis* – to signify Christ, whose 'flight' is hidden from the eyes of unbelievers (633-658).[4] Like Gregory, he develops this metaphor at some length without ever suggesting that Christ is literally a bird. A bit further on, he follows Gregory's interpretation of Habakkuk 3 : 11 – *Elevatus est sol, et luna stetit in ordine suo* – and tells us that the 'holy gems' in the heavens 'are' God Himself. He develops the metaphor to show that Christ-God is the holy radiance of the sun, and His Church the moon which in varying degrees reflects His radiance (691-711). Cynewulf then enumerates the six 'leaps' of Christ predicted in Canticles 2 : 8 – *Ecce iste venit saliens in montibus, et transiliens colles.* Gregory lists only five leaps, but Cynewulf adds the harrowing of hell to the 'leaps' of conception, birth, crucifixion, deposition and burial, and ascension (712-743). No one, on the basis of these passages could, I think, attribute to Cynewulf (or Gregory) either sun-worship or a peculiar predilection for athletics; Cynewulf is using language figuratively and expects his audience to recognize it as such. It makes little difference that these passages do not originate with Cynewulf; if he had not felt comfortable about using figurative language or had felt that such language would be misinterpreted by his audience, he would surely not have borrowed them at all.

The angels' song of welcome to Christ upon His ascension (558-585), which has no counterpart in Gregory's sermon, is couched in heroic diction which makes Christ appear momentarily as a Germanic warrior returning from a successful military campaign. He has 'plundered' (*bireafod* – 558) hell of all the 'tribute' (*gafoles* – 559) which had been gathered there, leaving the 'devil's warriors deprived of prosperity' (*duguþum bidæled,   deofla cempan* – 563). 'Nor might His enemies succeed in battle, in casting of weapons, after the King of Glory, the Protector of Heaven, did battle against His foes with the might of one'[5] (564-567). He returns to his 'city' (*ceastre* – 578) after the 'war play' (*guðplegan* – 573) with a great host, and resumes his *giefstol* (572). Cook

---

[4]   Line references are to *The Exeter Book*, ed. George Philip Krapp and Elliott Van Kirk Dobbie (New York, 1936), pp. 15-27.
[5]   I.e., 'with his own might', 'alone'.

points out several general parallels between this passage in *Christ II* and the Ascension Hymn of Bede,[6] including the angelic *þreat* and the 'throne',[7] but nevertheless Cynewulf's language comes primarily from heroic poetic tradition. In spite of his use of heroic diction, Cynewulf clearly indicates in this same passage that he does not literally conceive of Christ as the superhuman leader of a *comitatus* which goes off on raiding parties. The *gafol* which Christ wins is the souls of the Old Testament saints; He is *sawla nergend* (571), and his 'troop' (*here* – 574) consists not of Germanic warriors but of blessed souls. His seat in heaven is a *gæsta giefstol* (572), but here *giefstol* means no more than 'throne', and lacks the heroic connotations of gift-giving. Cynewulf is employing heroic terminology to describe the spiritual victory of Christ, and His subsequent glory.

A homiletic passage near the end of the poem (756-782) which, like the account of the harrowing of hell, has no counterpart in Gregory's sermon, helps to support the assumption that Cynewulf's language is indeed figurative. Cynewulf tells his audience that God sends His messengers to Earth to shield mankind from the arrows of its enemies:

> He his aras þonan,
> halig of heahðu,   hider onsendeð,
> þa us gescildaþ   wið sceþþendra
> eglum earhfarum,   þi læs unholdan
> wunde gewyrcen,   þonne wrohtbora
> in folc godes   forð onsendeð
> of his brægdbogan   biterne stræl.   (759–765)

The diction of this passage is heroic, but the 'attacks' are obviously spiritual rather than physical. The wounds against which we need protection are 'wounds of sin' (*synwunde* – 757) which, Cynewulf suggests, are more dangerous than mere physical injuries: *þæt bið frecne wund, / blatast benna* (770-771). The metaphor of spiritual warfare is derived ultimately from Saint Paul (Ephesians 6 : 11-17) but not surprisingly, when it appears in an Old English poem it usually takes on Germanic coloring from the heroic diction,

---

[6] Cook, p. 131.
[7] Cf., *cohortes* (33), *coetus* (51), *agminum* (52); *thronum* (4), *altithroni* (50).

which carries connotations of the heroic concepts inherent in the poetic tradition. When Cynewulf's choice of words in *Christ II* suggests the system of *comitatus* relationships and martial activity which we find in poems like *Beowulf*, we must recognize that he is using these words and the concepts which they imply figuratively, as metaphorical approximations of spiritual phenomena.

The final passage of *Christ II* provides an excellent example of Cynewulf's facility in using a heroic concept as a metaphor for a spiritual condition. He takes up a single word, 'anchor', from Gregory,[8] and constructs upon it an extended simile:

> Nu is þon gelicost   swa we on laguflode
> ofer cald wæter   ceolum liðan
> geond sidne sæ,   sundhengestum,
> flodwudu fergen.   Is þæt frecne stream
> yða ofermæta   þe we her on lacað
> geond þas wacan woruld,   windge holmas
> ofer deop gelad.   Wæs se drohtað strong
> ærþon we to londe   geliden hæfdon
> ofer hreone hrycg.   þa us help bicwom,
> þæt us to hælo   hyþe gelædde,
> godes gæstsunu,   ond us giefe sealde
> þæt we oncnawan magun   ofer ceoles bord
> hwær we sælan sceolon   sundhengestas,
> ealde yðmearas,   ancrum fæste.
> Utan us to þære hyðe   hyht staþelian,
> ða us gerymde   rodera waldend,
> halge on heahþu,   þa he heofonum astag.   (850–866)

The life of Man is like a dangerous sea-journey. In heroic poetic tradition, a sea-journey, especially if it is difficult, usually suggests exile, and that concept seems to be implied here. The point of Cynewulf's comparison of human life to exile is that life is filled with suffering and danger, particularly spiritual suffering and danger, which will pass when life ends and one reaches the 'harbor' of salvation which Christ has prepared for the blessed. Cynewulf does not suggest that every man is an exile in the heroic sense of his being lordless; he suggests that every man resembles

---

[8] *Hom. in Evang.*, 29 : 11: "Quamvis adhuc rerum perturbationibus animus fluctuet, jam tamen spei vestrae anchoram in aeternam patriam figite, intentionem mentis in vera luce solidate."

a heroic exile insofar as he is separated from his spiritual 'lord', God, who awaits him at 'home', in heaven. Thus the heroic concept of exile functions here as a metaphor for the spiritual condition of humanity.

Much of the vocabulary in *Christ II* which Cynewulf uses to describe Christ, His followers and His enemies is recognizably the same as that used by heroic poets to describe Germanic lords, retainers and exiles but, in most instances, the heroic connotations of the words seem minimal or non-existent. For example, in the space of three lines (456-458) Cynewulf calls Christ *se brega mæra and þeoden þrymfæst,* and his disciples *þegna gedryht,* and *leof weorud,* but these formulas do not seem here to carry any definite heroic overtones. They seem to mean no more than 'the famous Prince', 'glorious Lord', 'throng of followers', and 'beloved host', and the approximate in meaning *Rex, Dominus, cohortes,* and *agmen* in Bede's Ascension Hymn. *Sincgiefa* (460), 'treasure-giver', has definite heroic connotations, but seems to be meant here figuratively; the 'treasure' which Christ gives to His followers must either be the 'word' mentioned in the previous line, or salvation in general, or both.

As one might expect, *Christ II* contains few traces of the heroic concept of treasure. Cynewulf's attitude toward earthly riches is a commonplace one in Christian thought – on the Day of Judgment *frætwe sculon / byrnan on bæle* (807-808), and consequently a man should not concern himself with the treasures of this world (807ff.).[9] God 'honors' His creatures with gifts, but these gifts are not treasures in the narrower heroic sense of the term. Rather, they are all of the good things which men possess in this world and the next (600-626, 659-691).[10] The one unquestionable reference to treasure in its heroic sense is to Christ as *mægna goldhord* (787), and here again the heroic concept functions metaphorically. Christ is figuratively a 'goldhoard', a repository of something

[9]   The sentiment of lines 807-849 is found in Gregory, *Hom. in Evang.,* 29 : 11. Cook, p. 164, takes *frætwe* (805, 807) to be equivalent to the 'ornaments' of the Earth, citing Genesis 2 : 1, "Igitur perfecti sunt caeli et terra, et omnis ornatus eorum."

[10]   Lines 659-690 are based upon Gregory's statement, "Dedit vero dona hominibus . . .".

supremely valuable.[11] Furthermore, although it would not be in-consistent with scriptural tradition to speak of God's vengeance upon the sinful, Cynewulf never really suggests that Christ takes heroic vengeance upon His enemies, nor does he even use a word which could be translated as 'avenge' or 'vengeance'.

Like *Christ II, Guthlac A* tells an essentially Christian story and is thoroughly permeated by and dependent upon Christian doctrine and the Christian view of the universe. The poem tells the story of the temptation of Saint Guthlac. The poet concen-trates primarily upon the spiritual growth of the saint, and conse-quently Christian spiritual ideals control the narrative. Heroic values, and the concepts in which they are embedded, are almost totally submerged beneath the Christian surface of the poem, and appear only occasionally, as a kind of residue from heroic tradi-tion. The poet does not employ heroic concepts in such a way as to form a consistent view of the secular, temporal world of the poem, but he does use them at times as metaphors in order to describe the extra-terrestrial, spiritual world of Christianity.

The question of whether or not *Guthlac A* has a literary source has not yet been satisfactorily resolved. The poet claims that the saint lived 'in [his] own time' (753-754),[12] leading one to believe that he is working with orally-transmitted traditions. However, Gordon Hall Gerould, in an article published in 1917,[13] argues that *Guthlac A* is based upon the Latin *Vita Sancti Guthlaci* by Felix of Crowland, and Bertram Colgrave, the most recent editor of the *Vita,* concurs: ". . . no real additional information is given beyond what could have been derived from life. It is therefore pretty clear that the poet had a vague knowledge of Felix's work and that for the rest he depended upon his own invention."[14] Claes Schaar, on the other hand, does not think the *Vita* is the

---

[11]   Cook cites two passages from the *Blicking Homilies* (9.28, 11.29) in which 'goldhord' is used in reference to Christ.
[12]   Line references are to *The Exeter Book*, ed. George Philip Krapp and Elliott van Kirk Dobbie (New York, 1936), pp. 49-72.
[13]   "The Old English Poems on Saint Guthlac and their Latin Source", *MLN* XXXII (1917), 77-89.
[14]   *Felix's Life of Saint Guthlac*, ed. Bertram Colgrave (Cambridge, 1956), p. 20.

poet's source.[15] It is certainly clear that if the poet followed the
Vita, he did not follow it at all closely. Since we cannot be certain
that the *Vita* is the source of *Guthlac A*, we cannot be certain
that the material found in the poem but not in the *Vita* is indeed
the poet's "own invention". Nevertheless, it will be useful in the
course of the discussion to refer to the *Vita* for purposes of comparison.[16]

The Christian values which dominate and control the action in
Guthlac A are stated explicitly at the beginning of the poem. As
it stands in the manuscript, the poem begins with a passage on
the progress of a blessed soul after death (1-29). Thematically,
these lines are only tenuously connected to the earlier portions
of *Guthlac A*, and consequently it has been suggested that they
are either an epilogue to *Christ III* (which precedes *Guthlac A* in
the *Exeter Book*) or a separate poetic fragment. However, the
evidence of capital letters in the manuscript and, more important,
the virtual identity of the ideas in this prologue with those stated
elsewhere in the poem, indicates that the poet (or the compiler
of the manuscript) intended it to introduce *Guthlac A*.[17] In essence,
the prologue sets up an opposition between the transitory joys of
this world (*þas eorþan wynne* – 2, *þas lænan dreamas* – 3) and
the eternal joys of heaven (*engla dream* – 11, *ece lean* – 15) available after death to those who serve Christ during their lives (*þa
þe her Cristes æ / lærað and læstað,   ond his lof rærað* – 23-
24). This initial emphasis upon a Christian after-life sets the tone
for the entire poem.

The poet continues in somewhat the same homiletic vein to
discuss the conditions of men in this world (30-93). Here the
emphasis is more specifically upon the steady decay, both physical
and spiritual, of the world and its creatures, and upon the final

[15]   Claes Schaar, *Critical Studies in the Cynewulf Group*, pp. 39-41.
[16]   If the poet's sources are oral traditions, it should perhaps be dated shortly after the death of Guthlac in 714 or 715; if the *Vita* is a source, the poem
must have been composed after ca. 730-740 (Colgrave, p. 19). The 'Cynewulfian' nature of *Guthlac A* by itself suggests a ninth-century date.
[17]   Krapp, *The Exeter Book*, pp. xxx-xxxi; L. K. Shook, "The Prologue of
the Old English 'Guthlac A'", *MS*, XXIII (1961), 294-304; S. B. Greenfield,
Critical History, p. 120.

Judgment of God. This world, he says, will bring us no relief from the miseries which we daily suffer while we dwell here. He goes on to take the conventional attitude toward the material treasures dear to Germanic heroes by implying that God will reject those men who place their hope in earthly wealth (*eorðwela* – 62) while, conversely, He will save those who abandon worldly treasure (*woruldgestreon* – 70). 'Right treasure' (*ryhtra gestreona* – 78) is not that which is hoarded, but that which those who desire heavenly glory give away to the poor. Such philanthropy is quite distinct from the heroic practice of treasure-giving insofar as there is no suggestion that the recipient of 'alms' (*ælmessan* – 77) has any claim to them other than the fact of his poverty, or that he gives any sort of service in return. Germanic heroes reveal their moral worth by accumulating treasures, Christian heroes reveal theirs by giving all of their treasures away.

As he draws nearer to the point at which he will introduce Guthlac into the narrative, the poet focuses next upon holy men who not only give up worldly wealth, but leave the world of men altogether to dwell as hermits (81-92). In heroic terms, such men are exiles, for they live in wastelands (*on wæstennum* – 81), in dark places (*on heolstrum* – 83), where they are subject to the persecutions of terrifying creatures (84-88). Here, however, as in *The Seafarer*, the condition of exile is affirmed rather than lamented; indeed, these holy hermits choose exile *sylfra willum* (82). Such men are not Germanic exiles in *Guthlac A*; rather they are 'tested warriors' (*gecostan cempan* – 91) who serve God and whom angels protect with 'spiritual weapons' (*gæsta wæpnum* – 89) from demonic assaults. Thus, by affirming the hermit's condition as being spiritually beneficial, the poet implicitly denies the validity of the heroic view of exile as the worst of all possible fates.

The 'spiritual warfare' metaphor at times calls to the reader's mind the heroic concept of loyalty and the general pattern of *comitatus* relationships by implying that Guthlac and the angels are God's retainers. The spiritual or psychological nature of the 'warfare' in which 'God's warriors' engage, however, makes it clear that the heroic diction is for the most part figurative. For example, the 'strife' (*gewin* – 115) in which the good and bad angels contend for Guthlac's allegiance is clearly a *psychomachia* which takes place in Guthlac's mind immediately prior to his final decision to serve God rather than the World (114-140). The poet develops his allegory in enough detail to ensure that his audience could not mistake this psychological conflict for a physical encounter between angel and devil. The good angel advises Guthlac to reject the transitory world and serve God; the bad angel advises him to seek worldly prosperity and disregard the welfare of his soul. Finally, God decides the 'battle' in favor of the good angel; the psychological fiend is 'put to flight' (*geflymed* – 136) not, apparently, by any physical action, but by the force of Guthlac's decision to serve God. The *Vita* (XVI-XIX) gives an account of Guthlac's psychological conversion in which he contemplates *contemtibile temporalis vitæ gloriam* and *proprii obitus sui forma,* but this account contains no hint of a pair of contending angels, nor does there appear to be more than minimal conflict in his mind. Felix says only that a *spiritalis flamma* burned suddenly in the saint's breast; the 'warfare' metaphor may well be the poet's own contribution to the story here.

Formulas like *Cristes cempa* (153) and *dryhtnes þegn* (693) frequently suggest a lord-thane relationship between God and Guthlac. The 'God's warrior' metaphor is suggested several times in the *Vita*,[18] although it is only developed at some length in one passage:

Deinde praecinctus spiritalibus armis adversus teterrimi hostis insidias scutum fidei, loricam spei, galeam castitas, arcum patientiae, sagittas psalmodiae, sese in aciem firmans, arripuit. Tante enim fiduciae erat, ut inter torridas tartari turmas sese contemto hoste iniecerit.   (XXVII)

Rosemary Woolf finds this warfare metaphor much more pronounced in *Guthlac A* than in the *Vita*:

Among the differences in emphasis the most important is that of the heroic idea. The Latin *Guthlac*, like so much hagiographical literature, contains the image of the saint as the *miles Christi*, the warrior of God equipped with the spiritual armour described by

---

[18] See, e.g., *militis sui* (IV), *Domino militavit* (XLV), and the 'arrow of despair' metaphor in XXIX.

St. Paul. But in the Latin this occurs in an isolated passage, while in the poem phrases such as *Cristes cempa* or *eadig oretta* occur with refrain-like insistence. [19]

At times the metaphorical function of the martial, heroic diction of *Guthlac A* is made explicit by the language itself. At one point, for example, the poet describes Guthlac as a 'blessed warrior, hard in battle' (*eadig oretta,   ondwiges heard* – 176), but in the succeeding lines we learn that he girds himself with 'spiritual weapons' (*gæstlicum / wæpnum* – 177-178) and raises Christ's cross at the 'battle-station' (*ætstælle* – 179) where he will overcome 'great danger' (*frecnessa fela* – 181). At other times the distance between the heroic diction, with its associations of physical battle, and the events which are being described underscores the figurative nature of the language. The devils, for example, threaten Guthlac with physical battle, with an attack by 'troops of horses and armies' (*meara þreatum   ond monfarum* – 286) but apparently this is merely a threat intended to frighten Guthlac since nothing ever comes of it. A few lines later Guthlac denies the possibility that he will have to bear a 'worldly weapon' in physical combat against his foes (302-307), and his statement proves correct. He is never forced to fight the devils, nor is he subjected to real physical abuse.

It seems possible that the poet may have gotten his idea for the devils' threat of military assault from chapter XXXIV of Felix's *Vita*. In this chapter the demons take the form of Briton soldiers in an unsuccessful attempt to convince Guthlac that his dwelling is being attacked by a hostile army. In Chapter XXXI of the *Vita* he is actually subjected to physical punishments at the hands of his tormentors. If the poet were using some form of the *Vita* as his source, he would thus find adequate justification for a literal threat of demonic attack. The poem, however, contains considerably less actual physical violence than the *Vita*. In *Guthlac A*, the saint's body is never abused by demons, nor is he ever attacked by a sword-wielding assassin like Beccel (*Vita*, XXXV). Hence, the threat of military attack, which could easily be taken

---

[19]   "Saints Lives", *Continuations and Beginnings*, p. 55.

literally if it were found in the *Vita,* seems much less likely to be intended literally in the poem.

The 'strife' in which Guthlac actually engages in *Guthlac A* consists primarily of two psychological temptations. The poet prefaces the first of these (412ff.) by the observation that God protected Guthlac's soul, rather than his body, from danger (407-411), an observation perhaps prompted by the fact that the poet's portrayal of Guthlac's temptations are more exclusively spiritual and psychological than those of Felix, which usually include either physical violence or the threat thereof. The devils take Guthlac up into the air and reveal to him the widespread corruption prevalent in monasteries. The poet states explicitly that their purpose is to cause the saint mental anguish:

>   Bonan gnornedon,
> mændon murnende   þæt hy monnes bearn
> þream oferþunge,   ond swa þearfendlic
> him to earfeðum   ana cwome,
> gif hy him ne meahte   maran sarum
> gyldan gyrnwræce.   (429–434)

The *Vita* contains no specific temptation which parallels this one, in which the devils seem to be attempting to discourage Guthlac by suggesting that he is somehow responsible for the trespasses of the younger monks (488-493).[20]

For his second (and final) temptation, the devils carry Guthlac to the entrance of hell, where they show him the torments of the damned and attempt to convince him that he is doomed to spend eternity there because of his sins (557ff.). This, the poet tells us, is an attempt to make Guthlac despair of salvation:

> Woldun hy geteon   mid torncwidum
> earme aglæcan   in orwennysse,
> meotudes cempan.   (574–576)

The journey to hell parallels closely a similar account in the *Vita* (XXXI), where Guthlac is shown and threatened with the tor-

---

[20] The *Vita* does, however, contain two episodes (XLIII, XLIV) in which Guthlac encounters (and exposes) clerical dishonesty. In the second of these he pardons the culprits just as he does in the poem (495-504), although not for the same explicit reason.

ments of the damned. His rather lengthy reply in the poem to the threats of his tempters (590-684) could be simply an amplification of his terse reply in the *Vita,* in which he scorns the *semen Cain* and challenges them to do as they have threatened. In the *Vita,* however, Felix does not suggest that this is a temptation to despair, since Guthlac has already weathered one temptation to despair of salvation in chapter **XXIX**. Furthermore, in the *Vita,* Guthlac endures a series of physical torments prior to his visit to hell, but in the poem he does not. If the poet has used the *Vita* as his source, it seems that he has consolidated two temptations into one; by applying the rationale of spiritual despair to the journey to hell, and at the same time omitting the element of physical violence present in the *Vita,* he has made his version of the temptation thoroughly spiritual and psychological.

At no point in *Guthlac A* does the hero's behavior suggest that he is literally a warrior engaged in physical warfare for his Germanic lord, even though the heroic vocabulary does at times suggest that this is the case. Indeed, the relationship between God and Guthlac throughout the poem is not that of a lord and his retainer but that of a lord and his servant. The poet calls Guthlac God's 'servant' (*þeow* – 314, 386, etc.) about as frequently as His 'thane' or 'warrior'. Guthlac himself describes his relationship to God as one of subjection, obedience and devoted worship (599-611). It seems reasonable to assume that words like *þegn* in this poem have lost their heroic connotations to the degree that they mean little more than 'follower' or 'disciple'.

Heaven functions as if it were an ideal *comitatus* by implication when the poet makes use of the heroic concept of exile as a metaphor for the spiritual condition of the devils. The devils, unlike Guthlac, frequently appear as 'exiles'. In the most literal sense, they are geographically displaced, 'exiles' (*wræcmæcgas* – 231, 263) from the land which Guthlac has appropriated. When, however, the poet describes them specifically as exiles from heaven, the heroic concept of exile as a state of utmost deprivation and misery appears to function as a metaphor for their spiritual situation. This figurative use of the theme of exile is probably inherent in Guthlac's final taunting speech to his tempters (590-

684). Guthlac describes the *wræcsiðe* (623) from heaven of the devils as a punishment for disloyalty to their lord: *ge wiðhogdun halgum dryhtne* (631). While blessed souls enjoy the glory of *þam betran ham* (654), the damned suffer the torments of hell which, in spite of the physical details, are primarily spiritual torments. They have lost 'spiritual joy' (*gæstlicne goddream* – 630) and have gained 'spiritual death' (*gæstcwalu* – 679). The devils themselves point out that the requital which God gives His enemies is spiritual punishment for sin (582-589). In general, heroic concepts scarcely appear in *Guthlac A*, apparently because the poet does not need them to express Christian ideas of spiritual faith, reward and punishment.

The preceding detailed examination of *Christ II* and *Guthlac A* should leave one with the distinct impression that heroic concepts are much less in evidence in these two poems than they are in any of the poems which we have considered previously. The concepts, and motifs which are directly related to the concepts, appear in isolated passages throughout these poems, but they do not themselves form a consistent, fully developed view of the world, nor do the poets depend upon them to express their own moral ideals and attitudes. The poets frequently employ the same heroic locutions which, in poems like *Genesis B, Andreas, Juliana* and *The Seafarer*, express heroic concepts but, in *Christ II* and *Guthlac A*, heroic diction is not a reliable guide to the ideological content of the passage in which it is employed. A vocabulary which must originally have evolved to express Germanic, pre-Christian customs and ideals has been largely drained of its heroic associations. In these Christian contexts *þegn* usually implies little more than 'follower' or 'subordinate' and *gestreon* little more than 'something of value'.

When, in passages scattered through *Christ II* and *Guthlac A*, heroic concepts do appear, their function is essentially metaphorical. The poets employ them to depict spiritual or psychological phenomena, rather than physical situations or genuine heroic attitudes. The concept of loyalty, along with the ideals of the Germanic *comitatus* relationship which depend upon this concept, appears frequently, primarily because the martial basis of the lord-thane relationship makes it useful to poets who wish to develop the 'spiritual warfare' metaphor. Thus Christ at times appears in the guise of a victorious Germanic lord, and Guthlac in that of God's warlike retainer, even though neither hero ever participates in physical warfare. In the same manner, the concept of heroic exile is occasionally employed to express the spiritual condition of mortal humanity or the immortal souls of the damned in a Christian universe. The concepts of treasure and vengeance appear infrequently, if at all, in the two poems and, indeed, none of the concepts functions, even figuratively, in a consistent manner throughout an entire poem; Christ is not always described as a heroic lord, nor Guthlac always as a fierce retainer. The poets do not depend upon heroic concepts to express Christian ideals and consequently these concepts seem to be disappearing from their poetry.

XI

CHRIST III, GUTHLAC B, JUDGMENT DAY II;

CONCLUSIONS

In *Christ II* and *Guthlac A*, one still finds traces of the concepts which permeate heroic Germanic poetry, even though these concepts by no means control the moral climate of the poems. The two poets occasionally employ heroic concepts, or at least motifs which are directly related to these concepts, but they do not depend upon them to express their ideas, as do the *Genesis B*- and *Andreas*-poets. They are capable of employing heroic concepts as metaphors for spiritual phenomena, without having to fear that their audiences will erroneously take their figurative language literally.

If one turns from *Christ II* and *Guthlac A* to *Christ III* and *Guthlac B*, he finds that the poets who composed the latter poems seldom employ heroic concepts and motifs, even as metaphors. Indeed, if he should compare the former pair of poems with the latter, he might well be struck by the infrequency with which even the most remote suggestions of heroic concepts and motifs appear in the latter poems. When such suggestions do appear, they are usually the merest vestiges of heroic themes which, in the poems which we have discussed previously, have been employed by other poets to express the most common and basic ideas inherent in Germanic heroic tradition. Seldom does one find more than a single, isolated half-line formula which appears to be left over from heroic tradition, and frequently he finds only a single word from the heroic vocabulary where he might expect the poet to have developed a heroic concept in some detail. As in *Christ II* and *Guthlac A*, the primary meanings of many of the key words from heroic poetry have changed in such a way that these words seem to be devoid of all heroic connotations whatsoever, and therefore closer to their modern English equivalents.

Christ III, probably a ninth-century poem,[1] tells of the Day of Judgment, when Christ will return to judge the souls of the living and the dead, and issue rewards and punishments according to their deserts. Albert S. Cook pointed out long ago that a principal source for *Christ III* is the alphabetic hymn quoted by Bede in his *De Arte Metrica* which begins, *Apparebit repentina dies magna Domini*.[2] The Old English poem is scarcely a close translation of the forty-six-line Latin hymn, but undeniably a number of verbal resemblances and a good deal of structural similarity exists between the two. One of the most recent literary historians to deal with the poem, Stanley B. Greenfield, accepts Cook's judgment concerning the sources of *Christ III*: "What structure [the poet] has seems in the main to follow the sequence of ideas in the alphabetic poem. . . . But the piece, with its many hypermetric lines, is a tissue of poeticized material from Gregory, Augustine, Caesarius of Arles, and other Christian writers on the great theme of Judgment."[3]

In spite of its Latin source, and in spite of the body of Christian doctrine which traditionally informs the theme of Judgment, the subject matter of *Christ III* is no more abstract and no less inherently capable of being expressed by means of the language and concepts of heroic poetry than the subject matter of *Christ II*, the Ascension, or that of *Genesis B*, the Creation and Fall of Man. Nevertheless, almost nothing from the secular, heroic system of values appears in this Christian narrative. The relationship of Christ and Man, for example, is nowhere clearly depicted in such a way as to suggest that of a Germanic lord and his retainers. A few words and phrases like *Þrymfæst þeoden* (943), *frean* (945)

---

[1] See, e.g., Greenfield, *Critical History*, p. 131. This date can presumably be justified by the 'Cynewulfian' quality of the poem.
[2] *The Christ of Cynewulf*, pp. 171-177. First suggested in *MLN* IV (1889), 341ff.
[3] *Critical History*, p. 131.

and *folca weard* (945), all of which refer to Christ, no doubt come to the poet from the vocabulary of Germanic heroic poetry, where they appear as epithets for secular lords, but in *Christ III* they do not seem to carry their heroic connotations.[4] Christ judges Man from His *cynestole*, a *heahsetle* (1216-17), but in the absence of other details which might suggest a similarity between Christ's position and that of a Germanic giver-of-rings, these words must mean no more than 'throne', a seat of honor befitting a ruler. This detail appears to come directly from the Latin hymn: *Gloriosus in sublimi Rex sedebit solio* (13). Christ sends the souls of the damned to hell by a swing of His *sigemece* (1530), but again there are no other elements of the military motif, either literal or figurative, present; no 'strife' of any kind occurs. The 'sword of victory' functions not as a military weapon, but as an emblem of Christ's omnipotent authority. Cook cites a parallel instance in Prudentius (*Cathemerinon*, 6:85ff.) in which the sword of Revelations 1:16 is transferred to the hand of Christ the Judge.[5]

Just as the poet refrains from portraying Christ as a Germanic lord, so he avoids suggesting that the blessed souls are His retainers. Many of the words he uses in referring to the angelic host come from heroic tradition; *þreat* (927), *scolu* (928, 1534, 1607), *hergas* (929), *heapum geneahhe* (929), *gedryht* (941, 1013), *þegna* (943), *hreþeadig heap* (944), *æþelduguð betast* (1011), *herefeðan* (1012) *and dugduð* (1062) all can be used to describe a heroic *comitatus*. Here, however, none of these words and phrases suggests much more than 'a group of followers'. The Latin hymn affords the poet ample precedent for the vaguely military language he uses to describe the blessed souls: *claris angelorum choris comitatus aderit* (8), *angelorum . . . agmina* (14), and *beatorum agmina* (42). Heaven, the home of this blessed company, bears little resemblance to the hall of a Germanic lord. The *dream* (1636) of the inhabitants of heaven is eternal, and includes angelic song, the sight of God's bright face, eternal love, life, youth, glory,

---

[4] Line references are to *The Exeter Book*, ed. George Philip Krapp and Elliott Van Kirk Dobbie (New York, 1936), pp. 27-49.

[5] Cook, p. 216.

health, rest, daylight, bliss and peace, and freedom from hunger, thirst, sleep, sickness, heat, cold and care (1634ff.). This is the *gaudia* suggested in a general way in the hymn (37-42) and supplemented by material like that which Cook finds in the writings of Augustine and Gregory.[6]

The poet's descriptions of the damned souls do not depend upon the heroic concept of exile to express either their misery or their spiritual separation from God. *Wræc*, as it is used in line 1271 (*wræc winnende*) and line 1514 (*wræc mid deoflum geþolian*) may mean 'exile', 'punishment', or 'misery', but 'wræce' in line 1601 (*hwæt him se waldend   to wræce gesette*) and line 1606 (*synna to wræce*) can mean only 'punishment'. Christ's description of Man's fall and loss of Paradise, his 'spiritual home', (*gæsta eþel* – 1406), may retain some vestiges of the concept of exile – Man's failure to serve his Lord, his loss of *dugeþum ond dreamum* (1408), his removal to a 'dark world' (*þeostran weoruld* – 1409), an 'unknown land' (*uncuðne eard* – 1417), and his general state of misery. However, the reminiscenses of the heroic concept seem here to be incidental to the dominant theme of Christ's sacrifice to save Man from death and, indeed, the entire passage (1399-1418) may be derived from Caesarius of Arles.[7]

The poet's description of Christ's Judgment upon the souls of the sinful perhaps contains some vague echoes of the heroic concept of vengeance, but here 'vengeance' seems to have been subsumed under the Christian idea of righteous 'punishment'. Thus, the heroic concept is not usually distinguishable from the punishment in hell meted out as an *eftlean* to the damned (1099ff., 1362ff.). A vestige of the heroic concept of vengeance perhaps inheres in Christ's comment at the end of His enumeration of the crimes for which the sinners are to be damned:

> Eall ge þæt me dydan,
> to hynþum heofoncyninge.   þæs ge sceolon hearde
>   adreogan
> wite to widan ealdre,   wræc mid deoflum geþolian.
>   (1512–1514)

---

[6] Cook, pp. 222-223.
[7] Cook, pp. 207-211.

The suggestion that Christ repays 'humiliation' with torment recalls the customary heroic sensitivity to personal insult, although Christ's words to the sinners in the Latin hymn— *me sprevistis improbi* (32) – appear to be the source of the Old English. If the poet intends to introduce the idea of vengeance in this passage, he probably does so because it is suggested by his source and not because he desires to portray Christ as a Germanic hero.

Some slight vestiges of the heroic concept of treasure appear in *Christ III*, in spite of the orthodox attitude toward worldly wealth which pervades the poem. The rewards of the blessed are of course spiritual joys in heaven, and have nothing to do with heroic 'treasure', while the fate of *goldfrætwe, . . . eall ærgestreon eþelcyninga* is that it will be consumed by fire on Judgment Day (994-996). *Ealdgestreon* (1570) likewise carries negative connotations when, near the end of his description of the final Judgment, the poet remarks that the damned souls 'lament their old treasures', that is, the possessions which they mistakenly held dear in their lives. When, however, the poet describes the thoughts of the blessed as *breosta hord . . ., feores frætwe* (1072-1073), the word 'treasure' has positive connotations.[8] The heroic concept of treasure as a man's most important possession is being employed with figurative, spiritual implications. Again the detail of the chosen bearing *beorhte frætwe* (1635), which Cook takes to mean their holy works,[9] before Christ in heaven depends for its efficacy upon a positive, heroic conception of treasure.

The ninth-century poem *Guthlac B*, like *Christ III*, contains a few traces of heroic concepts which, upon careful examination, appear to be for the most part mere verbal echoes, almost entirely divorced from the complex of ideas which in heroic poetry forms a consistent view of the secular world. Words and phrases which have definite heroic connotations and which imply heroic concepts in poems like *Beowulf* and *Genesis B* seem to have lost these connotations and implications, and have either gained new,

---

[8] Cook, p. 189, likewise takes *breosta hord* and *frætwe* to refer to the thoughts and deeds of the blessed, although there is no apparent reason why the poet could not just as well mean their souls.

[9] Cook, p. 221.

non-heroic meanings or else appear to be used as if they have no very definite meanings at all. In a context such as this, one should not expect any of the heroic concepts which I have discussed to be developed very fully, either for literal or figurative purposes.

While considerable doubt persists among scholars as to whether the poet who composed *Guthlac A* relied upon Felix's *Vita* for his story, no such doubt exists concerning the source of *Guthlac B*.[10] The Anglo-Saxon poet follows the account of Guthlac's holy death which he found in Chapter Fifty of the Latin *Vita*: *Quanta egrotus temtamenta pertulerit aut quid de sua commendaverit sepultura; quæ novissima mandata sorori commendaverit; inter verba orationis spiritum quomodo emiserit.*[11] Before describing Guthlac's death, he recapitulates in a very abbreviated, general manner the material dealt with in *Guthlac A*, the temptations and holy life of the hermit, as it appears in the earlier chapters of Felix's work.[12] He has added a good deal of poetic elaboration to Felix's single chapter on Guthlac's death, but the subject matter of the poem is essentially that of the prose version.

In the discussion of *Christ II* and *Guthlac A*, it was suggested that the heroic concept of loyalty, which underlies the *comitatus* relationship portrayed in heroic poetry, functions metaphorically in passages where the Christian hero appears as 'God's warrior', participating in 'spiritual warfare' against God's enemies. Figuratively, the hero is a Germanic retainer, God is his lord, and the host of heaven his *comitatus*. In Old English poetry, the more fully the poet develops his 'spiritual warfare' metaphor, the more points of correspondence between the heroic world and the spiritual world appear and, consequently, the more fully is the concept of loyalty stated, so long as the metaphor does not break down. The *Guthlac B*-poet describes his hero as 'God's warrior', but he scarcely develops his metaphor at all in terms of 'spiritual warfare' or a heavenly *comitatus*, and so one finds little suggestion of

---

[10] Gerould, "The Old English Poems on St. Guthlac and their Latin Source", 77-89. Greenfield, *Critical History*, pp. 120-121. Greenfield, p. 123, takes this dependence on the *Vita* and the 'Cynewulfian' quality of the poem as indications of a ninth-century date.

[11] *Felix's Life of Saint Guthlac*, ed. Bertram Colgrave, pp. 150-161.

[12] *Guthlac B*, 878-932. References are to *The Exeter Book*, pp. 72-88.

the heroic concept of loyalty and the relationship of lord and thane. In the *Vita,* the 'spiritual warfare' metaphor appears several times, but never in the chapter on Guthlac's death. It seems that the poet likes this metaphor well enough to transfer it from the *Vita* to his poem, but not well enough to attempt to develop it very carefully or consistently.

Indeed, the 'God's warrior' metaphor seems quite lifeless when it appears in *Guthlac B.* For example, the poet introduces the metaphor early in the poem when he describes the devils' attacks upon Guthlac:

> Dryhtnes cempa,
> from folctoga, feonda þreatum
> wiðstod stronglice. (901–903)

The introduction of this metaphor seems mechanical and largely gratuitous here, however. The poet does not describe the devils' attacks in terms of warfare, nor does he elaborate at all upon Guthlac's role as a 'warrior' or even mention his spiritual armaments. The devils make noise, change their shapes occasionally, and threaten Guthlac with death, while he simply endures these disturbances with patience and fortitude. A bit later, the poet speaks of *se halga þeow* as being *deormod, heard ond hygerof* (951-953); formulas associated in heroic poetry with warriors are here applied to a 'servant', and are appropriate because they no longer carry exclusively martial connotations.

A more striking example of the use of heroic vocabulary in a context in which no heroic connotations are implied occurs when the poet applies the epithet *duguþa hleo* to Guthlac (1061). In heroic poetry this epithet means 'protector of (tested) warriors', and is synonymous with 'lord', but this meaning makes no sense in *Guthlac B,* for Guthlac is obviously not the leader of a *comitatus* of any sort. Indeed, in neither the poem nor the *Vita* does he have a permanent group of followers, although in the *Vita* he does have numerous visitors who seek spiritual consolation and physical relief for their various afflictions (Ch. XLV). Either the poet intends the epithet to mean something like 'shepherd of the (spiritual) flock', or he has employed it, without particular regard

for its meaning, because it is a conventional epithet for a prominent hero. If the latter explanation is the proper one, then the
epithet is essentially meaningless here, but in either case it carries
no heroic connotations whatever. It is vestigial in the same way
that *dryhtnes cempa* is vestigial in this poem   it is a conventional
formula which the poet uses with little or no regard for its suit-
ability to its context.

The poet's use of the vocabulary of heroic poetry suggests that
the relationship between Guthlac and the man who attends him
in his last hours is that of a Germanic lord and his retainer. Thus
Guthlac is called, either by this man or by the poet, *mondryhten*
(1007, 1051, 1151, 1337), *winedryhten* (1011, 1202), *freodryh-
ten* (1021), *sigedryhten* (1375), *þeoden* (1014, 1198), *hlaford*
(1053, 1357), *frean* (1200) and *sincgiefan* (1352). The only justification for such titles in the *Vita* is that the man, there identified as Beccel, twice addresses Guthlac as *domine*. In the poem,
Beccel is in fact Guthlac's pupil and servant (*ombehtþegn* –
1000, 1199, etc.), who dwells nearby and visits the saint daily for
spiritual guidance (999ff.). Aside from heroic epithets, the poet
offers no information which suggests that Beccel is Guthlac's
retainer, even though the two men seem devoted to the welfare
of one another. Nor is there any overt indication whatever that
the heroic vocabulary is being used figuratively, and that Guthlac
is Beccel's 'lord' in some spiritual sense. Here again, the heroic
vocabulary has either lost its connotations of loyalty in battle,
vengeance, and the exchange of treasure, in which case the various epithets mean little more than 'leader', or it is being used by
the poet with little or no regard for its inherent heroic meanings.

After Guthlac's death, his faithful disciple Beccel rushes to the
saint's sister to deliver the sad news. In the *Vita* we learn only
the barest details; Beccel goes by boat to the sister, Pega, tells
her that Guthlac is dead, and then disappears from the story.
Felix neither describes Beccel's voyage, nor reports his words to
Pega, nor mentions his grief. The poet, however, develops this
portion of the story at some length (1326-1379), and in so doing
he relies heavily upon the diction of heroic poetry. As a reader
familiar with the conventions of heroic poetry might expect, it is

the diction associated with the theme of heroic exile which the poet employs to describe Beccel's melancholy sea-journey and his grief over the loss of Guthlac. Indeed, it might well have been the single, minor detail of Beccel's boat in the *Vita* which prompted the poet to employ the exile-theme at this point in his narrative. Beccel's voyage is as sorrowful as that of any Germanic exile:

> . . . gewat þa ofestlice
> beorn unhyðig,   þæt he bat gestag,
> wæghengest wræc,   wæterþisa for,
> snel under sorgum.   (1327–1330)

Like an exile, he grieves over the death of the man who was most dear to him:

> Gnornsorge wæg
> hate æt heortan,   hyge geomurne,
> meðne modsefan,   se þe his mondryhten,
> life belidenne,   last weardian
> wiste, wine leofne.   (1335–1339)

His report to Guthlac's sister is essentially the lament of an exile, *wineþearfende* (1347), over his wretched fate:

> Ellen biþ selast   þam þe oftost sceal
> dreogan dryhtenbealu,   deope behycgan
> þroht þeodengedal,   þonne seo þrag cymeð,
> wefen wyrdstafum.   þæt wat se þe sceal
> aswæman sarigferð,   wat his sincgiefan
> holdne biheledne.   He sceal hean þonan
> geomor hweorfan.   þam bið gomenes wana
> ðe þa earfeða   oftost dreogeð
> on sargum sefan.   Huru, ic swiðe ne þearf
> hinsiþ behlehhan.   Is hlaford min,
> beorna bealdor,   ond broþor þin,
> . . . .
> . . . .
> . . . .
> gewiten, winiga hleo,   wica neosan
> eardes on upweg.   (1348–1366)

If they appeared in a heroic poem, one could unhesitatingly identify the description and lament quoted above as those of an exile, and could assume that the unstated aspects of the concept of exile should apply to this wretched man. In *Guthlac B*, however, Beccel is not really an exile in the heroic sense of that term, and it is perhaps significant that neither the poet nor he himself ever says that he is. In spite of his lament that he is 'lordless' now that his 'loyal giver-of-treasure' is dead, Beccel appears not as a warrior bereft of the joys of the *comitatus* but as a humble Christian who has lost his spiritual advisor. As I pointed out earlier, the poet does not present the relationship between Guthlac and Beccel consistently as that of a Germanic lord and his retainer in either a literal or a figurative sense, and, consequently, we cannot assume that his use of heroic vocabulary implies the presence of heroic concepts in *Guthlac B*. By the same token, the poet's use of the diction of the theme of exile in this passage does not imply the heroic concept which such diction was originally intended to express. The diction seems to be intended to describe Beccel's sea-journey and to express his grief and nothing more.

I have suggested that key words and phrases which originally arose to express heroic concepts and motifs in heroic poetry appear in *Guthlac B* without their traditional heroic associations. Such words and phrases seem to persist in the Old English poetic vocabulary as the vestigial remains of a complex of concepts and ideals which, at least in Christian poetry, may no longer be present. For example, some of the vocabulary used in *Guthlac B* to describe the devils who annoy the saint comes from heroic poetry, where it appears in conjunction with the concept of exile. The devils are *herehloðe   helle þegna* (1069), *duguþa byscyrede* (895), *dreamum bidrorene* (901), and they lament their *wræcsið* (1074). In the context of *Guthlac B*, however, these devils do not appear as exiles in the heroic sense of the term. The poet offers no definite suggestions of either a heavenly *comitatus* from which they are excluded or a hellish *comitatus* in which they are 'thanes'. If the poet does not intend his vocabulary to carry its original, heroic connotations, then *wræcsið* must mean no more than 'geographical displacement' or 'miserable journey', *helle þegna* 'inhabitants of hell', *duguþa bescyrede* 'cut off from prosperity', and *dreamum bidrorene* 'deprived of happiness', none of which need apply exclusively to the exiles of heroic tradition.

Perhaps a more striking example of a word which carries specific heroic connotations is the word *sincgiefa* (1352), which Beccel employs in referring to Guthlac. The word means 'giver-of-treasure', and consequently it seems a rather incongruous epithet for the saint. One might explain the presence of this word by ignoring the elements of which it is compounded and translating it as 'leader', or by assuming that the poet intends it metaphorically as 'giver of valuable spiritual gifts'. Whatever we do with the word, however, we cannot escape the fact that it must originally have been intended to express one aspect of the concept of heroic loyalty, the generosity of a lord to his retainers. In *Guthlac B*, it appears independent of the concept of loyalty; it is vestigial, a verbal remnant of a complex of ideas which does not inform the poem in which we find it.

Greenfield, in the course of his discussion of *Guthlac B*, remarks that, "The lord-thane relationship – at heart a Germanic concept – is developed gradually as the poem proceeds, culminating in the end (though the last few lines are missing in the manuscript) as the servant flees to his ship to seek the saint's sister and reports to her in exile-elegiac fashion."[13] I have suggested, on the contrary, that the lord-thane relationship not only is not developed, but that it is not really present at all. Greenfield has, I think, mistakenly assumed that the presence of vocabulary which, in a poem like *Beowulf*, would certainly express aspects of the concepts of loyalty and exile, must indicate the presence of the identical concepts in *Guthlac B*. It is my contention that, in poems like *Christ III* and *Guthlac B*, the vocabulary has been for the most part drained of its heroic implications, and that the concepts of loyalty, vengeance, treasure and exile do not appear in any significant way. In poems where the concepts with which we have been dealing no longer form a consistent, coherent matrix of secular ideals, the diction which once expressed those concepts cannot by itself be taken as a firm indication that any one concept or any aspect of a concept is being alluded to by the poet.

In *Christ III* and *Guthlac B*, slight and infrequent suggestions

[13] Greenfield, *Critical History*, p. 122.

of heroic concepts appear primarily as a result of the presence of various heroic words and phrases in the traditional poetic diction employed by the poets. These words and phrases, usually drained of the conceptual implications which they carry in heroic poetry, remain as vestigial elements in the diction of Christian verse. If we turn finally to the late poem known as *Judgment Day II*,[14] we find that even these last vestiges of the heroic concepts have disappeared. The vocabulary of *Judgment Day II* is almost entirely free of words which might even remotely suggest heroic concepts.

This absence of heroic vocabulary can be partially accounted for by the fact that this late tenth-century poem [15] is a rather close translation of a Latin poem, *De Die Judicii*, frequently attributed to Bede.[16] However, as we have seen previously, a Latin source is in itself no guarantee that an Old English Christian poem will be free of heroic elements. Anglo-Saxon poets often alter and elaborate upon their sources freely and, indeed, the poet who translated *De Die Judicii* added several details to the speaker's description of his situation at the beginning of the poem (Latin 1-11, O. E. 1-25). In the Latin poem, the speaker describes himself sitting in a flowery field, alone and unhappy, under a tree through which the wind blows; the setting and his own mood lead him to consider his sins and the Final Judgment. The Old English poet adds a grove (*bearwe* – 1), a brook(*wæterburnan* – 3) and a turbulent sky (*wolcn wæs gehrered* – 8). Bernard F. Huppé attributes these additional details to a desire on the part of the poet to emphasize traditional Christian symbols present in his Latin source.[17] Be that as it may, the poet had a splendid opportunity to intensify his portrait of a solitary, dejected man by employing some of the vocabulary which is usually associated with the theme

[14] *The Anglo-Saxon Minor Poems*, ed. Elliott Van Kirk Dobbie (New York, 1942), pp. 58-67. All references are to Dobbie's text.

[15] See, e.g., Dobbie, *Minor Poems*, p. lxxii; Greenfield, *Critical History*, p. 133.

[16] Bedae Venerabilis, *Opera Rhythmica*, ed. J. Fraipont (= *Corpus Christianorum*, Series Latina, CXXII) (Turnholti, 1955), pp. 439-444. The most thorough study of the Old English poem and its source is L. Whitbread, "The Old English Poem *Judgment Day II* and its Latin Source", *PQ* XLV (1966), 635-656.

[17] Bernard F. Huppé, *Doctrine and Poetry* (New York, 1959), pp. 80-94.

of exile. Yet even here, where he elaborates upon his source, he employs none of the traditional heroic language.

The poet describes his hero, Christ, in language which suggests that He is, at least in some respects, like a human king, but not a particularly Germanic king and certainly not a lord modeled upon those in heroic poetry. The elements which seem reminiscent of details in descriptions of lords in heroic poetry come, almost without exception, from the Latin source. Thus, the poet's description of Christ sitting on His 'high throne' (*heahsetle* – 118) surrounded by His 'retinue of angels' (*engla werod* – 115) depends not upon traditional heroic conceptions of lordship, but upon the corresponding lines of the Latin:

> Tum superum subito veniet commota potestas,
> Coetibus angelicis regem stipata supernum.
> Ille sedens solio fulget sublimis in alto . . . .   (57–59)

The choice of the word *domsetle* (124) a bit later is an accurate translation of the Latin 'tribunal' (62), 'judgment seat'. The 'helmet' which Christ wears (*helme beweorðod* – 118) seems to be the contribution of the Anglo-Saxon poet, but we are, I think, justified in assuming that it is some sort of crown rather than a piece of war-gear.[18] Generally speaking, no attribute of the Christ of *Judgment Day II* seems particularly warlike or Germanic, whether it can be accounted for in the source or not.

Heaven, as the poet describes it in the Old English poem (247ff.), has almost nothing in common with the dwelling places of the heroic *comitatus*. He follows his source (124ff.) in portraying heaven as a place where the blessed souls suffer none of the afflictions which oppress men in this world, and partake of all the wondrous joys of the next. God, we learn, *fægere frætuað* heaven's inhabitants (277), but this phrase seems to be the equivalent of the Latin *ornat* (140), 'adorns', and has nothing to do with

---

[18] There is no mention of a 'helmet' in the Latin, but in the Latin lines which supply the next four lines of the Old English (119-122) the word *capiat* appears. It is possible that the 'helmet' is the product of some sort of conflation of *capiat* and *caput* in the manuscript which the poet had before him. Whitbread, *op. cit.*, points out that no printed text of the Latin poem includes a collation of the many manuscripts extant; perhaps one of them is corrupted in such a way as to account for this detail.

heroic customs of treasure-giving. Likewise, the rewards which Christ bestows are *ece mede / heofonlice hyrsta* (280-281), the spiritual rewards which the poet found in his source: *Collocat altithrona laetosque in sede polorum / Praemia perpetuis tradens caelestia donis* (141-142).

The torments of hell are described at some length in *Judgment Day II* (176-246), but none of the concrete details which the poet enumerates particularly suggest that hell is more than superficially akin to the lands of exile in heroic poetry. The extreme heat and cold, darkness, foul stench and perpetual lamentation all come directly from the Latin poem (87-123). The various allusions to Christ's vengeance likewise depend not upon the heroic concept but upon the Christian material which the poet is translating. Sinners suffer 'avenging fires' (*wrecende bryne* – 155), the *vindex ardor* (77) of hell, which was itself created 'to repay sins' (*weana to leane* – 184), as the Latin implies clearly enough. Christ comes on the Day of Judgment 'as an avenger' (*vindice* – 44) to 'punish' (*vindicat* – 45, *wrecan* – 89) the guilty, but of course this Christian concept of divine retribution is quite independent of heroic tradition.

Certainly Judgment Day II owes nothing conceptual to Germanic heroic tradition, nor is its vocabulary colored by the language of heroic verse to any significant degree. Apparently, the translator of *De Die Judicii* felt no need to embellish or expand the statements of the Latin poem with allusions to heroic concepts or motifs. Neither was he forced by a paucity of appropriate Old English equivalents of Latin words to utilize the somewhat specialized vocabulary of heroic verse. It would, I think, be difficult, if not impossible, to find a poem written in the language and native meter of Old English verse which revealed less of the influence of Germanic heroic tradition than *Judgment Day II*.

This study began with the commonly accepted view that two distinct literary traditions, the native Germanic and the Latin Christian, contribute to the content and character of extant Old English poetry. The oral-formulaic theory of composition helps to account for the persistence of ideals, concepts and verbal motifs from Germanic heroic tradition in Old English poetry long after Christianity and Christian literary tradition had become firmly entrenched in England. The pre-Christian concepts of loyalty, vengeance, treasure and exile form a consistent, unified view of the secular world which is independent of Latin Christian tradition and which forms the ideological matrix underlying Germanic heroic poetry. Heroic concepts and the values which they embody dominate poems like *Beowulf* and *Widsith,* which treat basically heroic, Germanic subjects and themes, and they also play roles of varying importance in poems which treat essentially non-Germanic, Judaeo-Christian subjects and themes. This phenomenon suggests that the displacement of heroic values by Christian values was not an abrupt event but rather a gradual process; that the religious conversion of Old English poetic tradition was a process of slow transition rather than sudden illumination.

I have attempted to differentiate between various Old English poems on the basis of the ways in which their poets employ pre-Christian, heroic materials in them. If the reader accepts the validity of the distinctions which I have made, then I have accomplished my primary purpose. I should like now to go a bit further and suggest that it is possible to employ these distinctions as a criterion for defining a pattern of development for Old English Christian poetry. I would postulate the following general theory of the successive stages in the movement from Germanic heroic to Christian poetry in England: At the earliest stage, shortly after the conversion of the English to Christianity, poets began to embellish the old songs of pagan Germania, as well as the new heroic songs which they made, with Christian allusions and sentiments in order to make these songs acceptable to a Christian audience. *Widsith,* a poem given its final form around the end of the seventh century, but containing material of perhaps much greater antiquity,[19] contains a small amount of apparently Christian material, while *Beowulf,* which was probably composed in the earlier half of the eighth century,[20] is a fully Christianized, but essentially

---

[19] On the date of *Widsith* see Malone, *Widsith,* pp. 51-57.

[20] So Klaeber, *Beowulf,* pp. cvii-cxiii, and most subsequent scholars. Whitelock, *Audience,* pp. 4-30, 64, 82-85, 99-105, argues that the poem could have been written as late as the end of the eighth century.

heroic, poem. At the next stage, poets began to tell stories from Christian Latin tradition by grafting Christian subject matter onto the framework of concepts and values which they inherited more or less intact from pre-Christian Germanic tradition. Thus, the same ideological framework which dictates the shape of *Beowulf* underlies *Genesis B* as well. Later still, this heroic conceptual framework begins to lose its significance for the poet and his audience, and to disintegrate under the prolonged influence of Christianity. Poets no longer use the heroic poetic tradition intact in Christian poems, but they still depend upon individual concepts and motifs for a variety of poetic effects. *Andreas* could well represent a stage of development in which heroic and Christian poetic traditions are mixed together but not really integrated with one another.

Eventually, poets who wish to compose Christian poems in English no longer need to fall back upon heroic concepts and motifs to express their ideas directly and to gain emotional effects, and they no longer accept the validity of any sort of heroic system of values. Like Cynewulf in *Juliana* and like the *Seafarer*-poet, they examine heroic concepts and values from a firmly Christian point-of-view and reject these concepts and values unequivocally. However, even after heroic concepts have been rejected by Christian poets because they no longer provide a valid system of values by which to live, they remain useful for purposes of figurative expression. Concepts and motifs from heroic tradition may be employed as metaphors for non-heroic concepts and abstractions. In *Genesis B* and *Andreas*, God's followers ARE the warrior-thanes of a Germanic lord; in *Christ II* and *Guthlac A*, they are merely LIKE heroic thanes in their devotion. At this stage, the heroic concepts are no longer treated as a coherent matrix of ideas, and the vocabulary which originally evolved to express these concepts has begun to lose its heroic connotations. Gradually, Christian poets cease to employ heroic concepts and motifs even for figurative expression. As the concepts themselves drop out of Christian poetry, all that remains is the vocabulary which once expressed them, and this vocabulary therefore becomes vestigial. It is left over from the earlier tradition and largely devoid of its original meanings. One may observe this stage in *Christ III* and *Guthlac B*. Finally, even the vestigial vocabulary of heroic poetry disappears from Old English Christian verse, as it appears to have done in *Judgment Day II*.

The highly speculative chronology of the poems which I have chosen to demonstrate these stages in the development of Old English Christian poetry lends at most tenuous support to this reconstruction. While *Widsith* might antedate the 'Caedmonian' Christian narrative poems of the Age of Bede *Beowulf,* according to what seems to be the prevalent scholarly opinion, does not.[21] Even so, this is no great obstacle since Christianized heroic poems could have been produced continuously until long after the advent of poems on Christian subjects. *Genesis B* was probably composed in Old Saxon in the earlier ninth century, but it is modeled upon the earliest English poems on Christian subjects, the 'Caedmonian' poems, and comes ultimately from an area which, like Caedmon's England, had been converted fairly recently to Christianity. *Andreas* seems to have been composed around the middle of the ninth century, but its stylistic affinities with *Beowulf* might suggest that it should be placed closer in time to that eighth-century poem than to the later, more sophisticated Christian poems of the Cynewulf-group with which it is usually associated. *Juliana* and *Christ II* are signed by Cynewulf, who wrote no earlier than the last quarter of the eighth century, and probably a bit later than that. *Guthlac A* could have been composed in the eighth century, but its 'Cynewulfian' qualities suggest a ninth-century dating, as do similar qualities in *Christ III* and *Guthlac B*. *The Seafarer* seems roughly contemporary with the poems of the Cynewulf-group. Indeed, the safest statement possible about the dates of the last six poems mentioned is that they are all 'roughly contemporary', probably composed in the ninth century, later than *Beowulf* and, perhaps, *Andreas*. *Judgment Day II*, a product of the late tenth century, is certainly later than the other poems I have considered.

Of course, few of the approximate dates of these poems are

---

[21]   See, e.g., Klaeber, *Beowulf*, p. cxiii; Whitelock, *Audience*, pp. 8-12; Wrenn, *Old English Literature*, p. 108.

much more than educated guesses, and no scholar would, I think, venture to propose at all dogmatically any specific relative chronology for them. It is not at all unusual or extravagant to allow a period of a hundred years during which a given Old English poem might have been composed. If the very vague chronology of these poems does not firmly support the theory of development I have suggested, at least it does not absolutely contradict it. *Beowulf* should, as a Germanic heroic poem, be associated with the earliest kind of English poetry; *Genesis B*, a 'Caedmonian' poem, with the earliest kind of English poetry which treats Christian subjects and themes. *Andreas* seems a little more sophisticated in theme and subject matter than the 'Caedmonian' poems, but more heroic and less theological than the poems of the Cynewulf-group, and could fall somewhere between the two groups in time. The 'Cynewulfian' poems and *The Seafarer* are always placed later in time by scholars than the 'Caedmonian', and *Judgment Day II* is certainly the latest of all.

The obstacles in the way of establishing external evidence to support the theory which I have tentatively proposed on the basis of internal evidence appear insurmountable; we have too few poems, and know too little about those we have. We cannot date most Old English poems with any precision at all, nor can we determine where they were composed, or by whom. This lack of factual information, along with the formulaic nature of Old English poetic diction, makes it all but impossible to speak with any confidence about the influence of one poem or group of poems upon another. The entire corpus of Old English poetry is so limited that even if one relies exclusively upon internal evidence it is extremely difficult to find many poems to exemplify the various stages which I have suggested form a pattern of poetic development. Many of the Christian poems we have seem to fall into the gray area between the black of one stage and the white of the next; in a larger corpus of poetry we might find more blacks and whites to set off the various shades of gray.

More poems and more precise information about the poems would alleviate but not eliminate the problems which stand in the way of an unqualified acceptance of this theory. As I remarked earlier, literary traditions do not develop in as orderly a manner as the literary historian would wish. No matter how closely the main stream of a poetic tradition seems to follow the general direction of a theory abstracted from it to describe its course, one can always find anomalous poems which run counter to the theorist's speculations. In describing a general pattern of poetic development, minor variations and discrepancies necessarily must be ignored. Furthermore, in a country like Anglo-Saxon England, locality probably made a considerable difference in the pace at which Christian poetic tradition developed. At any given time, the poets of one kingdom, for example Northumbria in the Age of Bede, might produce more sophisticated, 'advanced' Christian poems than their counterparts in less enlightened parts of the country, only to stagnate and be outstripped eventually by the poetic developments elsewhere. Ideally, we need not only dates but places in order to plot the course of development of Old English Christian poetry. Again, we should logically expect the various stages of development to overlap in time; Christianized heroic poems like *Beowulf* would not disappear immediately upon the emergence of 'Caedmonian' poems on Christian subjects. Indeed, their production could, and apparently did, continue unabated for some time.

These qualifications do not contradict the general theory which I have outlined; they merely suggest the sort of caution with which one must approach such theories and the difficulties inherent in attempts to verify them by the use of empirical data. But what is one to make of Bede's story of the poet Caedmon?[22] Bede's story might suggest that Old English Christian poetry emerged fully-developed from the mind of the divinely inspired shepherd, although that is not precisely what Bede says. A sceptic might relegate the entire 'miracle' to the realm of fiction and simply ignore it, but Bede is considered a rather reliable historian by many scholars. Wrenn considers the miraculous element in the story to be the fact that "a peasant, lacking entirely in that kind of upbringing and training which could have given him the ability to

---

[22]   *Historia Ecclesiastica Gentis Anglorum*, IV, xxiv.

employ the essentially aristocratic technique of the Germanic heroic diction and style, should suddenly have produced a poem in which all this 'educated' technique was demonstrated with exact correctness . . . what Caedmon did was – so far as we know, for the first time – to apply the whole technical apparatus of that Germanic heroic poetry which the Anglo-Saxons had brought with them from their Continental homelands to a specifically Christian version of the story of Creation." [23] This reading of the miracle does not apparently, preclude the possibility that Christianized heroic poems were already in existence. Magoun, on the basis of the formulaic character of Caedmon's *Hymn*, argues that Caedmon must have known the formulas and techniques by which he composed the *Hymn* before his dream. He takes the miracle to be the poet's conquest of his fear of singing before an audience.[24] Certainly the diction of the *Hymn*, the one poem we can definitely attribute to Caedmon, is traditional and formulaic, but it is too brief for us to draw conclusions about the heroic content of Caedmon's other poems from it. Even if we take Bede's story as unvarnished truth, the possibility remains that the poems on Old and New Testament themes mentioned by Bede depend, like *Genesis B*, upon heroic concepts and a heroic view of the world for their coherence, and thus represent the earliest stage in the development of Old English poetry on specifically Christian subject matter.

The pattern of development which I have proposed for Old English Christian poetry is rather speculative but, I think reasonable and credible. If one acknowledges the probability that there existed a pre-Christian, heroic tradition of Germanic poetry, it seems logical to hypothesize *a priori* that, as Anglo-Saxon poets became more and more adept at the art of composing poems upon Christian themes and Christian subjects, they should become less dependent upon, and ultimately reject, the pre-Christian concepts and values which they originally inherited along with the techniques of composition which they employ. If we had a larger

---

[23] *Old English Literature*, p. 102.
[24] Francis P. Magoun, Jr., "Bede's Story of Caedman: The Case History of an Anglo-Saxon Oral Singer", *Speculum* XXX (1955), 49-63.

corpus of Old English Christian poetry, we might discover more poems which fit into one or another of the stages of development which I have defined. On the other hand, we might discover that some poets use heroic concepts and motifs in ways which I have not considered. We should, I think, on the basis of their use of heroic materials, be able to place all of the Christian poems in Old English somewhere in the pattern of development which I have suggested.

One more loose end remains to be considered in order to make the theory I have offered viable. *The Battle of Maldon*, a poem composed sometime after the actual battle of 991, certainly qualifies as a heroic poem. E. V. Gordon calls it "the only purely heroic poem extant in Old English", and "the clearest and fullest expression known in literature of the ancient Germanic heroic code".[25] Kemp Malone observes that the poem contains one truly Christian passage, Byrhtnoth's dying prayer for his soul (173-180), but his evaluation of the heroic quality of the poem agrees with that of Gordon: "The poem belongs to the tradition of the scops, and most of it might be put back into heathen times with little or no change in word or thought."[26] Most scholars who have written on Maldon express similar views, and dissenters are few.[27] Earlier in this study I used *Maldon* as a principal source for examples of the concepts of loyalty, vengeance and treasure as they appear in heroic poetry and, clearly, these concepts control the action of the poem. The viking invaders demand *beagas* from the English *on hyra sylfra dom*, (29-41), but Byrhtnoth refuses to surrender treasure in a shameful manner (45-61) and battle is soon enjoined. The English fight for worldly 'glory' (*tir* – 104, *dom* – 129). Byrhtnoth falls, and some of his followers flee the

[25] E. V. Gordon, ed., *The Battle of Maldon* (London, 1937), pp. 24, 26.
[26] "The Old English Period", *A Literary History of England*, ed. Albert C. Baugh (New York, 1948), p. 58.
[27] N. F. Blake, "*The Battle of Maldon*", *Neophil.* XLIX (1965), 332-345, argues that the poet draws upon saint's lives like that of St. Edmund for his portrayal of Byrhtnoth; but see esp., J. E. Cross, "Oswald and Byrhtnoth: a Christian saint and a hero who is Christian", *English Studies* XLVI (1965), 93-109; and George Clark, "*The Battle of Maldon*: A Heroic Poem", *Speculum* XLIII (1968), 52-71.

battlefield, presumably to their everlasting shame (181-201). His loyal retainers remain on the field, mindful of their oaths of service to their lord, to either avenge him or die in the attempt (207-208). Ælfwine's speech, which echoes that of Wiglaf to Beowulf's retainers (*Beowulf*, 2631-2660), typifies the attitude of Byrht-noth's loyal followers and epitomizes the heroic code of Germania:

> Gemunan þa mæla   þe we oft æt meodo spræcon,
> þonne we on bence   beot ahofon,
> hæleð on healle,   ymbe heard gewinn;
> nu mæg cunnian   hwa cene sy.
> Ic wille mine æþelo   eallum gecyþan,
> þæt ic waes on Mycron   miccles cynnes;
> wæs min ealda fæder   Ealhelm haten,
> wis ealdorman,   woruldgesælig.
> Ne sceolon me on þære þeode   þegnas ætwitan
> ðæt ic of ðisse fyrde   feran wille,
> eard gesecan,   nu min ealdor ligeð
> forheawen æt hilde.   Me is þæt hearma mæst;
> he wæs ægðer min mæg   and min hlaford.   (212–224)

The heroic quality of *The Battle of Brunanburh*, a slightly earlier battle poem than *Maldon*,[28] is usually attributed by scholars to a kind of antiquarian revival of interest in the early heroic poetry of England.[29] This theory gains support primarily from the rather artificial 'correctness' of the poem's meter and style when judged by the standards of earlier English heroic poetry, together with a bookish reference at the end of the poem (65-73). *Brunan-burh* contains a few clear suggestions of heroic concepts, but its brevity and panegyrical nature make it impossible to say much about the precise role of heroic values in the poem. *Maldon*, on the other hand, is much less technically 'correct' than *Brunan-burh*,[30] and is quite thoroughly and clearly controlled by heroic concepts and values. These factors suggest that *Maldon* is the product of a still living poetic tradition rather than an antiquarian revival. Poets working in a living poetic tradition sometimes take

---

[28]   It appears as the entry for the year 937 in the *Anglo-Saxon Chronicle*.

[29]   See, e.g., Alistair Campbell, ed., *The Battle of Brunanburh* (London, 1938), pp. 34-42; C. L. Wrenn, *Old English Literature*, pp. 182-185.

[30]   See, e.g., E. D. Laborde, *Byrhtnoth and Maldon* (London, 1936), pp. 73-78; C. L. Wrenn, *Old English Literature*, p. 186.

metrical and stylistic liberties; antiquarian poets strive for 'correctness', for fidelity to the ancient manner which they are attempting to imitate. Again, it seems unlikely that a poet attempting to imitate a moribund kind of poetry should be quite so successful in resurrecting a defunct ideological system and spirit as is the *Maldon*-poet. The paucity of heroic poems in the extant corpus of Old English poetry, together with the difficulties attendant upon dating the few extant poems and fragments, makes it impossible to prove the unbroken continuity of the secular, heroic verse tradition in England. Nevertheless, the very existence of *Maldon* suggests that this tradition, colored to be sure by Christianity but based upon pre-Christian concepts and values, survived in England through the tenth century.

It would appear, then, that by the end of the Old English period we have two distinct poetic traditions, the heroic and the Christian, which spring from a single root. The heroic tradition has its origins far back in the pre-literate, pre-Christian Germanic past. Transplanted to England from the Continent, it seems to have flourished even after the appearance of Latin Christianity, which influenced but never dominated it. Although Christian allusions and sentiments appear in the Old English heroic poetry preserved today, the diction and values remain essentially Germanic and secular as late as *The Battle of Maldon*. The Christian poetic tradition in English begins as an offshoot of the heroic tradition, with the addition of Christian material to originally secular Germanic poems. As poets turn to specifically Christian subjects and themes, the Christian branch of English poetry grows steadily farther away from the Germanic stalk. Poets become less dependent upon the concepts and diction of heroic poetry, and become more adept at expressing Christian concepts and sentiments in a poetic language suited to such expression. One can only with difficulty imagine two poems composed at about the same time in the same place and the same language with less in common conceptually, and with less similar values than *The Battle of Maldon* and *Judgment Day II*.

BIBLIOGRAPHY

PRIMARY SOURCES

The Acts of Andrew and Matthew in the City of the Man-Eaters. Ed. Alexander Roberts and James Donaldson, The Ante-Nicene Fathers, VIII. Buffalo, 1886.

Andreas and the Fates of the Apostles. Ed. Kenneth R. Brooks. Oxford, 1961.

Andreas and the Fates of the Apostles. Ed. George Philip Krapp. Boston, 1906.

The Anglo-Saxon Minor Poems. Ed. Elliott Van Kirk Dobbie, The Anglo-Saxon Poetic Records, VI. New York, 1942.

The Battle of Brunanburh. Ed. Alistair Campbell. London, 1938.

The Battle of Maldon. Ed. E. V. Gordon. London, 1937.

Bedae Venerabilis. *Opera Rhythmica.* Ed. J. Fraipont, Corpus Christianorum Series Latina, CXXII. Turnholti, 1955.

Bede's Ecclesiastical History of the English People. Ed. Bertram Colgrave and R. A. B. Mynors. Oxford, 1969.

Beowulf and the Fight at Finnsburg. Ed. Fr. Klaeber. 3rd ed. Boston, 1950.

The Christ of Cynewulf. Ed. Albert S. Cook. Boston, 1900.

Cynewulf. *Juliana.* Ed. Rosemary Woolf. London, 1955.

Cynewulf. *The Juliana of Cynewulf.* Ed. William Strunk. Boston, 1904.

Deor. Ed. Kemp Malone. New York, 1966.

The Exeter Book. Ed. George Philip Krapp and Elliott Van Kirk Dobbie, The Anglo-Saxon Poetic Records, III. New York, 1936.

Felix's Life of Saint Guthlac. Ed. Bertram Colgrave. Cambridge, 1956.

Gregorii Papaei. *Opera Omnia,* II. Ed. J. P. Migne, Patrologia Latina, LXXVI. Parisiis, 1844-1864.

Heliand und Genesis. Ed. Otto Behaghel. Halle, 1903.

The Junius Manuscript. Ed. George Philip Krapp, The Anglo-Saxon Poetic Records, I. New York, 1931.

The Later Genesis. Ed. B. J. Timmer. Oxford, 1948.

The Seafarer. Ed. Ida L. Gordon. London, 1960.

Tacitus. *Germania.* Ed. M. Hutton, The Loeb Classical Library. Cambridge, Mass., 1914.

Three Old English Elegies: The Wife's Lament, The Husband's Message, The Ruin. Ed. Roy F. Leslie. Manchester, 1961.

The Vercelli Book. Ed. George Philip Krapp, The Anglo-Saxon Poetic Records, II. New York, 1932.

Waldere. Ed. Frederick Norman. London, 1949.

Waltharius. Ed. Karl Strecker. Berlin, 1947.

The Wanderer. Ed. Roy F. Leslie. Manchester, 1966.

Widsith. Ed. Kemp Malone. London, 1936.

SECONDARY SOURCES

Anderson, G. K., *The Literature of the Anglo-Saxons.* Princeton, 1949.

Bambas, Rudolf C., "Another View of the Old English *Wife's Lament*", *JEGP* LXII, 303-309.

Benson, Larry D., "The Pagan Coloring of *Beowulf*. In: Robert P. Creed (ed.), *Old English Poetry: Fifteen Essays*, 193-213. Providence, R. I., 1967.

—, "The Literary Character of Anglo-Saxon Formulaic Poetry", *PMLA* LXXXI, 334-341.

Bessai, Frank, "Comitatus and Exile in Old English Poetry", *Culture* XXV, 130-144.

Blake, N. F., "*The Battle of Maldon*", *Neophil.* XLIX, 332-345.

Bonjour, Adrien, "*Beowulf* and the Beasts of Battle", *PMLA* LXXII, 563-573.

—, "*Beowulf* and the Shares of Literary Criticism", *Etudes Anglaises* X, 30-36.

—, "Monsters Crouching and Critics Rampant: or The *Beowulf* Dragon Debated", *PMLA* LXVIII, 304-312.

Bosworth, J. and T. N. Toller, *An Anglo-Saxon Dictionary.* Oxford, 1882-1920.

Bright, James W., *An Anglo-Saxon Reader.* New York, 1917.

Brodeur, Arthur G. (ed.), *The Art of Beowulf.* Berkeley, 1959.

Cabaniss, Allen, "*Beowulf* and the Liturgy". In: Lewis E. Nicholson (ed.), *An Anthology of Beowulf*, 223-232. Notre Dame, Indiana, 1963. Originally published in: *JEGP* LIV, 199-201.

Campbell, Alistair (ed.), *The Battle of Brunanburh.* London, 1938.

Cassidy, Frederic G., "How Free Was the Anglo-Saxon Scop?" In: Jess B. Bessinger, Jr., and Robert P. Creed (eds.) *Franciplegius: Medieval and Linguistic Studies in Honor of Francis Peabody Magoun, Jr.*, 65-85. New York, 1965.

Chadwick, H. Munro, *The Heroic Age.* Cambridge, England, 1912.

Chambers, R. W., *Widsith: A Study in Old English Heroic Legend.* Cambridge, England, 1912.

Cherniss, Michael D., "*Beowulf*: Oral Presentation and the Criterion of Immediate Rhetorical Effect", *Genre* III, 214-228.

Clark, George, "*The Battle of Maldon*: A Heroic Poem", *Speculum* XLIII, 52-71.

Cross, J. E., "Oswald and Byrhtnoth: A Christian Saint and a Hero Who Is Christian", *English Studies* XLVI, 93-109.

Crowne, D. K., "The Hero on the Beach", *Neuphilologische Mitteilungen* LXI, 362-372.

Culbert, Taylor, "The Narrative Functions of Beowulf's Swords", *JEGP* LIX, 13-20.

Curschmann, Michael, "Oral Poetry in Mediaeval English, French and German Literature: Some Notes on Recent Research", *Speculum* XLII, 36-52.

Curtius, Ernst Robert, *European Literature and the Latin Middle Ages.* Translation William R. Trask. New York, 1963.

Das, S. K., *Cynewulf and the Cynewulf Canon.* Calcutta, 1942.

260 BIBLIOGRAPHY

Diamond, Robert E., "Heroic Diction in the Dream of the Rood". In: Wallace A. Doyle and Woodburn O. Ross (eds.), *Studies in Honor of John Wilcox*, 3-7. Detroit, 1958.

Diamond, Robert E., "Theme as Ornament in Anglo-Saxon Poetry", *JEGP* LXIV, 645-659.

Donahue, Charles and Larry D. Benson, "*Beowulf* and Christian Tradition: A Reconsideration from a Celtic Stance", *Traditio* XXI, 55-116.

Elliott, Ralph W. V., "Byrhtnoth and Hildebrand: A Study in Heroic Technique", *CL* XIV, 53-70.

Evans, J. M., "*Genesis B* and Its Background", *RES* XIV, 1-16, 113-123.

Fisher, Peter F., "The Trials of the Epic Hero in Beowulf", *PMLA* LXXIII, 171-183.

French, Walter H., "Widsith and the Scop", *PMLA* LX, 623-630.

Gang, T. M., "Approaches to *Beowulf*", *RES* III.

Goldsmith, Margaret, "The Christian Perspective in *Beowulf*". In: Arthur G. Brodeur (ed.), *The Art of Beowulf*, 71-90. Berkeley, 1959.

—, "The Christian Theme of *Beowulf*", *MAE* XXIX, 81-101.

—, "The Choice in *Beowulf*", *Neophil.* XLVIII, 60-72.

—, *The Mode of Meaning of 'Beowulf'*. London, 1970.

Gordon, E. V. (ed.), *The Battle of Maldon*. London, 1937.

Greenfield, Stanley B., *A Critical History of Old English Literature*. New York, 1965.

—, "*The Wife's Lament* Reconsidered", *PMLA* LXVIII, 907-912.

—, "The Formulaic Expression of the Theme of 'Exile' in Anglo-Saxon Poetry", *Speculum* XXX, 200-206.

Gummere, Francis B., *Founders of England*. With supplementary notes by Francis P. Magoun, Jr. New York, 1930. Originally published as *Germanic Origins*, 1892.

—, "MIN, SYLF, and the 'Dramatic Voices in *The Wanderer* and the Seafarer'", *JEGP* LXVIII, 212-220.

Halverson, John, "*Beowulf* and the Pitfalls of Piety", *University of Toronto Quarterly* XXXV, 260-278.

Hart, Walter M., *Ballad and Epic*. Boston, 1907.

Henry, P. L., *The Early English and Celtic Lyric*. London, 1966.

Hulbert, J. R., "The Genesis of *Beowulf*: A Caveat", *PMLA* LXVI, 1168-1176.

Kennedy, Charles W., *The Poems of Cynewulf*. New York, 1910.

Ker, W. P., *Epic and Romance*. New York, Dover Publications, Inc., 1957. Original edition 1896.

Laborde, E. D., *Byrhtnoth and Maldon*. London, 1936.

Leisi, Ernst, "Gold und Manneswert im *Beowulf*", *Anglia* LXXI, 259-273.

Lord, Albert B., *The Singer of Tales*. New York, 1965. Original edition Cambridge, Mass., 1960.

Lucas, Angela M., "The Narrator of *The Wife's Lament* Reconsidered", *NM* LXX, 282-297.

Magoun, Jr., Francis P., "The Oral-Formulaic Character of Anglo-Saxon Narrative Poetry". In: Lewis E. Nicholson (ed.), *An Anthology of Beowulf Criticism*, 189-211. Notre Dame, Indiana, 1963. Originally published in: *Speculum* XXVIII, 446-462.

—, "Bede's Story of Caedman: The Case History of an Anglo-Saxon Oral Singer", *Speculum* XXX, 49-63.

Malone, Kemp, "Symbolism in *Beowulf*: Some Suggestions". In: G. A. Bonnard (ed.), *English Studies Today*, second series, 81-91. Bern, 1961.

Nicholson, Lewis E., *An Anthology of Beowulf Criticism*. Notre Dame, Indiana, 1963.

Peters, Leonard D., "The Relationship of the Old English *Andreas* to *Beowulf*", *PMLA* LXVI, 844-863.

Pope, J. C., "Dramatic Voices in *The Wanderer* and *The Seafarer*". In: Jess B. Bessinger, Jr. and Robert P. Creed (eds.), *Franciplegius: Medieval and Linguistic Studies in Honor of Francis Peabody Magoun, Jr.*, 164-193. New York, 1965.

Renoir, Alain, "The Heroic Oath in *Beowulf*, the *Chanson de Roland*, and the *Nibelungenlied*". In: S. B. Greenfield, *Studies in Honor of Arthur G. Brodeur*, 237-266. Eugene, Oregon, 1963.

Robertson, D. W., "The Doctrine of Charity in Mediaeval Literary Gardens: A Topical Approach Through Symbolism and Allegory". In: Lewis E. Nicholson (ed.), *An Anthology of Beowulf*, 165-188. Notre Dame, Indiana, 1963. Originally published in: *Speculum* XXVIII, 24-49.

Rogers, H. L., "Beowulf's Three Great Fights". In: Lewis E. Nicholson (ed.), *An Anthology of Beowulf Criticism*, 233-256. Notre Dame, Indiana, 1963. Originally published in: *RES* IV, 339-355.

Schaar, Claes, *Critical Studies in the Cynewulf Group*. Lund, 1949.

—, "On a New Theory of Old English Poetic Diction", *Neophil.* XL, 301-305.

Sisam, Kenneth, "Cynewulf and His Poetry". In: *Studies in the History of Old English Literature*. Oxford, 1962.

—, *The Structure of Beowulf*. Oxford, 1965.

Skemp, A. R., "The Transformation of Scriptural Story, Motive and Conception in Anglo-Saxon Poetry", *MP* IV, 427-470.

Smithers, G. V., *The Making of Beowulf*. Durham, 1961.

Stanley, E. G., "*Haethenra Hyht* in *Beowulf*". In: Arthur G. Brodeur, *The Art of Beowulf*, 136-151. Berkeley, 1959.

Stevens, Martin, "The Narrator of *The Wife's Lament*", *NM* LXIX, 72-90.

Stevick, Robert D., "Christian Elements and the Genesis of *Beowulf*", *MP* LXI, 79-89.

Taylor, Henry Osborn, *The Emergence of Christian Culture in the West*. New York, 1958. Original edition 1901.

Taylor, Paul Beekman, "Themes of Death in *Beowulf*". In: Robert P. Creed (ed.), *Old English Poetry: Fifteen Essays*, 249-274. Providence, 1967.

Timmer, B. J., "Heathen and Christian Elements in Anglo-Saxon Poetry", *Neophil.* XXIX, 180-185.

Tolkien, J. R. R., "*Beowulf*: The Monsters and the Critics". In: Lewis E. Nicholson (ed.), *An Anthology of Beowulf Criticism*, 51-103. Notre Dame, Indiana, 1963. Originally published in: *Proceedings of the British Academy* XXII, 245-295.

—, "The Housecoming of Beorhtnoth Beorthelm's Son", *E&S* IV, 1-18.

Van Meurs, J. C., "*Beowulf* and Literary Criticism", *Neophil.* XXXIX, 114-130.

Watts, Ann Chalmers, *The Lyre and the Harpe: A Comparative Reconsideration of Oral Tradition in Homer and Old English Poetry*. New Haven and London, 1969.

Whallon, William, "The Christianity of *Beowulf*", *MP* LX, 81-94.

—, "The Idea of God in *Beowulf*", PMLA LXXX, 19-23.

—, "The Diction of *Beowulf*", *PMLA* LXXVI, 309-319.

Whitelock, Dorothy, "The Interpretation of *The Seafarer*". In: Sir Cyril Fox and Bruce Dickens (eds.), *The Early Cultures of North-West Europe*, 261-272. Cambridge, 1950.

—, *The Audience of Beowulf*. Oxford, 1951.

—, *The Beginnings of English Society*. Baltimore, 1952.

Woolf, Rosemary, "The Fall of Man in *Genesis B* and the *Mystère d'Adam*". In: Arthur G. Brodeur (ed.), *The Art of Beowulf*. Berkeley, 1959.

—, "Saints Lives". In: Eric Gerald Stanley (ed.), *Continuations and Beginnings: Studies in Old English Literature*. London, 1966.

—, "The Devil in Old English Poetry", *RES* IV, 1-12.

Wrenn, C. L., *A Study of Old English Literature*. New York, 1967.

INDEX

Acta Sanctorum, 195
Acts of Andrew and Matthew (Greek), 172, 174, 176, 177, 178, 180, 182, 185, 188
Aeneid, 132, 137, 173-174
Alcuin, 8
Alfred (King of England), 7, 152
allegory (in *Beowulf*), 129-131
Anderson, G. K., 9
Andreas, 83n., 171-193, 196, 197, 198, 206, 207, 233, 235, 250, 251
    relationship to *Beowulf*, 173-174
Andrew, Saint, Old English prose legend of, 172
Anglii, 27
Antony, Saint, see Athanasius
Athanasius, 118
Augustine (missionary to England), 10
Augustine, Saint, 127, 139, 146, 236, 238
avarice, sin of, 80-81, 145-146, 149
Avitus, 153

Bambas, Rudolph C., 117
Battle of Brunanburh, see *Brunanburh*
Battle of Finnsburh, see *Finnsburh*
Battle of Maldon, see *Maldon*
battle, unfair advantage in, 69-70
Baugh, Albert C., 255n.
Bede, 221, 223, 225, 236, 237, 238, 239, 246, 247, 248, 253-254
Bede, Age of, 251, 253
Behaghel, Otto, 155
Benson, Larry D., 17n., 20n., 129

Beowulf, 11, 11-12, 16, 17, 22, 23, 25, 28, 30, 31, 32, 33, 34, 36-58 *passim*, 60-77 *passim*, 79-99 *passim*, 104-117 *passim*, 120, 121, 122, 124-150, 156, 157, 158, 159, 165, 173-174, 182, 184, 191, 192, 196, 210, 214, 224, 239, 249, 250, 251, 252, 253, 256
Bessai, Frank, 103n.
Bessinger, Jess B., Jr., 17n.
Blackburn, F. A., 126, 134, 142
Blake, N. F., 255n.
Bolton, W. F., 124n.
Bonjour, Adrien, 22n., 86, 130, 131, 132
Bosworth, J., 36n., 42n.
Bowra, C. M., 143-144n.
Bright, James W., 172n.
Brodeur, Arthur G., 17n., 128-129, 142-143, 145-146
Brooks, Kenneth R., 172, 173, 195
Brown, Arthur, 125n.
Brunanburh, 28, 74, 96, 256-257

Cabaniss, Allen, 129
Caedmon, 126, 253-254
Caedmonian poetry, 24, 137, 150, 152, 172, 251, 252, 253, see also *Genesis A, Genesis B*
Caesarius of Arles, 236, 238
Cain passages (*Beowulf*), 115, 138-140
Campbell, Alistair, 256n.
Cassidy, Frederic G., 17n.
Chadwick, H. Munro, 10n., 11n., 16, 34, 45, 87, 126, 131, 133, 134, 137